D1584822

𝕽𝖔𝖒𝖆𝖓𝖎𝖘𝖒

Published for the furtherance of the Gospel by:

White Horse Publications
PO Box 2398
Huntsville, AL 35804-2398
1-800-867-2398

-and-

PEACEWAY Productions
Defending the Gospel of Jesus Christ

PO Box 9064
Austin, TX 78766
1-512-346-6771

About this book: *Romanism* has been written to aid the serious student of Scripture. It is hoped that all those seeking truth will benefit from its contents. We have labored to present an accurate portrait of the Roman Catholic religion. We have labored as well to be consistent and sound in our interpretation of the Holy Scriptures. May God be pleased.

About this ministry: We believe that Christians should witness the truth of Christ's gospel. We are dedicated to a defense of the gospel. There are millions caught up in the Roman Catholic religion who do not hear or know the glorious gospel of our Lord Jesus Christ. *A Christian Witness to Roman Catholicism* seeks to remedy this fact. May God be pleased.

—Robert M. Zins, Director
A Christian Witness to Roman Catholicism
PO Box 6409
Rutland, VT 05702

𝕽omanism

*The Relentless
Roman Catholic Assault
on the Gospel of Jesus Christ!*

by Robert M. Zins, Th.M.

White Horse
Publications
Huntsville, Alabama, USA

Romanism: The Relentless Roman Catholic Assault on the Gospel of Jesus Christ!
second edition

First edition published in 1994 with the generous assistance of PEACEWAY PRODUCTIONS, PO Box 9064, Austin, TX 78766

Cover design by Kevin Xiques

For copyright information, write to White Horse Publications, Copyrights and Permissions, P.O. Box 2398, Huntsville, AL 35804-2398.

Unless otherwise noted, all Scripture texts in this work are taken from the *King James Version* (*Authorized Version*, UK) of the Bible

Library of Congress Catalog Card Number: 95-60418
ISBN 0-9637141-4-7

Second Edition   0 9 8 7 6 5 4 3 2 1

Additional copies of *Romanism* may be obtained by using the order forms at the back of this book, or by writing to:

White Horse Publications
P.O. Box 2398
Huntsville, AL 35804-2398
1-800-867-2398

This book is dedicated to the English martyrs
of the Protestant Reformation.

Their faithfulness, to the death, of simple trust and
full assurance in Christ beckons our imitation.
Through faith, though they are dead, they yet speak.

Contents

"At a time when evangelical leaders want to wed Roman Catholicism and Biblical Christianity, Rob Zins unashamedly states the critical differences. Must reading for all those who would 'earnestly contend for the faith that was once for all delivered to the saints.'"

Kathy McDonnell
Homemaker, Mother
Groveland, MA

"Who will stand in the day of battle? With the worldwide ecumenical tide of 'unity' and 'reconciliation,' with the Church of Rome moving at an ever-increasing pace, where are those men willing to stand for the uncompromised truth of God regardless of the cost?

"Did Jesus and the Apostles create ecumenical councils in order to get along with the Scribes and the Pharisees?

"Did Luther or Calvin agree to compromise the Gospel for the sake of unity with the Pope at Rome?

"Author Rob Zins cries out, just as the Reformers of old did, to turn men's hearts back to God's eternal truth.

"Rob's fine book deserves to be on the shelf of every 'defender' of the faith!"

Larry Wessels
Christian Answers, Inc.
Austin, TX

Acknowledgments

IT IS difficult to know where to stop in my thanks and appreciation for all those who have made this book possible. Certainly all those involved in witnessing the gospel to the Catholic community have to be mentioned for their encouragement and example to my life. Also, all the untold thousands who have been given eyes to see the finished work of the Lord have been a wonderful motivation to me as I have heard and read of their testimony.

But God always raises up certain people when He orders a task to be done. These special people are the ones so closely related to the progress of this writing that without them it could not have been done. I wish to thank first and foremost my wife, Nancy, for her patience and constant encouragement not to mention many long hours of typing. She is a special lady and her care has gone into this book. Also, I would like to thank Al Angell, my dear friend and business partner, who has been a steady influence and steadfast supporter of my writing and ministry efforts. He has done more than mere words can record to see us through this project. In addition, I would like to say a hearty thanks to all the wonderful people of Reformed Bible Church. There simply could not be a finer support Body in all the world. Likewise, I wish to mention all those who are continuing to give their support to *A Christian Witness to Roman Catholicism.* We labor together to set forth the truth. Special thanks to Jon Limmer, without whose diligence and expertise on the technical end of a computer I would have been imprisoned to a pen and pad in the writing of this book! My special thanks also to Timothy F. Kauffman, without whose diligence and special care, this book would not have survived.

For those of you who take the time to read this book I assure you the emphasis is on the religion of the Roman Catholic community, not individual Catholics. There are, no doubt, many fine citizens and exemplary personalities within Roman Catholicism. But such can be said of all religions including those of the first century. The issue here is the truth of the gospel, not the relative merits of lifestyles. This book is devoted to exposing what a man believes in relation to God Almighty. This is the issue. The issue is not what a man does relative to his fellow man. For in the final analysis there are none who are good men. To deny the need for the Savior is the folly of mankind in general. To deny the gospel of the Savior is the folly of the Roman Catholic religion.

Introduction

O N THE first page of his book entitled, *Catholicism and Fundamentalism: The Attack on "Romanism" by "Bible Christians,"* Karl Keating quotes the following from Acts 18:9,10;

> "Do not be afraid, speak out, and refuse to be silenced; I am with thee, and none shall come near to do thee harm; I have a great following in this city."

This encouragement was given to the apostle Paul as God came to him by night in a vision. Finding solace in the above passage of Scripture, Keating has catapulted himself into the foray of defending his religion against those whom he calls "Bible Christians." In light of the popularity of his book, we have chosen Keating as an example of modern Catholic writing. We have selected Keating not only because of the reputation of his book, but also due to his magazine, *This Rock*, which is so well-respected in the Roman Catholic community. We learn more about Keating from the back cover of his book:

> "Karl Keating is the director of *Catholic Answers*, a lay organization which explains and defends the beliefs, history and practices of the Catholic Church. He engages in debates with leading anti-Catholics, and edits *Catholic Answers*, a monthly journal of apologetics."[1]

In the main, Keating represents historical Romanism and is faithful to the decrees and canons of the Council of Trent. His defense of Roman Catholicism has been widely acclaimed and he is well-read. However, we have not limited this book to interacting with Keating alone. Where it is necessary, we have always gone straight to the highest sources of Roman authority both to check Keating, and to display accurately Roman Catholic doctrines.

We hasten to add that we have to remain cautious about the content of Keating's book. He is a lay person and has no real teaching authority in the

---

[1] Keating, Karl, *Catholicism and Fundamentalism*, (San Francisco: Ignatius Press, ©1988) back cover

11

Roman Catholic religion. However, his book has been given the *Nihil Obstat* and *Imprimatur* from a Monsignor and an Archbishop with the following explanation of what this means.

> "The *Nihil Obstat* and *Imprimatur* are official declarations that a book is considered free of doctrinal or moral error. No implication is contained therein that those who have granted the *Nihil Obstat* or the *Imprimatur* agree with the contents, opinions or statements expressed."[1]

We shall use Keating as a convenient backdrop to facilitate our purpose in writing this book. However, we will back him up with higher sources of authority where necessary. One unique aspect of Keating's work is his strategy. He is not afraid to name names! He also launches a blistering assault on Loraine Boettner's standard Protestant resource entitled *Roman Catholicism.*[2] It is Keating's purpose to dismiss Boettner's work and then pursue whom he calls the "fundamentalist." We presume Boettner is the target of Keating because Boettner has written such a comprehensive work against the Roman Catholic religion. Keating has convinced some that Boettner's work has been thrown down. One Roman Catholic sympathizer endorses Keating's book with the following warning!

> "I strongly advise honest fundamentalists not to read this book. They might find their whole position collapsing in ruins."[3]

This is strong language and typifies the style of Keating's writing. The result of his book has been a fairly clear presentation of Romanism as well as a poignant criticism of what he calls "Bible Christians." For this we are grateful. The Christian community should be more aware of the Roman religion and their peculiar beliefs. Keating has given us a very lucid picture of the differences that exist between Rome and Christianity.

---

[1] Keating, *Catholicism and Fundamentalism*, inside cover page

[2] We have available, in separate booklet form, a special printing of Keating's treatment of Boettner and a vindication of Boettner. It is entitled *Formidable Truth* and is available upon request. It is included in this work as an appendix.

[3] Keating, *Catholicism and Fundamentalism*, back cover, as contributed by Sheldon Vanauken, author of *A Severe Mercy*

Chapter 1

The Essence of the Roman Catholic Religion (Romanism)

WHEN we are asked to give a short summary of the Roman Catholic religion and the best way to contrast the gospel of Jesus with the Catholic system, we begin with the sacraments. The Roman religion is based 100% on the notion that Jesus Christ came and left His own with an elaborate *system*. These religious rituals are to be performed in hopes of achieving salvation. They are administered through the power of Catholic priests who, by virtue of the sacrament of holy orders, take Catholic initiates through the sacraments. These sacraments are administered from the cradle to the grave.

The word "sacrament," from the Latin word *sacramentum*, generally means secret or rite. It is used to convey the "mysterious." The Catholic religion uses this word to describe rituals that are a means of grace. In its elaborate forms of endless rituals and traditions, Romanism may well represent the pinnacle of man's attempt to arrive at God. But is it the gospel left to us by Jesus Christ?

At the outset, we question the entire sacramental system, beginning with baptism. Does the Bible teach that the Holy Spirit can be called down from Heaven by a man priest in the waters of baptism? Can we believe baptism is the beginning of justification? Are we to believe baptism is the entry into the Body of Christ? Is it not true that entry into the Body of Christ is by faith in the finished work of Jesus Christ on the cross?

We further question the Catholic teaching that the Holy Spirit is manipulated through water baptism. Is not the Spirit free and Spirit baptism the free gift of God which makes alive, seals and sanctifies those who are redeemed?

We also question the second Roman Catholic sacrament of confirmation. The Catholic religion believes that their bishops have the authority to summon the Holy Spirit. We believe the Holy Spirit cannot be manipulated by a human bishop in order to leave a "footprint" on the heart. Does the Bible speak of an anointing with chrism (a mixture of oil and balm) for such a purpose? The Holy Spirit is given for life to all those believing on the Lord Jesus Christ. What does this have to do with the Catholic sacrament?

We also turn away from the third Roman Catholic sacrament of the Eucharist. The Romanist religion affirms that a priestly class has the power to transform a simple piece of bread and a cup of wine into the actual body and blood of Jesus. It is equally asserted that participation in the Mass brings about forgiveness of sins. The Roman Catholic contends the Mass is the representation of the once-for-all sacrifice of Christ as a continuing sacrifice for sins. Is this true?

We further question the fourth Roman Catholic sacrament of Penance. The Catholic religion affirms the Lord Jesus gave special powers of forgiveness to a priestly class to confer forgiveness on the basis of penance. Yet it seems plain that the Bible teaches direct access to God the Father through Jesus Christ. Forgiveness of sin and guilt is absolutely free without need of further "penances."

The Roman Catholic religion also confesses faith in a final ritual to cleanse sin. This seventh sacrament of Rome is Extreme Unction. The Roman religion teaches a ritual of cleansing from sin at the death bed. Where can we find scriptural justification for such a ritual?

The fifth sacrament of marriage in the Catholic religion is not of consequence to the gospel unless one is confronted with Catholic religious intolerance. Normally, Catholics are taught to convert perspective spouses or marry within the Catholic community.

The sixth sacrament is Holy Orders. The Catholic religion believes that Jesus Christ conferred onto men the ability to change bread and wine into His actual body and blood. To continue the Mass, the sacrament of Orders is maintained in the Roman religion. In essence, Roman Catholicism is a giant religious system. It contains millions of adherents in virtually every country of the world. It claims to be *the* representation of Jesus Christ and the gospel! The heart of this religion is its sacramental system. It is obvious that due to the current views of Romanism on married priests and women in the priesthood no one can normally partake of all seven sacraments. Holy Orders is critical to the ongoing sacramental system. It is from the ranks of the priests that bishops and cardinals are selected. Ultimately, the Catholic pope emerges through this hierarchy.

'Sacramental Salvation'

There is no reason to depart from the basics of the Catholic religion when trying to define it. It would be a mistake to parade around countless stories of popish intrigue or doctrines of Mary. At heart, the Catholic religion is a sacramental religion administered by an army of priests, bishops, cardinals, prefects, theologians, and ultimately the pope.

Christians can affirm the proper meaning and place of baptism. Christians can affirm the reality of the Holy Spirit and the attending gifts of the Spirit. Christians can affirm the death of Christ and the wonderful gift of His sacrifice. Christians can affirm confession of sin directly to God and to one another, and repentant hearts. Christians can affirm Church leadership and "elders that rule well." But can we confuse the gospel of Christ with the Roman Catholic system?

We ask, in the final analysis, did Christ leave a *message*, or a *method* for salvation? Did He leave us with the promise of His Person indwelling in the form of the Holy Spirit, or rituals? Did He leave us with a completely finished work, or an ongoing reconstituted sacrifice by a priestly class? Did He leave us with a personal relationship or a personal system of obedience?

There are many other facets of the Catholic religion upon which we could dwell. The doctrine of purgatory, the history of the popes, the testimony of Catholic traditions which are put on a par with Scripture could all fill volumes. In our day and age we see the elevation of the person of Mary by the Roman religion. There is also the widespread ecumenical movement spearheaded by the Vatican. But none of these is the heart of the issue. The heart of the matter is Roman "sacramental salvation." This is the essence of Rome. It is a heartbeat that has not changed throughout the centuries.

We need to evaluate any reforms coming out of Vatican II as they relate to Christianity. Has Vatican II shifted Rome from its original moorings and widened the margins of Catholicism in an attempt to absorb pagan religions? Likewise, has Rome confounded the world by calling Christians "separated brethren"? Is this a maneuver designed to give Rome credibility and a broadened voice in the marketplace?

In the following pages, we will be dealing with Rome in a somewhat unique way. We will interact with a number of modern-day Roman Catholic defenders. We shall discuss the main sacraments of the Catholic religion. We will finish this book with some thoughts on justification and the future direction of Rome in light of Vatican II. We have chosen this format because we are most anxious to help the reader understand the differences between Christianity and Romanism. Also, it is very important to listen carefully as modern Catholics give their defense.

Chapter 2

Some Observations

TODAY, as was true when Paul stood up to teach the Word of God, there is a certain danger. Paul ended up being hounded by religious leaders to such an extent that he was forced to flee to Syria. It is interesting that accusations made against Paul may be likened very much to wars fought over truth in every generation. Paul was accused of misrepresenting God. The Jewish community accused Paul of misinterpreting the prophets and usurping the authority of Moses. Of course, Paul was in good company. They did the same to Jesus. It was the focus of criticism of both Paul and Jesus that they were misrepresenting God.

History teaches us that there has been standing room only in the stadium of all those who wish to speak on behalf of God. The advent of the Savior opened the flood gate for not only those who stood against Him, but also those, in subsequent years, who *claimed* to speak for Him.

At the outset we should not be surprised that many have travailed in the enterprise of speaking for God. The Roman Catholic community has been anything but silent in their estimation of the gospel of Jesus Christ! Likewise many throughout the ages have stood up and joined in chorus against Rome. The issue has always been, "What is the true gospel?"

As in other generations, we dare not be silent in our assessment of Roman Catholicism. We disagree wholeheartedly with the Roman Catholic understanding of the gospel. While Rome indeed defends some portions of biblical truth, this remnant of light is soon swallowed up in a vast network of confusing religion. This religion bears little resemblance to the name of the Lord Jesus Christ. The words of Paul come to mind from a portion of the book of Acts:

> "Take heed therefore unto yourselves, and to all the flock, over the which the Holy Ghost hath made you overseers, to feed the church of God, which he hath purchased with his own blood. For I know this, that after my departing shall grievous wolves enter in among you, not sparing the flock. Also of your own selves shall men arise,

speaking perverse things, to draw away disciples after them." (Acts 20:28-30)

Herein lies the battle! Who is telling the truth when speaking of the gospel of the Lord Jesus Christ? Indeed, what is the gospel of Christ? Where can we find it? What can be said about it? With whom has it been entrusted? For the Roman Catholic there is but one answer. Rome has the gospel! Rome has been given charge of the mind of Christ! It is through Rome that we must travel on our way to the heavenly city! Such is the claim.

Against such a claim is the testimony of many throughout the centuries. Myriads have spoken and written contra Rome. This book seeks a clearer definition of this chorus of dissent. We are not so willing to acquiesce to the presumption of some who insist that "Romanism" be given the title of Christianity.

Questions faced by every generation since the first century face us today. Who speaks for the gospel of Jesus Christ? A corollary question will be one of authority and the interpretation of that authority. This book is generally a response to the relentless Catholic assault on the gospel of Jesus Christ. Roman Catholic sources will be cited so as to give the reader an honest presentation of Romanism from their *own* sources.

What about Ecumenism?

We are aware that the official posture of the post-Vatican II papacy is one of reconciliation. Protestants are to be considered "separated brethren" who must be patiently brought back to the fullest expression of Christ's revelation in Romanism. Protestants are given credit for having some truth, albeit not full, as it is in Rome. Thus, due to this spirit of reconciliation, there are many voices in both the Catholic community and the Christian community who are clamoring for unity and peace. Many have gone so far as to determine that doctrine is absolutely irrelevant and the only thing that matters is "love" and "unity."[1] While this may be the sentiment of popular and naïve modernists, it is not the sentiment of either Rome or the Christian community. Vatican II did not rescind the doctrines of the Catholic religion as they pertain to the gospel of Christ and salvation. On the contrary, the great Council upheld and reaffirmed their central doctrines. We must ask if

---

[1] We recommend a careful reading of Keith Fournier's *Evangelical Catholics* to begin to grasp the depth to which some have gone to obscure the gospel and sugar-coat Romanism in hopes of unity. Keith A. Fournier, *Evangelical Catholics*, (Nashville: Thomas Nelson Publishers, ©1990)

opposite and radically different concepts of the gospel can somehow co-
exist under the same umbrella.

We are equally aware and even less encouraged by well-meaning professing
Christians who seem to be insisting on a *third* gospel. This *third* gospel
wishes to take two absolutely contradictory views of the gospel and mesh
them together as one. This is done in the name of "love" and "unity." We
confess that those who insist on this romancing of strange doctrines will in
some measure incur the same judgment which Paul reserved for the like-
minded of his own day. The apostle Paul would have nothing to do with
any attempt to compromise, add to, diminish, blend or confuse the gospel
of the grace of Christ with any other philosophy or religion. All such
attempts to redefine the gospel through syncretism met with his stern
warning:

> "But though we, or an angel from heaven, preach any other gospel
> unto you than that which we have preached unto you, let him be
> accursed." (Galatians 1:8)

The fact that Paul would bother with such a warning is proof that there will
be many "gospels" vying for the heart and soul of mankind. We simply do
not have the right to think that we can dismiss the difference between a true
faith and a false faith by blanketing that which is false with "love" and
"unity." Let the professing Christian be reminded of wolves in sheep's
clothing. Let the professing Christian be attentive that Satan still disguises
himself as an angel of light. Let all be careful to give somber and grave
consideration to the words of our Savior as found in the 16th chapter of
John:

> "...yea, the time cometh, that whosoever killeth you will think that
> he doeth God service." (John 16:2)

We purpose to clarify the absolutely irreconcilable differences between
standard Catholic dogma and the Christian gospel. And yet, even as we do
this, there appears to be a willingness on the part of some to dismiss all
doctrine and forge a religious consensus around the concepts of "love" and
"unity." With respect to the above quote by Paul, found twice in the first
chapter of Galatians, we compare the philosophy of this age:

> "I believe that we must respect a person's faith in God to the extent
> that we are relaxed that he will attain salvation in his own
> denomination or religion. As long as he responds to God to the best
> of his ability, he can be saved. As a Catholic I believe that salvation

comes through Jesus. But Jesus can express Himself to others in ways that are richer and deeper than I can imagine."[1]

We sincerely doubt the author of this quote reflects either historic or modern Catholicism. He certainly does not represent the Christian gospel. It awaits perhaps another book to delve into this third gospel which is neither Roman nor Christian.

Meanwhile, when one plays fast and loose with the biblical evidence of the gospel of Christ there needs to be criticism from knowledgeable Christians that no amount of "love" and "unity" can eliminate. Jesus Christ came with a profound message to mankind. Part of that message was that He is the way and the truth and the life. No one goes to the Father except through Him. In his zeal to jump on the bandwagon of ecumenism, the above quoted modern Roman Catholic writer seems willing to forsake the exclusivity of the gospel of Christ for his own ideas about salvation. This may represent new Catholic thinking on the doctrine of salvation. If so, we find it just as disturbing as the old hard line Council of Trent Romanism. Both are equally misunderstanding of the Bible and what it means to be a Christian.

---

[1] Manning, Michael, *Questions and Answers for Today's Catholics*, (Nashville: Thomas Nelson Publishers, ©1990) pg. 229

Chapter 3

Clearing the Air

THERE is a religious undercurrent in America which gives the impression that there are many "types" of Christianity. By this, it is not to be assumed that "types" represent shades of interpretation on difficult portions of the Bible, but rather, that Christianity is something of a giant umbrella under which sit any number of ideas and philosophies. Somehow the word "Christian" has become a catch-all phrase for anyone who has a remote interest in God or the Bible or Jesus Christ. Thus, in some minds, there are Lutheran Christians, Baptist Christians, Methodist Christians, Presbyterian Christians, Catholic Christians, Fundamentalist Christians, etc.. Now, while it is true that there may be Christians involved in many of these religious organizations, it does not follow that those involved are Christians for the fact of involvement. One can be a part of a denomination his entire life and not be a Christian. Christianity is not to be differentiated from non-Christianity by virtue of denominational affiliation. Christianity is rather a matter of one's relationship with God through the gospel of His Son, Jesus Christ, as revealed in the Bible.

It is wise to refrain from identifying the body of Christ on the basis of religious organizations. Christianity comes down to the individual and the gospel. What a person believes about the gospel of Jesus Christ is the question. This alone will be the basis upon which all mankind will be held accountable. Paul puts it succinctly:

> "In the day when God shall judge the secrets of men by Jesus Christ according to my gospel." (Romans 2:16)

Because of this, we are hard pressed to believe that Christianity can contain radically divergent views as to the nature of God, the mission and work of His Son, Jesus Christ, and the gospel message itself. In our analysis, one is either a Christian or not. It has been that way since the beginning of the gospel. The only bearing this has on the history of denominations is that Christians historically leave denominational structures that deny the essential truths of Christianity. To be sure, there is a history of fragmentation or hair-splitting which is not complimentary to Christianity but the Christian need not be defensive over this. The centrality of the gospel message has re-

20

mained the focus of even diverse Christians who differ in areas of freedom. We ask the reader to review Romans 14 for a good discussion of liberty within the bounds of Christianity.

When a Christian views the Body of Christ, which is *the Church*, he has in mind only those for whom Christ has died and subsequently made alive through the regeneration of the Holy Spirit. The Christian would shudder to think someone born into a denomination or religion is a Christian simply on that basis. Contrary to the teaching of other religions, sacraments cannot make one a member of the *Church*, the Body of Christ. One has to be born from above, by the free work of the Spirit, to be a part of the *Church* of Christ.[1]

In this study we must analyze if Roman Catholicism is but one more "color" on the rainbow of Christianity, or is it to be regarded as a non-Christian religion. Christians may practice their faith differently but they practice the same faith. It remains to be seen if the Roman Catholic faith is the same faith as that of the Christian.

Fundamentalism

The name "fundamentalism" has been used in a negative sense to label Christians who assert that Roman Catholicism is not Christianity. The label "fundamentalist" grew out of the Modernist/Fundamentalist controversy, which took place at the close of the 19th Century. Controversy is not something new to Christianity. Ever since Paul penned these words to Timothy in 2 Timothy 2:2, the Body of Christ has been cleansing itself from error.

> "And the things that thou hast heard of me among many witnesses, the same commit thou to faithful men, who shall be able to teach others also." (2 Timothy 2:2)

Yet, some Roman Catholic writers have enlisted the use of the term "fundamental" to describe what appears to them as a small and recent "wing" of evangelicalism. One is asked to conclude that "fundamentalism" is some sort of moss growing on the generally acceptable stone of American evangelicalism. One assessment that, "It is easy to find people who call themselves Evangelicals, who disdain fundamentalists, who are reasonably friendly with Catholics,"[2] helps us to understand what some Catholics hope

---

[1] *Ex opere operato*, the idea that sacraments bring about the new birth, is a Romish idea which we will discuss in our chapter on Baptism

[2] Keating, *Catholicism and Fundamentalism*, pg. 11

to be true but is not. What they hope is to give the appearance that Evangelicals side with them against the dreaded "fundamentalists" who are cast as the *only* ones standing against Rome. But, as we shall see, the word "fundamentalist" was historically a good word to describe Christian tenacity in holding onto the "fundamentals" of the faith.

We consider the Modernist/Fundamentalist controversy to have served a valuable purpose in God's protection of the gospel of Jesus Christ. This is essential for the safeguarding of the Church. Some wish to conclude that fundamentalism is a new kid on the block of Christianity. Some then ask, "If it is new, how can it have a mooring in Christianity?" Also, some may ask, "How is it that those defending fundamentalism are able to trace its teachings to the first century?" But wait! Let us not confuse the name given to a movement with the elements of the movement. We may agree that "fundamentalism" is a modern *term* but it is not a modern *movement*. It is correct to note the word "fundamental" is new to Church history. But to say that fundamentalism is,

> "...mainly an American phenomenon influenced by British evangeli-calism, and it would be difficult to trace its antecedents beyond that of the Great Awakening."[1]

is a mistake! Roman Catholics admit to at least five elements of fundamentalism. These are:

> "(1) the inspiration and infallibility of Scripture; (2) the deity of Christ, including his Virgin Birth; (3) the substitutionary atonement of his death; (4) his literal resurrection from the dead; and (5) his literal return in the Second Coming."[2]

We would ask the reader to examine whether the elements of fundamentalism are modern or recent to the history of the Church. The point is that such beliefs are not something new to Christianity. Neither are those who believe them to be considered as a fringe of Christianity. These fundamental principles represent a good part of biblical revelation and have served all generations in some form or another in ferreting out heresy.

We find it equally odd that some would find remotely tangential to the gospel varying interpretations of such things as "millennialism" or "dispensationalism." We know of not one Pre-Millennialist or Dispensationalist who would use their particular school of eschatology as a litmus test for

---

[1] Keating, *Catholicism and Fundamentalism*, pg. 18
[2] Keating, *Catholicism and Fundamentalism*, pg. 17

Christianity. It appears to us that some wish to create a group of "straw men" to blow away. If we are not careful, the straw man may be the use of the term "fundamentalist." Let us rather be honest and say the issue is between Christianity and Roman Catholicism. Christians throughout the centuries have been fighting heresies of all types. In the sense of the *elements* of fundamentalism, as listed above, both our Lord and His disciples would have born the name *fundamentalist*. Thus, we are disturbed by the effort of Rome to reclassify Christians into another category. It is not that *fundamentalists* believe this or that. Rather it is that *Christians* believe this or that!

We really think the issue is whether or not to resist attempts by Roman Catholics to include themselves under the umbrella of Christianity. Are the two systems of belief compatible within one Christianity? Can Rome warrant an entry into the Christian world without changing its belief system? We also need to clear the air. Those resisting Roman Catholicism are not some fringe group known as "fundamentalists." "Fundamentalism" was a very good word at one time. It described those who stood for the x αβ gospel of Jesus Christ in an uncompromising fashion.

The Belief System of Rome is Sacramentalism.

Sharper Focus

An additional undercurrent in America is to present the Christian community as nothing more than a massive tangle of theological subtleties—a sort of free-for-all, loose association whereby everyone does what is right in his ∧β own eyes. This is then contrasted with the alleged pristine beauty of order and hierarchical machinery which rules in the Roman Catholic community. But one need only look at the preponderance of differences which exist between the Catholics of America and Rome to sober the notion of lock-step Catholicism. Insofar as the Christian world is concerned, there is not the loose latitude that some hope for. When one sets aside the various liberal elements—which have long ago forfeited the Bible to higher criticism, humanism—and the fringe elements, there is, not surprisingly, unanimity when it comes to the gospel of Christ. The comments of James R. White are helpful with respect to Christian unity:

> "Surely there are many interpretations around—but does this mean that the Bible is not clear in its teaching? When one discounts all those interpretations that accept human traditions as authoritative, as well as those who reject the authority, inspiration, and the resultant inerrancy of the text, you don't have nearly as wide a field of interpretation as at first. And, when one begins to ask which of those interpreters left has given the most serious study to the

language and structure of the text as well as the historical back-grounds, the range gets even smaller."[1]

This is to say that there are various and in some cases serious differences of opinions among Christians concerning some portions of God's inspired text. Even Peter says that some things which Paul writes are hard to understand (cf., 2 Peter 3:15,16). However, it is an unwarranted assumption to say that because there are differences on such things as eschatology that there are many gospels!

Furthermore, it serves no purpose to say that there are some "Christians" who do not have a problem with Roman Catholicism. We would have every reason to question whether or not some are, in fact, educated enough to make such a decision! The gap between Roman Catholicism and Christianity is very severe. However, it takes more than a casual look to penetrate the depth of difference. Having done our homework, we do not hesitate to draw, what may appear to some, critical conclusions!

Some Catholics may wish to isolate those whom they view as a few cantankerous dissidents who have a grudge with Rome. It shall be our goal to repair some of the damage which may have resulted from this false bifurcation between *fundamentalism* and Christianity. We shall also main-tain that the "war" for truth is not being waged between a characterization of Christianity called *fundamentalism* and the so-called "Christian Catholic Community." Rather, the battle is between Christians and the Roman Catholic religion. Any attempt to camouflage this stark battle by denigrating it to a modern movement is a denial of Church history. This is illustrative of the problem we as Christians have with the Roman Catholic religion. We are sure it would be of great interest for men such as John Huss, John Calvin, Martin Luther, Theodore Beza, Philip Melanchthon and John Knox to find out that they were nothing more than forerunners of a 20th century group of fanatics called *fundamentalists*. We, as they, would prefer not to give up the title of our Lord and Savior. We simply wish to preserve the dignity of the gospel and be called "Christians."[2]

---

[1] White, James R., *The Fatal Flaw*, (Southbridge, MA: Crowne Publications, ©1990) pg. 11

[2] A "Christian" must be defined in terms of faith. Assurance of Heaven is the essence of the Christian's faith. Good works *necessarily* flow out of his faith. The finished work of Christ is the only object of his faith. The Bible is his sole authority and sufficient for knowledge of salvation and sanctification. His faith is not a frivolous confidence in religious affections. His is a dynamic trust that the righteousness of Jesus Christ is gained by faith *apart from works of any law*. It is this righteousness which will be the Christian's "grace gift" ensuring him Heaven. To add anything to his faith by way of merit or works defeats the gospel message. To subtract the necessity of fruit from his

continued on following page

We hasten to reiterate that no amount of restructuring of history will convince the Christian that this battle is a "new" battle waged between *fundamentalists* and Catholics. We urge the reader to examine the historical stakes in this struggle for the truth of God. Despite revisionist attempts to rewrite history and modern "gloss over" techniques by ecumenists, the war fought over the right meaning of the gospel continues as something ongoing! As such, this struggle will not go away by trying to minimize it through redefinition.

Roman Ritualism

Ask the common, everyday Roman Catholic what he/she believes to be true about Jesus Christ and the Bible and you will most likely receive a somewhat bewildered look followed by a hasty retreat into a defensive posture. Ask any professing Christian what he/she believes to be true about Jesus Christ and the Bible and you will be invited into a lively discussion with a follow-up invitation to his/her local Church. This does not prove that the Christian is an authority on everything in the Bible. But it does illustrate the willingness to show one's faith *from* the Bible. The Roman Catholic, on the other hand, will generally answer, "I'm a Catholic," or, "I was born a Catholic." When asking a Romanist to show forth his faith from the pages of the Bible one is soon left with an empty sense of sadness. It generally comes down to "the priest says this," or "the priest says that."

In the Roman Catholic religion the ritual begins at the cradle (infant baptism) and ends at the grave (extreme unction). Catholics are indoctrinated into their system from birth. With respect to this point, we should mention that the child growing up in Rome has little opportunity to learn the Scriptures. So complete is the indoctrination that Catholics are unable, even as adults, to explain their religion or defend it from Scripture. This brings up the question of Roman Catholic doctrine. From where do all the Romish doctrines emanate? As will be illustrated later, the Catholic religion relies heavily on the traditions of the early Church as well as the authority of the councils for their sources of authority. It has never been, and is not now today, *Sola Scriptura* (Scripture only) in the Catholic religion. This is not to

---

faith robs the gospel of its transforming power and reduces it to intellectual assent only. Between these two thieves (licentiousness and legalism) hangs the Prince of Glory!

A "Christian" must never be defined in terms of confidence in any religious system. Be it Romanism, Hinduism, Buddhism, Animism or Humanism, they all fall short of absolute confidence in the finished work of Christ for forgiveness of sin. The profound and yet simple words of John 6:47, "Truly, truly, I say to you, he who believes has eternal life," refer to Christ's mission on the cross. They do not, as the Romanist might say, refer to believing in a system of merit salvation!

say that Rome denies the Bible as the foundation for their religion. Later on we shall examine several examples of their interpretation of the Scriptures. But, let us be content for now to see that when it comes to biblical interpretation, a modern Catholic is very much like a school child who realizes that he has missed the bus to school. Off he goes trying to flag down the bus. Finally he succeeds in stopping the bus and gets on only to find he is on the wrong bus. Thus it is for those Catholics who are now taking some pride in the "availability" of the Bible. Christians can find little to cheer about upon hearing that Catholics are reading the Bible! As long as the doctrines of Rome remain above the Scriptures, there is little hope of reconciling the gospel of Jesus Christ with the Catholic religion.

Some Catholics rail against Christians, blasting them for not really interpreting the Bible literally except when it is to their advantage to do so.[1] Such accusations are, generally, much easier to allege than to prove. We will have opportunity to test the waters of John 6, among other texts of Scripture, to see if this allegation is valid.

Catholic Authority

Roman Catholics are quite right in their assumption that the Christian regards the Bible as the keystone of his faith. However, it is not B. B. Warfield or any other modern writer that informs Christians of the authority of the Scriptures. A Christian, by faith, trusts the Words of Christ given to His apostles and later written down. This Word of Christ has been recognized by the people of Christ throughout the ages. The key term is "recognized." Contrary to Roman Catholicism, which insists that the Church established the canon, the Christian believes that the Word of the Lord established the Church! This is a critical point in the Christian's departure from Rome. Christ spoke the truth to many men and women during His incarnation. However, it was only those to whom the Father revealed the Word of Christ who became His true followers. Not even Peter could have understood and *recognized* the truth of what Christ was saying unless the Father in Heaven revealed it to him (cf., Matthew 16:17, 11:25,26). The stage was set by Christ for the "recognition" of the truth by

---

[1] We find this scornful analysis of how Christians interpret their Bibles from Karl Keating. "Fundamentalists use the Bible to protect beliefs that are, in fact, antecedent to the Bible, which is interpreted so it justifies what they already hold, although most fundamentalists think what they believe comes straight out of the sacred text and that they are merely acknowledging its plain meaning. This confusion on their part is matched by one on the part of most nonfundamentalists, who think fundamentalists interpret Scripture in a strictly literal manner. This is incorrect." (Keating, *Catholicism and Fundamentalism*, pg. 26)

the will of the Father. This "recognition" of the truth is the way in which the Scriptures have come to us. Our Lord promised that He would send the Holy Spirit to guide men to the truth. It is indefensible to say that a Church council could sit in judgment on the very thing (the *Word of God*) by which it has been established. Think about the claim that the Catholic Church decided the text of Scripture. Did the Church exist before the Word? This would be impossible for it was the Word preached which formed the Church. Therefore the Word itself formed the Church. There was *recognized* truth quite apart from any Church council. This *recognition* of the truth was prior to the establishment of the canon. It can be no other way! The Word of Christ established His followers long before any council sat in judgment on it. It is this same Word received by those at Thessalonica from Paul.

> "For this cause also thank we God without ceasing, because, when ye received the word of God which ye heard of us, ye received [it] not [as] the word of men, but as it is in truth, the word of God, which effectually worketh also in you that believe."(1 Thessalonians 2:13)

It is the consistent theme of the Scriptures that God moved men by the Holy Spirit to write the truth about Jesus Christ. Examine 2 Peter 1:20,21 along with 2 Timothy 3:16. The writing of this truth and the *recognition* of it are under the authority of the Holy Spirit. This ensures a Bible that is free from error in its original autographs. Subsequent translations may contain minor error but not to the point where the message of truth is compromised. Christians believe that God superintends the administration of His economy when it comes to the Bible. While admitting the fallibility of the translators, Christians have been given the truth preserved by God and brought to light through the Holy Spirit.

It is at this juncture that we must not overlook our differences with Rome. Rome believes just the opposite. Rome holds a "rationale" belief in the infallibility of the Catholic religion. Instead of relying on the inner conviction of the Holy Spirit, the Roman Catholic falls back on his authoritative, infallible religion. We are hard pressed to see how blind faith in an institution is more rational than reading the Bible and believing it. The Romanist seems content to *not* measure everything according to the Word of God. This does not measure up well with the prayer of the Lord in John 17, wherein the Father might sanctify His own through the Word of Truth. The Christian arrives at doctrine through a careful examination of the Bible. We shall see many voices of authority in and throughout the Roman Catholic religion.

The Christian relies upon the Bible to the exclusion of all other sources of authority. In this sense the Christian is linked to the Words delivered to the earliest followers of our Lord. There is no safety in reliance on various Tribunals or councils of mere men who do not have apostolic authority. The battle cry of *Sola Scriptura* ever remains the unified voice of Christianity. "The Bible alone for faith and practice," is the Christian defense against councils. All Christians agree that unless a doctrine or practice can be proved from the Scriptures it is not mandatory to be believed or practiced. The decision for the resolution of differences among Christians is a matter for individual Church leadership and ultimately the conscience of each Christian.

Some would mock this position with discrediting language like "unalloyed Christian individualism" when describing individual Christian conscience. Such a description is not meant to be complimentary. It is rather a derogatory comment on what is not easily understood by Roman Catholicism. For the Christian, there is a point in his/her life where regeneration unto faith actually occurs. This is called "conversion" in biblical terminology (cf., Acts 15:1-3). We feel the terminology "personal" Savior may be overdone and may not be the best of terms to describe one's relationship with the Lord. But, nevertheless, the idea is the same. What could be more "personal" than coming to a point of faith where one believes that Jesus is the Christ and the Son of the living God? Herein lies the mystery to which Roman Catholicism cannot adhere. The Christian can harken to a point *when* he actually believed in the Lord for salvation. The Roman Catholic does not have contact with this kind of "personal" faith in the real *Person* of Christ. For the Catholic, there is no personal confidence in understanding the Word of God apart from hierarchy. To a large extent, the Catholic system of religion becomes a stumbling block in front of the simplicity of each individual's understanding of the Bible.

Chapter 4

Scripture Over the Church

FROM this point on we shall be examining exactly "what" the Roman Catholic religion holds to be true. We shall endeavor to quote the highest sources within the Roman hierarchy.

At the outset, we would have the reader understand why we consider the Christian and the Catholic positions to be diametrically opposed to each other in the most basic issues of truth. The reason these two systems cannot ever be reconciled is because the Christian and the Catholic have absolute contrary sources of authority to which they appeal for religious truth. The gap which exists between the Christian and the Muslim or the Mormon is no wider than that between the Christian and the Roman Catholic. It is the Christian position that the Bible and the Bible alone is the source of authority to which we can appeal for the truth of the revelation of God in matters pertaining to salvation. This is the doctrine of *Sola Scriptura*, i.e., the Bible alone. From this doctrine will come the complementary doctrine of salvation by faith alone, or *Sola Fide*. Christians believe that the Bible established the Church and the Church exists to obey the Lord through an obedience to His Word as found in the Bible. The Bible sits over the Church to protect the Church from the error to which all men are disposed in their reasoning. God established the Church through His infallible word. The Church is never to be considered infallible. Only the Word of the Lord is infallible and as such stands to correct and inform the Church—not vice versa. Clark Pinnock sums up for us the position we have believed:

"The text of Scripture must not be fused with the mind of the interpreter, whether that of church or individual. It is to stand over us. Denial of clarity reflects a refusal to be bound by Scripture and a determination to follow one's own inclinations. Whenever a church or a theologian takes it upon himself to define truth without reference to the objective authority of God's Word, he becomes demonically solipsistic. The Roman Catholic and liberal Protestant theologies are not so far apart as they seem at first glance. In one case the papal ego and, in the other, the theologian's are the lights which lighten Scripture. In each case something human is placed above Scripture. It is vital, therefore, for them to hold to the

solipsistic

obscurity of Scripture, lest its truth should break forth and challenge the interposed human authority. We have no right at all to place anything above God's Word. These 'Bibles to the second power' do not exist."[1]

We contrast this with the Council of Trent, in April, 1546.

"It also clearly perceives that these truths and rules are contained in the written books and in the *unwritten traditions, which, received by the Apostles from the mouth of Christ Himself,* or from the Apostles themselves, the Holy Ghost dictating, have come down to us, transmitted as it were from hand to hand. Following, then, the examples of the orthodox Fathers, it receives and venerates a feeling of piety and reverence all the books both of the Old and New Testaments, since one God is author of both; *also the traditions, whether they relate to faith or morals, as having been dictated either orally by Christ or by the Holy Ghost, and preserved in the Catholic Church in unbroken succession."*[2]

Lest the reader think that Vatican II may have altered the position of Rome on the authority of their traditions, we ask the reader to consider the following taken from the *Handbook for Today's Catholic*:

"The Second Vatican Council describes Tradition and Sacred Scripture as being 'like a mirror in which the pilgrim Church on earth looks to God' (Revelation 7). God's word of revelation comes to you through words spoken and written by human beings. Sacred Scripture is the Word of God 'inasmuch as it is consigned to writing under the inspiration of the divine Spirit,' (Revelation 9). Sacred Tradition is the handing on of God's Word by the successors of the Apostles. Together, Tradition and Scripture 'form one sacred deposit of the word of God, which is committed to the Church.'"[3]

One Roman Catholic writer states the case of the Roman Catholic succinctly:

"Catholics, on the other hand, say *the bible is not the sole rule of faith and nothing in the Bible suggests it was meant to be.* In fact, the Bible indicates it is not to be taken by itself. The true rule of faith is Scripture and Tradition, as manifested in the living teaching

---

[1] Pinnock, Clark, *Biblical Revelation*, (Chicago: Moody Press, ©1971) pp. 99-100

[2] Schroeder, H. J., *The Canons and Decrees of the Council of Trent*, (Rockford, IL: TAN Books, ©1978) pg. 17. From the 4th Session of Trent. Emphasis added

[3] *Handbook for Today's Catholic*, (Liguori, MO: Liguori Publications ©1978) pp. 24,25

authority of the Catholic Church, to which were entrusted the oral
teachings of Jesus and the apostles plus the *authority to interpret
Scripture rightly.*"[1]

We cannot for a moment minimize the huge differences which exist between
the Christian and the Catholic community at this juncture. It is a small
wonder that Catholicism looks different, worships differently, believes
differently and preaches a different gospel than the Christian gospel. Their
source of authority goes outside the revelation of the Bible and hence is
subject to the teachings of mere men.

With respect to this question of authority, it is not only the inclusion of
traditions that make up the Roman Catholic triumvirate of authority, but also
the ongoing authority of the Church found in the promulgations of the
councils as they interpret Scripture. Within this alleged Church authority is a
hierarchy upon which sits the infallible pope. The pope is the final authority
in matters of faith and doctrine. Hence, the light forbidden to individual
interpretation of the Bible is somehow vouchsafed to the pope of the Roman
Catholic religion. How ironic that the right given, by authority of the Bible,
whereby Christians may know and investigate firsthand the revealed will of
God is reserved, in the Roman religion, for a select few culminating in one
man.

We shall take up the issue of the infallibility of the pope in another chapter.
For now, we must consider the two claims of the Catholic apologist. The
first is the Roman claim that it has the authority to "declare" what is
inspired. The second is that "tradition" is to be considered on the same level
of authority as the Bible.

Who Inspired Whom?

It is the teaching of the Catholic community that the only way to satisfy the
intellect in believing that the Bible is inspired, is to swallow the Catholic
position. The Catholic position is that they have the authority to determine
which books belong in the canon of the text. The upshot of the Catholic
position is that Catholics are intellectually safer if they believe what the
"Mother Church" tells them to believe. The reason that this is the most
intellectually satisfying position is that the Catholic religious leaders are
inspired and sit in declaration on what else may be inspired. In other words,
Christ established an infallible Church from which came the inspired Word.
How did Christ establish this infallible "Church"? He allegedly did it

---

[1] Keating, *Catholicism and Fundamentalism*, pg. 134. Emphasis added

through His Word. But, we may ask, why was this Word trustworthy to begin with? The answer given is, "Because the Catholic religion said so." Thus, we have the startling claim that the Catholic religion decided on the inspiration of the Word! The Word, they say, did not determine the Church. The Church, they say, determined the Word. This, of course, is absolutely backward from the Christian position. The historic Christian position is that the Word gave formation and direction to the Church and lives ever to protect, guide and inform the Church.

For the Roman Catholic affirmations to be plausible, they have to build some straw men and set them on fire. Ridicule is cast upon those who cling to the inspiration of Scripture for reasons other than those of Rome. They are jeered as having to do so on the basis of habit, culture, family background or an unfounded claim, says Rome, to the inspirational nature of the Bible. This ridicule is not *because* one believes in inerrancy; rather *why* one holds to inspiration is held up for mockery. If someone holds to the inspiration of the Bible for reasons other than *because the Roman Catholic religion says so*, they are scorned. It is clear that Christians and Catholics not only radically disagree with the *extent* of and *source* of authority, but also the basic *reason* why the Scriptures are viewed as inspired. This is no small disagreement. The Catholic is convinced that a source outside of Scripture always has authority to both declare Scripture to be inspired and also add to it! The Christian finds the Bible as his one and only source of authority. The Scriptures are inspired because they are "God-Breathed." The Bible is found to give its own claim to such authority and inspiration. Lest the reader think that we are in some sense exaggerating this point of difference, let us ponder these words of the Roman apologist.

> "What about the Bible's own claim to inspiration? There are not many places where such a claim is made even tangentially, and most books in the Old and New Testaments make no such claim at all. In fact, no New Testament writer seemed to be aware that he was writing under the impulse of the Holy Spirit, with the exception of the author of Revelation."[1]

Before refuting this Catholic claim, we might ask some questions. If the Bible itself does not claim any special authority as coming from God, then does it deserve to be considered inspired? If the Bible lays no claim to inspiration and nothing in it carries the weight of special "God-Breathed" revelation, then why indeed should it be labeled "inspired" by anyone? Also, given the Catholic position that the Bible makes no such claim for itself, then on what basis or criteria did the Catholic religion decide that such and such a book would be part of an inspired canon?

---

[1] Keating, *Catholicism and Fundamentalism*, pg. 123

It really comes down to the issue of either trusting the Catholic religion or the internal claim of the Scriptures. But do the Scriptures claim for themselves such "God-Breathed" authority? The Christian answers a resounding *Yes!*

We agree heartily with Clark Pinnock who quotes James Orr:

> "It may surprise those who have not looked into the subject with care to discover how strong, full, and pervasive, the testimony of Scripture to its own inspiration is."[1]

We shall start by letting the Scriptures speak for themselves in four main passages which present a foundation for the self-authentication of the Bible as the inspired Word of God. The first passage is found in the third chapter of the second letter of Paul to Timothy.

> "But continue thou in the things which thou hast learned and hast been assured of, knowing of whom thou hast learned [them]; And that from a child thou hast known the holy scriptures, which are able to make thee wise unto salvation through faith which is in Christ Jesus. All scripture [is] given by inspiration of God, and [is] profitable for doctrine, for reproof, for correction, for instruction in righteousness: That the man of God may be perfect, throughly furnished unto all good works." (2 Timothy 3:14-17)

Paul uses the term here *theopneustic* which means literally "God-Breathed." Paul is not saying that the writers are inspired but rather *what they wrote* is inspired. It is the text, not the man, which is inspired. Paul understood that the Scriptures, which Timothy was raised upon, were in fact the deposit of "God-Breathed" words. This realization of inspiration existing for the Old Testament canon gives rise, in the New Testament, to equal footing for the words of Christ and the words of Paul. Paul quotes the words of Jesus in 1 Timothy 5:18;

> "For the scripture saith, Thou shalt not muzzle the ox that treadeth out the corn. And, The labourer [is] worthy of his reward."

The latter part of this verse is found in the words of our Lord as recorded in Luke 10:7. These words are put on a par with the Old Testament citation in the first part of the verse. Thus, the words of our Lord are placed in the category of "God-Breathed" by Paul in his writing to Timothy. This gives the New Testament writings a similar footing as the Old Testament insofar as inspiration is concerned.

---

[1] Pinnock, pg. 54

In 2 Peter 3:15,16 Peter places the writings of Paul on the same level that Paul had placed the writings of Luke when he says:

> "...even as our beloved brother Paul also according to the wisdom given unto him hath written unto you; As also in all [his] epistles, speaking in them of these things; in which are some things hard to be understood, which they that are unlearned and unstable wrest, as [they do] also the other scriptures, unto their own destruction."

Peter includes the writings of Paul as part of what he considers to be "the Scriptures." But what of the Roman Catholic claim that "no New Testament writer seemed to be aware that he was writing under inspiration"? Does this spell the death knell for the inspiration of the New Testament? We answer No! It is not necessary that a writer of Scripture be aware of anything other than that he spoke with authority the Words of God. Paul was absolutely convinced that he was carrying the authority entrusted to him by Christ (cf., 1 Corinthians 15:37,38 along with 1 Thessalonians 2:13). This apostolic authority, when inscripturated to the New Covenant community, was received as the inspired Word of God. Scripture carries with it its own authority and that authority is "received" or "recognized" by men. Men do not give the Scripture authority, they merely "recognize" it. Herein lies the difference between the Catholic and Christian community.

The notion that Scripture is not generated nor subject to the whim of men is given to us by Peter:

> "Knowing this first, that no prophecy of the scripture is of any private interpretation. For the prophecy came not in old time by the will of man: but holy men of God spake [as they were] moved by the Holy Ghost." (2 Peter 1:20,21)

It is intrinsic to the nature of revelation that it must carry a weight of its own, not a derived weight from a body of men. Men have not been given authority to invest into a collection of writings any importance which cannot be challenged by the next group of men who come along. There must be a supernatural character to the writings that declare for themselves such intrinsic value. The ability to place faith in such writings must also be controlled by the same authority. This is why the value of the Scriptures are not trusted or believed in by every one. What we are driving at is that it does not take a supernatural revelation to see that the Scriptures wish to authenticate themselves as the inspired Word of God. Scriptures do testify of their own inspiration, but that fact alone does not guarantee they will be believed. Belief in the content of the Scriptures must not be confused with the simple grasping that the Scriptures do validate themselves as the "God-Breathed" writings. For them to be believed requires the illumination of the

, intellect by the One who authored them in the first place. The same author of the writings reveals their witness as truth.

To further our case, we would ask the reader to consider the words of Jesus Christ as written in Matthew 5:17,18;

> "Think not that I am come to destroy the law, or the prophets: I am not come to destroy, but to fulfil. For verily I say unto you, Till heaven and earth pass, one jot or one tittle shall in no wise pass from the law, till all be fulfilled."

The "law" and the "prophets" of which Jesus spoke are the entirety of the Old Testament. Our Lord recognized the value of the Word and considered it to be the Word of His Father (cf., Mark 7:13). No one in the entirety of the New Testament had a higher view of the Old Testament writings, as the inspired Word of God, than did the Son of God. Witness His statement in John 10:35;

> "If he called them gods, unto whom the word of God came, and the scripture cannot be broken..."

It is important to understand that the Christian is in good company when he begins to partake of the doctrine of inspiration. The testimony of the Lord as to the veracity of the unbroken Word of the Old Testament is the pattern for our acceptance of the same authority imparted the New Testament Scriptures. We are encouraged to take such a posture by the fact that Paul raises Luke's writing to such an extent and that Peter raises Paul's writing onto the same plane. Taking as our pattern the Old Testament, which was recognized and received as authoritative by Jesus Christ and His apostles, we can better understand New Testament authority. Jesus left with His apostles the immediate charge of teaching and preaching all that they had heard and learned from Him (cf., Matthew 28). This task was to be carried out under the auspices of the Holy Spirit and the words that the apostles were to speak were pre-authenticated by the Lord to give gravity and weight to the apostles' mission. It would be the work of the Father through the Holy Spirit to prepare the hearts of those who would receive this word (cf., Acts 16). That which the apostles spoke originally would soon be written down and received. That which Christ spoke originally would be written down so as to safeguard the deposit of revelation from those who would distort the truth in the absence of those commissioned to safeguard it. Through a time process, guided and directed by the Holy Spirit, the full writings of the New Testament canon were "recognized" as coming into existence by those whom the Spirit of God had prepared to listen. In commenting on the role of men, in the writings of the Old Testament, James White captures the heart of "recognition":

"The role of the people of God in the formation of the Old Testament canon cannot be over-emphasized. It was not simply a group of crusty old men who sat down one day before a pile of would-be-canonical writings and decided, by vote or by lot, which would be included and which would not. God's people, as they experienced God's leadership and providence in the course of history, 'recognized the inherent inspiration and authority of the books of the Bible.' Certainly there was dissension and discussion about certain books—the so called 'anti-legomena'. But there is everything right in carefully examining, for example, Esther, to determine whether it should be canonical or not. God's people were not, by so doing, placing themselves as 'judges' over those materials. They were, rather, seeking to recognize that which was already done in God's providence. They sought to be custodians of the oracles of God and as such to be good stewards in not delivering to the rest of the world writings that did not live up to the standards and content of the inspired Writ. We shall see a very similar process taking place in the New Testament."[1]

Catholic Objections

We turn our attention now to the objections which may be raised by Catholic apologists to our understanding of inspiration. The Catholic does not like the idea of relying on the Holy Spirit to "impress" upon the mind that the Scriptures are inspired by God. They liken it to the way in which Christians seek guidance from the Holy Spirit in interpreting the Bible. But, in the first place, there is not a myriad of "Christian" interpretations as to who Christ is and what the gospel of Christ entails. The differences in various Christian interpretations of some things in the Bible should not be taken as a failure of the work of the Spirit to create an understanding of the basic truths of Christianity. One of the basic truths of Christianity is that the Bible is the inspired Word of God. To reject it as such is to create a human source of authority that sits in judgment on the Bible. This is something that the Holy Spirit forbids the Christian from doing. Besides, without the opening of the mind's understanding by the Holy Spirit there would be no apprehension of this truth. We cite Acts 16 where even a God-fearer, such as Lydia, had to have her heart opened to the words which Paul was speaking. We would ask the reader to consider 1 Corinthians 2:13f in this light also.

---

[1] White, James R., *Answers to Catholic Claims*, (Southbridge MA: Crowne Publications, ©1990) pp. 81, 82

We find it interesting that the Romanist would reject the "subjective" testimony of the Holy Spirit in determining that the Bible is the inspired Word of God. He does so while insisting that some men, somewhere, in some place, using their "reason," could determine which books were inspired. How would they know? Is this not a double standard? The leaders of the Catholic religion reserve for themselves the right to subjectively determine for the entire world both what constitutes the Bible and what is the interpretation of the Bible. To say that Christ founded the Word on the foundation of the Church is absolutely backwards and yet this is the Catholic claim. It is, evidently, to no avail that our Lord said: "Sanctify them through thy truth: thy word is truth" (John 17:17). Or that the writer to the Hebrews says: "For the word of God [is] quick, and powerful, and sharper than any twoedged sword, piercing even to the dividing asunder of soul and spirit, and of the joints and marrow, and [is] a discerner of the thoughts and intents of the heart" (Hebrews 4:12). Or that James says: "Of his own will begat he us with the word of truth, that we should be a kind of firstfruits of his creatures" (James 1:18). Passage upon passage on the primacy of the Word of God could be listed. And yet, the Catholic religion insists that Christ came to somehow establish a Church, presumably out of thin air, which would then make a determination as to what the Word of God might entail. Truly the tail wags the dog in the Romanist religion.

We read carefully their ultimate conclusion:

> "It reduces to the proposition that, without the existence of the Church, we could not tell if the Bible were inspired."[1]

We would assert just the opposite: *without the existence of the Word, there would be no Church.*

Before leaving this section, we would like to comment on a portion of Scripture. We ask the reader to consider the book of Jonah. Jonah is occasionally used to illustrate the Catholic religion's position of silence on the interpretation of "many biblical passages, readers being allowed to accept one of several understandings."[2] In the first place, we find this odd since the entire Catholic position rests on the "Mother Church" being the only one able to interpret the Bible correctly! Presumably, the Holy Spirit stopped short of giving the "Mother Church" too much authority when it comes to biblical interpretation. This coming from the same writer who one page earlier says,

---

[1] Keating, *Catholicism and Fundamentalism*, pg. 126
[2] Keating, *Catholicism and Fundamentalism*, pg. 129

"The Catholic believes in inspiration because the Church tells him to—that is putting it bluntly—and that same Church *has the authority to interpret the inspired text.*"[1]

We might ask, "What good is this alleged authority when, 'the Catholic Church is silent on the proper interpretation of "many biblical passages, *readers being allowed to accept one of several understandings.*'"[2] If the Romanist religion is able to be certain about the meaning of any one passage by way of "infallibility," then why not the rest? We find this interesting and revealing citation from a Roman Catholic priest which we think cements our point:

"Father (Francis X.) Cleary (S.J.), scripture scholar and professor in the Department of Theological Studies of St. Louis University, specializes in biblical theology of the Old Testament, writes, 'Many people think that the Church has an official 'party line' about every sentence in the Bible. In fact, only seven passages have been definitely interpreted. Even in these few cases, the Church is only defending traditional doctrine and morals. For example, Jesus' teaching in John 3:5 that we must be born of water and of the Spirit means that real ('natural') water must be used for a valid baptism. When Jesus, after instituting the Eucharist, commanded His disciples to 'Do this in memory of me' (Luke 22:19; 1 Corinthians 11:24), he meant to confer priestly ordination. Again, the power conferred on the apostles to bind and loose sins (see John 20:23) authorized them and their successors in the priestly office to forgive sins in God's name. These authoritative interpretations emphasize the biblical origins of sacramental life. (The three other defined texts are John 20:22; Romans 5:12 and James 5:14).'"[3]

Some Roman Catholics have a problem with the book of Jonah. In lamenting that "fundamentalists" do not take the Jonah episode as an allegory, we are told there is nothing to distinguish one interpretation over the other. The accusation is that "fundamentalists" have no *authority* to determine which is the correct interpretation. (It is already admitted that the Catholic Church is silent on the matter, although why an infallible "Church" will not give to her people the right answer is never answered). Perhaps if the Roman Catholic writers studied some of the rules for biblical interpretation they would arrive at the reason why Christians take the Jonah passage literally. One good reason to take the story of Jonah literally is the words of our Lord found in Matthew:

1 Keating, *Catholicism and Fundamentalism*, pg. 127. Emphasis added

2 Keating, *Catholicism and Fundamentalism*, pg. 129

3 Taken from *The Denver Catholic Register*, March 29, 1990, pg. 10

"For as Jonas was three days and three nights in the whale's belly; so shall the Son of man be three days and three nights in the heart of the earth." (Matthew 12:40)

Dictation

John Henry Newman's book, *On the Inspiration of Scripture*, is often quoted to show that the "dictation theory" of inspiration cannot be applied to Luke's prologue or some of Paul's writings. But it is difficult to respond to the word "dictation" when used in the context of inspiration. The term has to be defined before its validity can be ascertained. We would remind the reader that the Council of Trent used precisely this term when describing how the Catholic religion understands the inspiration of the Scriptures:

> "It (the Council) also clearly perceives that these truths and rules are contained in the written books and in the unwritten traditions, which, received by the Apostles from the mouth of Christ Himself, or from the Apostles themselves, the Holy Ghost *dictating*, have come down to us, transmitted as it were from hand to hand."[1]

Yet, here Catholicism has a bone to pick with those who hold to the "dictation" theory. We might ask, "Who speaks for Rome?" at this point. Either way, there have been direct attempts to explode the myth of inspiration through dictation by quoting 1 Corinthians 1:14-16 where Paul admits that he (Paul) could not remember exactly who or how many people he may have baptized at Corinth. To argue for "dictation" must mean that God temporarily forgot how many people Paul baptized, since God was whispering in Paul's ear as he was writing. Yet, we know of no theory of "dictation" that supposes that God becomes the person who is writing while that person slips off into a trance. Paul does not say that God does not remember. Under "inspiration" of the Lord, Paul is being honest with the Corinthians to prove a greater point on the issue of baptism. The inspiration of the Bible takes into consideration the personality and earthly experiences of the writers. They are not put to sleep and then overwhelmed by the Lord. Rather, the Lord superintends the writing to convey His truth while not betraying the style and personality of the person with whom he is dealing.

Canon

It has long been the Catholic position that the "Mother Church" gave birth to the Bible or else the so-called Protestants would not even have a Bible.

---

[1] Schroeder, pg. 17. Emphasis added

History paints a different picture. The establishment of the canon of the text took place over a period of time and was not put together by Catholic religious leaders. The canon emerges in Church history as a by-product of its being recognized as inspired. With this the early Church fathers are in agreement. Long before an official council formally recognized the canon, the books themselves were entertained as having inspired authority. Pinnock again, is helpful to us on this point:

"The early Fathers and apologists believed without hesitation in the divine inspiration of Scripture, and apparently considered it self-evident and incontrovertible. The fact of inspiration was never in doubt.

"Barnabas (1st century) cites Scripture as 'the Spirit of the Lord proclaims.'

"Clement of Rome (1st century) calls Scripture 'the true utterances of the Holy Spirit.'

"Athenagoras (2nd century) said, 'The Spirit using them (the biblical writers) as his instruments, as a flute player might blow a flute.'

"Irenaeus (2nd century) says the Scriptures are 'divine' and 'perfect,' being uttered by God. His view of plenary, verbal inspiration is impeccable.

"Tertullian (c. 200) equates scriptural teaching and true doctrine: 'For it is better to be ignorant when God has not spoken, than to acquire knowledge from man and be dependent upon his conjectures.'

"Clement of Alexandria (c. 200) says that all Scripture was spoken by the mouth of the Lord.

"Origen (3rd century) refused to accept 'a third scripture' (in addition to the two Testaments) because it would not be 'divine' like them. God himself is the Author of Scripture.

"St. Cyril of Jerusalem (4th century) said: 'The certitude of our faith does not depend on reasoning based on whim, but on the teaching drawn from the Scriptures.'

"Jerome (4th century): 'Ignoratio Scripturarum ignoratio Christi est (Ignorance of the Scripture is ignorance of Christ).'

"Theophilus of Alexandria: 'It would be acting according to demoniac inspiration to follow the thinking of the human mind and to think that there could be anything divine apart from the authority of the Scriptures.'

"Augustine (5th century) refers Scripture to 'the revered pen of the Spirit.' In a letter to Jerome he says, 'For I confess to your charity that I have learned to defer this respect and honour to those Scriptural books only which are now called canonical, that I believe most firmly that no one of these authors has erred in any respect in writing.'"[1]

From this we see a steady tide of desire to formally recognize the accepted writings as the canon of Scripture. White clarifies:

"It can be seen that prior to the Council of Nicea, there was a clear movement toward what we consider to be the modern New Testament canon. Though some books were less widely accepted than others, the vast majority of the material that comprises the 27 books was already in place and functioning as canon Scripture. It is important to note at this juncture that long before any 'church council' made any decisions about a 'canon' of Scripture, the Scriptures themselves were functioning with full and complete authority in matters of doctrine.

"Formalization took place first at the Council of Hippo in 393. The proceedings of this council are not extant, but its canon list was repeated as 'Canon 47' of the Third Council of Carthage in 397. The first of these was primarily a local council, overseen by Augustine. Carthage was a provincial council. The same canon is repeated in the sixth council of Carthage in 419, and is found to be identical, even in order, with the current English New Testament canon. As will be seen below, the men who made up these councils did not hold to many of the doctrines that Rome today believes to be 'inviolable.' They were not Roman Catholics in any proper definition of the term, and the church that existed at that time cannot logically be considered to be identical to, or the immediate ancestor of, modern Romanism."[2]

In closing this section it is necessary to respond to the allegation so casually made that, "...the Protestant Bible is an incomplete Bible."[3] We would rec-

---

[1] Pinnock, pp. 150, 151

[2] White, *Answers to Catholic Claims*, pp. 91-94

[3] Keating, *Catholicism and Fundamentalism*, pg. 132

ommend Boettner's summary of the apocryphal books.[1] However, the accusation that the Reformers removed the books of Maccabees because they teach the doctrine of purgatory is absolutely unfounded. I have mentioned as much in a published booklet on Roman Catholicism:

"Much of Rome's support for purgatory comes from the Apocryphal (hidden, obscure) writings. Rome accepts 2 Maccabees as part of the authoritative canon, whereas the Jews and the New Testament do not. Nevertheless, we cite the relevant section from Maccabees and let you judge whether it remotely teaches purgatory.

"'And the day following Judas (Maccabees) came with his company, to take away the bodies of them that had been slain, and to bury them with their kinsmen, in the sepulchers of their fathers. And they found under the coats of the slain some of the donaries of the idols of Jamnia, which the law forbiddeth to the Jews; so that all plainly saw, that for this cause they were slain. Then they all blessed the just judgment of the Lord, who had discovered the things that were hidden. And so betaking themselves to prayers, they besought him, that the sin which had been committed might be forgiven. But the most valiant Judas exhorted the people to keep themselves from sin, forasmuch as they saw before their eyes what had happened, because of the sins of those who were slain. And making a great gathering, he sent twelve thousand drachmas of silver to Jerusalem for a sacrifice to be offered for the sins of the dead, thinking well and religiously concerning the resurrection. For if he had not hoped that they that were slain should rise again, it would have seemed superfluous and vain to pray for the dead. And because he considered that they who had fallen asleep with godliness, had great grace laid up for them. It is therefore a holy and wholesome thought to pray for the dead that they might be loosed from Sin (2 Maccabees 12:39-45, *Douay-Rheims Version*).'

"We observe that the people in question were guilty of idolatry, which to Rome is a mortal sin worthy of hell, not purgatory. Also, nowhere is there a mention of any dead undergoing the pains of fire or torment for their sins. Even Rome's extra-Biblical evidence does not provide a foundation for the superstructure she builds on 'purgatory.'"[2]

---

[1] Boettner, pp. 80-87

[2] Zins, Robert M., *Salvation By Grace Or Merit?* (booklet) (St. Croix Falls, WI, ©1988) pp. 23, 24

Chapter 5

Who Speaks for Rome?

A SIDE from biblical and historical difficulties, Roman Catholicism cannot possibly be placed over the Bible due to the fact that Rome has too many voices claiming to speak with authority.

While discussing the question of inspiration and authority, it would be beneficial to show forth an example of the difference of opinions within the Roman Catholic community. Who really speaks for Rome? It appears to us that as men in authority change, so changes the theology of Rome. Robert L. Saucy has this to say about the Catholic theologian Hans Kung:

> "Despite the revocation of his status as an official Catholic theologian in December of 1979, Hans Kung continues as one of the most prominent and influential forces within the Roman Catholic church."[1]

Kung's influence on the Catholic community is undeniable. And yet his view of Scripture is anything but the teaching of the Council of Trent. It appears that a shift in thinking, away from the conservative Trent, served as a necessary prelude to the extremes of both Hans Kung and Karl Rahner. Saucy's citation of Raymond Brown, a preëminent Catholic theologian, is helpful for us to grasp the shift in Rome from conservative inspiration to modernistic thinking when it comes to the text of Scripture:

> "Signs of a change in Rome's stance toward critical biblical studies appeared in 1941 when the Biblical Commission 'condemned an overly conservative distrust of modern biblical research.' The Magna Charta for so-called progress in biblical studies came two years later in 1943 with the encyclical of Pius XII, *Divine Afflante Spiritu*. According to the Catholic biblical scholar Raymond Brown, in this statement the church 'made an undeniable about-face in attitude toward biblical criticism. The encyclical ...instructed

---

[1] Lewis and Demarest, *Challenges to Inerrancy*, (Chicago: Moody Press, ©1984) pg. 218. From an article by Robert Saucy

Catholic scholars to use the methods of a scientific approach to the Bible that had hitherto been forbidden to them. Within about ten years teachers trained in biblical criticism began to move in large numbers into Catholic classrooms in seminaries and colleges, so that the mid-1950's really marked the watershed. By that time the pursuit of the scientific method had led Catholic exegetes to abandon almost all the positions on biblical authorship and composition taken by Rome at the beginning of the century.'"[1]

An example of the teaching of Hans Kung is given below in an effort to show the rift existing within the Catholic community on this one question of inspiration. We would certainly not advocate the views of Hans Kung nor do we say they are the views of the Roman See. But they are the teachings of one of Rome's most influential writers.

"Thus the human weakness, autonomy, and historicity of the biblical writers remain completely untouched. They are never at any time made inerrant, almost superhuman: which would mean that they were not really human at all, but tools, without will and without responsibility. The operation of the Spirit excludes neither defects nor faults, excludes neither concealment nor dilution, neither limitation nor error. The testimonies of the New Testament, however much they all proclaim the God who acts on us through Jesus Christ, are neither uniform nor of equal value; there are brighter and darker, more clear and less clear, stronger and weaker, more original and more derivative testimonies: all in all, supremely variable testimonies, which can diverge, contrast and—up to a point—contradict one another."[2]

This quotation is representative of modern Catholic scholarship when centered on the inspiration of the Bible. One can readily see Kung does not hold to a view of inspiration even consonant with historic Catholicism.

Saucy's introduction to Karl Rahner is even more flattering:

"Karl Rahner stands as a giant among Catholic theologians, respected both inside and outside of the Roman church. When both the range and depth of his writings are considered, few theologians can be considered his peer. He has written on a vast array of subjects, many of which are not strictly theological. Nevertheless his primary interest has been contemporary theological problems, which he

---

[1] Lewis and Demarest, pg. 217
[2] Lewis and Demarest, pp. 224, 225

confronts with true profundity. His theology is marked by a tendency to affirm the essential traditional ideas while presenting them in new and creative forms. His thinking is truly systematic, with his view of God and His revelation being intrinsic to all of theology."[1]

And what precisely is Karl Rahner's view of inspiration? We give you below Rahner's comments on the first chapters of Genesis:

"How is one to conceive of this revelation to the 'first parents,' when they lived perhaps two million years ago, originated from the animal world by evolution and so must be imagined as 'primitive' beings? And yet they are supposed to recognize the path of 'supernatural salvation...' Furthermore what is one to make of this account if, with some justification, one assumes a state of polygenism with regard to the origins of mankind?"[2]

This is a far cry from the Christian understanding of inspiration and we might add the historic concept of inspiration taught by the early Church. It does, however, represent another modern Catholic scholar. We hasten to add that the views expressed by both Rahner and Kung are meant by them as a correction and a deepening of understanding of the Word of God. Both men seek to influence the Catholic Church away from the prejudice of the past toward a newer and better understanding of inspiration. They use the "system" against the "system." The teaching of the Catholic Church is always relative to the office holders in the Church. Thus, at any given point in time the relativistic truth can be expressed authoritatively. Without contradiction, it is alleged, the Catholic Church can make mistakes as the deeper revelations surface in the course of time. This is why Kung can say: "the errors of the ecclesiastical teaching office in every century have been numerous and indisputable."[3] This is altogether different from Karl Keating who has stated, "Christ's Church, to do what he said it would do, had to have the note of infallibility."[4] All three claim to speak for Rome as does the Council of Trent. Which one is the right source of authority? The only thing all agree upon is the authority of the Church over the Scriptures to shape them in interpretation and limit them to the desires of the Roman religion. Herein lies the precise danger we spoke of earlier. What are we to think if the forces of Rahner and Kung become the "indefectible" or "infallible" teachers of the Roman Catholic religion? We must deny the authority of

---

[1] Lewis and Demarest, pg. 227

[2] Lewis and Demarest, pg. 228

[3] Lewis and Demarest, pg. 245

[4] Keating, *Catholicism and Fundamentalism*, pg. 125

such men to make ruin of the doctrine of inspiration and in so doing we equally deny the original heresy that starts this fire ablaze, namely that the Church is over the Word! Saucy's choice of quoting Cullmann helps us to understand the absolute necessity of abhorring any undermining of the authority of the inspired Word of God:

> "There is an apostolic tradition which is norm because it rests upon eyewitnesses chosen by God, and because Christ speaks directly in it, and there is a post-apostolic tradition which is a valuable help for the understanding of the divine Word, but is not to be regarded as a norm. While accepting humbly the exegetical and dogmatic directives of the Church and its teachers, we must be ready to set ourselves directly before the testimony of the apostles, as the apostles themselves were confronted directly with the divine revelation (Gal. 1:12), without any intermediate interpretation."[1]

TRADITION vs. "tradition"

We come now to the second aspect of the Catholic claim vis-à-vis that "Tradition" (as defined by Rome) is on a par with scriptural authority. By "Tradition," Rome does not mean the tawdry traditions of men. Rome readily admits that there are, overthrown in Scripture, those who use their own tradition to escape the teachings of God. Rome wants to put as much distance between her teachings and these "traditions of deceit" as possible. So, for Rome, there is the bad tradition which is loudly decried in the Bible, and the good "Tradition" spelled with a capital 'T'! Rome is the depository of this good "Tradition," which may be defined as follows:

> "Tradition means the teachings and teaching authority of Jesus and, derivatively, the apostles. These have been handed down and entrusted to the Church (which means to its official teachers, the bishops in union with the Pope). It is necessary that Christians believe in and follow this Tradition as well as the Bible (Luke 10:16). The truth of the faith has been given primarily to the leaders of the Church (Ephesians 3:5), who, with Christ, form a foundation of the Church (Ephesians 2:20). The Church has been guided by the Holy Spirit, who protects this teaching from corruption (John 14:16)."[2]

Inherent within this definition of Tradition is the Roman Catholic commitment to apostolic succession. Whereas the historic Christian position would

---

[1] Lewis and Demarest, pg. 244
[2] Keating, *Catholicism and Fundamentalism*, pg. 137

stop at the teachings of Jesus and His apostles, the Romanist religion does not. Rather than allowing the Word of God to speak over and over again, through the teaching of Jesus and His apostles, the Catholic Church carries on into the future both the teachings and the authority of succeeding generations to make new teachings authoritative. The net result is the assumption that the authority of Jesus and His apostles was handed on to men who would then speak and write with the same authority. The Christian shows allegiance to the one Word delivered by the one Authority for all time. The Catholic shows allegiance to many more authorities throughout the centuries. These writings are the capital "T" of the Catholic Traditions. So then, the question is refined down to the point at hand. Did Christ give to His Church only the authoritative writings (the Bible) which speak over and over again so as to rule and control the Church? Or, did Christ give authority to men to pass along to succeeding generations who would write a trail of words adding new Scriptures throughout the years? In short, is the authority in the man or in the Word? The Catholic says the man. The Christian says the Word. In all this, the Catholic is convinced that the Word itself gives the authority to the man. The Christian objects. The two views cannot be reconciled.

What Says the Word?

Roman Catholics are taught that John 20:31 is *the* passage, along with 2 Timothy 3:16, upon which Christians rely for proof that the Bible alone is the sole rule of faith. So, they attempt to disassemble them and put them back together as supporting Rome. It is an accurate observation that Christians believe the Bible contains everything one needs to believe to be saved. We deny, however, the claim that Christians believe "the whole of Christian truth is found within its pages."[1] There is certainly "truth" found outside the written Word of God. None of this truth would add to what God has deemed necessary for salvation. Also, we are perplexed at the accusation that "anything extraneous to the Bible is simply wrong or hinders rather than helps one toward salvation."[2] To set the record straight, Christians believe all that is necessary to be saved is found in the Scriptures. Also, Christians believe all that is necessary to be sanctified unto God is found in the Bible. Also, Christians believe the Bible is the only reliable source of authority when keeping in check the formulation of doctrines and the setting forth of authority by men. In this sense the Bible is sufficient! John 20:30,31 supports and teaches the sufficiency of Scripture for the knowledge of salvation.

---

[1] Keating, *Catholicism and Fundamentalism*, pg. 134
[2] Keating, *Catholicism and Fundamentalism*, pg. 134

"And many other signs truly did Jesus in the presence of his disciples, which are not written in this book: *But these are written, that ye might believe that Jesus is the Christ, the Son of God;* and that believing ye might have life through his name." (John 20:30-31, emphasis mine)

A typical Roman Catholic understanding of this verse concludes: "The verse from John's Gospel tells us only that the Bible was composed so we *can be helped to believe* Jesus is Messiah."[1] This, however, is not what John has said. Let the reader make his own decision after reading the text.

2 Timothy 3:16 is an important verse to Christians as we have already mentioned. Let us visit the verse again to refresh our memory:

"All scripture [is] given by inspiration of God, and [is] profitable for doctrine, for reproof, for correction, for instruction in righteousness: That the man of God may be perfect, throughly furnished unto all good works." (2 Timothy 3:16-17)

Catholics wish to minimize the impact of this verse by saying,

"To say that all inspired writing 'has its uses' is one thing; to say that such a remark means that only inspired writing need be followed is something else."[2]

This is, in our opinion, begging the question. The text clearly states that the Scriptures, when believed (understood from context), have the effect of equipping the man of God adequately for every good work. It is highly gratuitous to say that something more must be necessary. What "good work" would the Catholic envision for which the Scriptures would not be able to adequately prepare a man?

A more serious challenge comes from the logic of John Henry Newman who takes the position that this verse would work against the New Testament as sole rule of faith since the Scriptures to which Paul refers are the Old Testament books. Thus, it is deduced that the New Testament is not necessary if Timothy was to have been instructed out of the Old Testament. But this is bringing foreign and extraneous thoughts to the passage. Paul was commending Timothy for his faithfulness to the inspired Word of God. This Word was sufficient as a guide to the faithfulness of God in sending His son as well as bringing salvation to Israel and all those who followed

---

[1] Keating, *Catholicism and Fundamentalism*, pg. 135. Emphasis added

[2] Keating, *Catholicism and Fundamentalism*, pg. 136

YHWH. It is ridiculous to say that the New Testament (the fulfillment of the Old) is unnecessary because Timothy was made wise unto salvation by giving careful attention to the Old. Both are the revealed will of God. Paul did not have in mind the cancellation of the New any more than he would have us to forget God's faithful dealing with His people in the Old. As the seed gives forth the fruit so does the Old make way for the New! As Timothy revered the Old Testament, he would be called upon to do likewise to the revelation of Christ as found in the New Testament. There is not a hint of insufficiency in the Old or the New.

Keating makes a rather startling statement with regard to the Bible's testimony of its own sufficiency. According to Keating, "The Bible actually denies that it is the complete rule of faith."[1] There are three passages which the Catholic uses to support such an outstanding claim. They are: John 21:25; 2 Timothy 2:2 and 2 Thessalonians 2:15. Let us examine all of these carefully and see if the contention can be maintained.

John 21:25 reads as follows:

> "And there are also many other things which Jesus did, the which, if they should be written every one, I suppose that even the world itself could not contain the books that should be written."

From this we are asked to deduce that the Bible claims it is not sufficient or complete as our rule of faith. But why not? It does not follow that just because Jesus could have had more written under inspiration, that what He has written is insufficient! That is tantamount to saying that one cup of arsenic is not sufficient to kill the body because there are many more types and kinds of poison which could have been used but were not. We might also add that what is given is sufficient. James tells us to "receive with meekness the engrafted word, which is able to save your souls" (James 1:21). Peter tells us that we were born again through the living and abiding Word of God. (cf., 1 Peter 1:23). Paul thanks God for the Thessalonians because they became imitators of Paul having received the Word in much tribulation. (cf., 1 Thessalonians 1:5,6,8). Throughout the New Testament there is not a *lack* of the Word. Rather, there is an emphasis on *doing* the Word. The central feature is an exhortation to understand better what has been given to the believer in Christ and to protect the *enough given* from unscrupulous men who would distort the truth revealed.

The next two passages may be taken together as the hinges upon which the Roman door of Tradition swings. They are 2 Timothy 2:2 and 2 Thessalonians 2:15. They read as follows:

[1] Keating, *Catholicism and Fundamentalism*, pg. 136

"And the things that thou hast heard of me among many witnesses, the same commit thou to faithful men, who shall be able to teach others also." (2 Timothy 2:2)

"Therefore, brethren, stand fast, and hold the traditions which ye have been taught, whether by word, or our epistle." (2 Thessalonians 2:15)

The contention is that the Bible is not the sole rule of faith because Paul tells Timothy to teach that which he "heard" from Paul. The Catholic wishes us to know that the text does not say: "teach that which he read" from Paul. Somehow Acts 2:42 is supposed to lend strength to the notion that we can differentiate between the "writings" of Paul and the "teachings" of Paul. In Acts, the brethren were devoting themselves to the apostles' "teaching." Furthermore, it is assumed by the Catholic religion that the "traditions" of which Paul writes in 2 Thessalonians are to be considered outside the closed canon of Scripture. This is maintained even though the verse itself organizes the content of the tradition to be in concert with the teaching of Paul whether spoken or written! The fact that something is given orally by the apostles does not substantiate the Catholic notion of Tradition outside the canon. It simply does not follow that "oral" transmission of the truth of the gospel of Christ is a compelling reason to suppose a body of Tradition which is allegedly separate from the Bible itself.

This whole concept of Tradition is elusive. What are these teachings that have been supposedly handed down throughout the centuries from the mouth of Christ? Indeed, where can we find such a body of literature? The answer to these questions is given to us from Rome by way of the magisterium. The magisterium is the official teaching authority of the Roman Catholic religion. It consists of bishops and cardinals, but ultimate authority has been given to the pope. It is in the magisterium of the Catholic religion where these Traditions are given form and substance. From time to time, the magisterium will pronounce upon a certain doctrine as having the full weight of Christ's authority. The proclamation of the Assumption of Mary is said to be a part of the oral Tradition of Christ which is now to be believed among the faithful. The veneration of Mary is another Catholic Tradition which is claimed to have equal authority as the Bible.

One cannot fully grasp the concept of Tradition in the Romanist system until one understands that the Catholic religion has proclaimed herself to be Christ on earth. When Rome speaks, Christ speaks. It is not surprising that the Romanist will claim for himself Tradition as part of the inspiration of Christ if the Catholic religion says so. None of the above mentioned texts remotely support the distinction between what Paul "said" orally and what Paul "wrote." The entire idea of a Tradition which has come down to us in the form of various Roman Catholic dogmas is indefensible from a Christian perspective. Yet we are to understand from the Catholic perspective that the religion of Rome is "non-correctable" since it has assumed the position of Christ on earth. The Catholic view and the Christian view can never be reconciled!

It is this critical assumption of the Catholic theologians which makes it almost impossible to bring the Catholic religion into conformity to the Bible. Subilia is helpful to us in citing the stark reality of Rome as evidenced at the disputation of 1536 at Lausanne:

> "The Church (Catholic) is both prior to and more potent than Scripture. This means that the Church is before Scripture and of more authority than Scripture. For the Church is the body of Jesus Christ."[1]

Subilia goes on to lament:

> "What is so perplexing in all the course of Catholic tradition is this too high exaltation of the ecclesiastical instruments till they seem to usurp the place of him who wields them, this too fluid continuity, this too easy, too unrestricted—one is tempted to say too irreverent—passage from the Lord to his human mediators, this too rigid, too logical sequence, which drains the essential dialectical tension from the relationships of God and man, imprisons the truth of God in a legalist straight-jacket and objectivizes God in the Church, in the magisterium and in dogma, and encloses him (as in a capsule) inside the sacred institution, its system and its function."[2]

The Christian must understand that Rome has taken the tool of God's revelation and fashioned it into God Himself. The Roman religion has become Christ. The magisterium speaks as though Christ was here now and speaking through it! Against this is the simple, and yet profound belief, that when a Christian holds his Bible he is lacking nothing to make him wise unto salvation and sanctification. The Bible is sufficient and represents all that Christ has for His Bride, the Church. The Christian does not demean the use of "tradition" in its proper place. We agree with Pinnock's overview of the importance of historical biblical interpretation:

> "While Scripture indeed has a normative authority shared by nothing else, it is not true that reason, tradition and conscience play no role

---

[1] Subilia, Vittorio, *The Problem of Catholicism*, (Great Britain: SCM Press, Ltd., ©1964) pg. 128. From *Il Problema del Cattolicesimo*
[2] Subilia, pg. 135

in the exercise of that authority. We read as intelligent men in a modern society. That is, we do not come to Scripture de novo. We stand on the shoulders of Christians before our time who reflected long upon God's Word. Peter Berger points out:

"'The fundamental questions of theology have been passionately considered for at least three thousand years. It is not only insufferable arrogance to think that one can begin theology in sovereign disregard of this history, it is also extremely uneconomical. It seems rather a waste of time to spend, say, five years working out a position, only to find that it has already been done by a Syrian monk in the fifth century.'

"To neglect tradition is often to fall prey to sectarian errors. He who ignores history is compelled to repeat history's mistakes. Tradition is an important commentary on the Bible. The sola scriptura principle does not exclude a respectful listening to the wisdom of the past. For we stand in a community of faith and cannot leap over two thousand years of Christian history in disregard of the prodigious labors already done. A careful, though critical, hearing is due the testimony of tradition because, despite heresies and declensions, there is a real doctrinal continuity in her history."[1]

In this posture, the Christian becomes correctable from *historical exegesis* of the Bible and also sets the Bible in its proper positioning. It stands above the Church which serves Christ through obedience to it. The gates of Hell will not prevail against the Church of Jesus Christ because He has given the truth of His Word to protect it! The Catholic religion is blind to this order of authority as evidenced by the writings of some modern Catholic theologians and the intrusion of the magisterium upon the supremacy of the Bible.

We find the Roman Catholic use of Acts 17:11 helpful in pointing out the blindness which exists among Catholics as to the divine order of authority. In the book of Acts, Luke recounts for us the story of Paul and Silas as they were sent away at night from Thessalonica to Berea. Upon arriving in Berea, Paul went into the synagogue of the Jews. Luke preserves for us the reaction of the Berean Jews in Acts 17:11-12;

"These were more noble than those in Thessalonica, in that they received the word with all readiness of mind, and searched the scriptures daily, whether those things were so. Therefore many of them believed; also of honourable women which were Greeks, and of men, not a few." (Acts 17:11,12)

---

[1] Pinnock, pg. 118

What did the Berean Jews examine? No doubt the answer is given to us earlier in the chapter where Luke tells us Paul reasoned with the Thessalonians from the Scriptures explaining and giving evidence that Christ had to suffer and rise again from the dead. Thus, wherever Paul went, he took with him the Old Testament and showed that the Jesus he preached was the Christ of God! The Berean Jews examined Paul from the Scriptures. The Scriptures were used as their source of authority. If what Paul said could not be supported or defended from the established authority he was to be rejected. The "norm" was Scripture and the apostle was under the scrutiny of the Jewish community as to whether or not his preaching could withstand the litmus test of the Word! Against this understanding of Acts 17 is the Catholic apologist. Sensing the obvious destruction of his own understanding of the Catholic religion being above the Word, at least one Catholic writer has this to say:

"What really happened is that these people first had been taught Christianity orally and now checked to see if its claims matched the Old Testament prophecies. This verse does not mean one uses the Bible as a checklist for all Christian doctrines."[1]

We will let the reader decide if this contention has any credibility. There is no other past record of the Bereans having been taught the gospel orally. Furthermore, Paul was teaching them the gospel orally and the Bereans were "checking it out" using nothing but the Bible!

We leave this discussion about authority with the sincerest hope that the Christian will have been better educated into the realities of the Roman Catholic world. We have endeavored in this book to keep track of two essential platforms. The first is an accurate portrayal of Catholicism. The second is the absolute irreconcilable differences which exist between Romanism and Christianity.

We continue our investigation by an analysis of the "bridge" which Catholics insist links their current doctrines with the apostolic doctrines of the first century. This "bridge" is something they refer to as the "development of doctrine."

What Says the Magisterium?

It is an inescapable fact of Roman Catholic teaching that the Bible alone is not the sufficient guide in matters pertaining to salvation and sanctification.

---

[1] Keating, *Catholicism and Fundamentalism*, pg. 140

The following, extremely assertive comment, is revealing.

> "Lloyd Jones' trouble, the trouble with all fundamentalists, is that he labors under the *misconception* that Scripture has the last word and that the Tradition built on oral teaching counts for nothing."[1]

Armed with this presupposition, the Catholic attempts to justify the introduction of Catholic religious beliefs by way of something which they call the 'development of doctrine.' By this terminology, the Catholic means a number of things. In the arena of application, it is a catch phrase which gives the Catholic religion authority 'to mature doctrines' to fit any particular period of history. The Roman apologist is quick to point out that the 'essence' of the doctrine does not change, just the clearing up of the obscurity of the doctrine. Thus, we are led to believe that the Catholic religion has been called by God to clarify, modify, bring to full understanding and establish the real meaning of the Scriptures. The assumption of the Romanist is that the Bible is hardly a guide unto itself capable of containing doctrine suitable for the Catholic religious enterprise. This is the first grievous error in the Catholic notion of 'development of doctrine.' The second grievous mistake of the Catholic community is the insistence upon the magisterium of Rome as the higher authority, which sits in judgment upon the doctrines of the Bible. For Rome it is simple: the Bible is as understandable as the Catholic religion says it is.

Given this backdrop, is it any wonder that we can find so little with which to agree with Rome? The Christian understands that there is a constant 'mining and refining' of the inexhaustible truths of the Scripture. The Christian is willing to accept a certain composition of doctrinal accuracy over the years as the Bible is used to combat heresy after heresy. But, the Christian is repulsed by the idea of having authority over the Bible. In Rome, the correction of heresy is performed by the magisterium sitting in council as equal with Scripture. For the Christian, heresy is dispelled from the Scripture with no outside source of authority. The difference with Rome at this juncture cannot be glossed over. Rome really and truly believes that *what* the magisterium decides is to be taken on a par with the Bible. It matters not if the teaching cannot be squared with the Bible or appears to be contrary to the Bible! Herein lies the rub. The Christian clings to the Bible and digs deep for understanding and further knowledge. It is the Christian's fervent hope and prayer that he or she has not done violence to the sacred Word in arriving at a conclusion and an application. The Christian is fearful of man's interpretation and proneness to wander. Therefore, the Christian checks his work with past and present theologians for the accuracy of his interpretations. Anything which is novel and cannot be substantiated by the

---

[1] Keating, *Catholicism and Fundamentalism*, pg. 151

words of the text, using all available scholarship and wisdom, is to be suspect.

In Romanism, the magisterium has presumed authority above the Scripture. There is no check to the magisterium other than the magisterium. Why would one fear a new or different interpretation to the Scripture, or even an idea outside of Scripture, if there was no way the Scripture could check you? Rome has no intention of subjecting her doctrines and ongoing 'development of doctrine' to the authority of the Bible. To do so would place the Catholic religion under the authority of the Word and put her subject to what every Christian in the world is subject, i.e., the Word of God as *Sola Scriptura.*

Some Roman Catholics point to the doctrine of the Trinity as proof of the need of the magisterium. They want us to know that without recourse to the magisterium one could not be certain of the teaching on the Trinity. They think that the doctrine of the Trinity is not obvious on the face of Scripture and therefore in need of a magisterium to identify it. We would ask, If the Bible is not clear on the Trinity then why should we believe it to be the teaching of the Lord and His apostles? The Catholic is quick to answer, because the Catholic religion says so. Yet, we would ask on what basis does the Catholic religion assume to speak for God? A quick check with the Church Fathers will show that those who labored to correct heresy did so from Scripture. All arguments against the heresies were founded on the Scriptures. Men of God were found to be digging for the right doctrines on their knees before God with the Bible as their source of authority. The formulation of the doctrines which are safeguarded in the Church of our Lord were forged from the refinery of biblical exegesis not a magisterium council. In the final analysis, it is not "What saith the council?" but rather, "What saith the Scripture?"

Catholicism is accurate when it understands that doctrinal clarification can and does await years to be admitted as truth to the Church. Yet, it is absolutely wrong in thinking that truth is independent from Scripture. In fact, it is only the Scripture which can defeat late arriving heresies. It is the Scripture which is the sword of the Lord to refute all manner of heresy. Nothing else will do. If one is to wage a war with an enemy of God, then one should use the weapon which has been entrusted to him. Christians understand the value of using non-biblical terminology to best describe biblical truth such as *homoousios* (the divine nature of Christ is the *same* as the divine nature of God the Father) versus *homoiousios* (the Arian error that the nature of Christ was only *similar* to God the Father). But if the distinction cannot be substantiated from Scripture (which it certainly can in every major doctrine of the Church, including this one) then it is better left alone. White summarizes succinctly the Christian understanding of doctrinal development from the Bible:

> "The guiding factor for development of Christian doctrine is the Bible itself! The text of Scripture provides the grounds, and most importantly, the limits for this 'development' over time. Rather than bringing in outside influences (such as Roman tradition), the Christian Church recognizes that no one has ever plumbed the depths of the revelation of God contained in the Bible. No one has ever come close to exhausting what is to be found in the pages of the Scriptures, which the writer of Hebrews called 'living' (Hebrews 4:12). Therefore, real development of Christian doctrine is simply the ever-increasing understanding of the Word of God. It is a delving deeper and deeper into the truths of the Word. It involves the recognition of how one passage is related to another, one truth to another. When Christian scholars discover more and more about the languages of the Bible, the meanings of words, the forms of expression, this brings about development of our understanding, and hence further definition of doctrine. On the spiritual level, it comes about through the Spirit's illumination of men of God who humbly submit themselves to the authority of the Bible, not men who arrogantly assume that they have a position of authority over the Bible."[1]

Before leaving this section it is important for us to analyze a rather lengthy quotation of Newman's argument on the rightness of the Catholic understanding of the prominence of the magisterium:

> "The argument is directed towards the Protestant critic of Tractarianism and in a simplified form goes like this. You criticize the Tractarians for teaching such doctrines as, for example, the Apostolic Succession of bishops or that the Eucharist is a sacrifice, and your criticism rests on the contention that these doctrines are not plainly and unambiguously contained in Scripture and may not indeed be in the Bible at all. I concede, goes the reply, that these doctrines are not to be found in the letter of Scripture or on its surface. But this is just as true of other doctrines you as an orthodox Protestant believe quite firmly; such doctrines as, let us say, the Godhead of the Holy Spirit or that Holy Scripture contains all that is sufficient for salvation. Neither of these doctrines is contained on the surface of Scripture, and there would even be logical difficulties in supposing that Scripture contained the latter doctrine. It seems to me that you ought in consistency to believe less than you do or more

---

[1] White, *Answers to Catholic Claims*, pg. 68

than you do. If you confine yourself to what is contained in Scripture then the content of your belief will be thin and even incoherent and you will have no rationale for giving the Bible this supreme position. What you do, inconsistently, believe (for you are not, thank God, a Unitarian) is a warrant for your going further and adopting as your criterion the tradition of the first few centuries and using this tradition, embodied in the formularies of the Church, as that in the light of which Scripture is to be read and understood. You must either move upwards into Catholicism or downwards into unbelief. There is no midway point of rest."[1]

The Tractarian movement is a reference to a mid-19th century group of Oxford students who wished to revert back to the ways and traditions of the Catholic religion. The name is taken from the 90 "Tracts for the Times" distributed during this period.

Notice carefully the argumentation. Newman castigates Protestants for looking down their noses at Catholic doctrines that are not plainly and unambiguously contained in Scripture. He even admits that some may not be found in the Bible at all. He does not labor to prove the opposite, that the Catholic doctrines *are* to be found in the Bible! Rather, he accuses the Protestants of being, as it were, hypocrites. The reason being that Protestants also believe things which are not readily and plainly taught in the Bible. He gives two examples of such beliefs. The first is the deity of the Holy Spirit and the second is the idea that the Holy Scriptures contain all that is sufficient for salvation. He concludes that anyone confining himself to only that which is taught in the Bible will be left with that which is thin and even incoherent. Thus, for Newman, the Bible does not deserve the status the Protestant gives it unless the Protestant is willing to believe less. He thinks we should be grateful for the Traditions which brought to us the fullness of our beliefs which the Bible could never do just standing alone! His incredible summary is that one is left either moving toward Catholicism (we presume the authority of the magisterium is meant by this) or toward unbelief.

It is beyond the context of this short book to prove from the Bible alone that the Holy Spirit is in fact taught by Scripture to be the third Person of the Godhead. We have already shown that the Scripture supports its own contention that it contains all that is necessary for salvation and sanctification. The main point is that all those who have proved the deity of the Holy Spirit appealed to the Holy Scriptures to do so! In addition, all those who were saved in the New Testament heard nothing but the words of salvation from the lips of the apostles. These very words are safeguarded

---

[1] Keating, *Catholicism and Fundamentalism*, pp. 151, 152

and speak as loudly and clearly today for salvation as did they in the first century!

As we have noted earlier, the only way for the Catholic religion to keep her adherents in the bondage of her theoretical religion is to heap obscurity upon obscurity when it comes to the Scriptures. The more one can be convinced that the Bible is unclear, the better a replacement system can be inaugurated. We find it absolutely inimical to Christianity that the champion thinker among Catholic theologians can boldly assert that the Bible does not contain all that is sufficient for salvation. We shall find in the upcoming chapters on Catholic dogma just how utterly foreign their understanding of salvation is to the Christian faith.

Chapter 6

Salvation and Security

WE HAVE arrived at a point in our analysis of Romanism where we can begin a thorough investigation into the heart of Roman Catholic teaching on various doctrines and dogmas. Undoubtedly, some of the readers of this book have been put off by our insistence in separating the term "Catholic" from the term "Christian." We have done so throughout the pages of this book for a very good reason. Although the Catholic religion does have an intellectual belief in the Trinity and the Person of Christ as the incarnate Son of God, the Catholic religion has failed to grasp or understand the gospel of Christ and the death of Christ on the cross. Without such an understanding, Roman Catholicism fails to measure up to the test of Christianity. It is therefore properly understood as a cult with a lot of Christian terminology. In this chapter, and the ones following, we will endeavor to showcase the actual teaching and belief system of the Roman religion. Our documentation will not be conditioned on what Christians say about Rome, but rather we are indebted to Catholic apologists who have been crystal clear in presenting their religion for all to see.

Person — Separated from His Work

Salvation

One of the foremost characteristics of the Christian faith is the assurance that God will never leave nor forsake all those who come to Him by faith in the finished work of Jesus Christ. We accept that Christians have for centuries debated among each other whether personal assurance of salvation is *necessary* for the sinner to be saved. However, the mighty testimony of the Christian Church is unified around the assurance that God will never forsake all those whom He has given to His Son. Some may have more assurance than others that they are, in fact, Christians, but both will agree that God never forsakes one of His own. Some Christians may be weak and frail, always consumed by their own sinfulness and loath to comprehend the love of Christ to a full measure of security. Yet, these very same Christians would disdain any and all attempts to please God for their own salvation by any works of merit or personal holiness. For the Christian, it is the work of satanic presumption to even suggest that anything could be added to the death of Christ for the salvation of a sinner. To dare to presume that God has considered the death of His own Son as insufficient to save the vilest of sinners is the height of presumption.

The Roman Catholic defines the sin of presumption in altogether different terms. This is where we must begin in our contrasting of the Roman Catholic religion with the faith of a Christian.

> "In Catholic theology, presumption is the attitude that one can gain heaven by his own merits or *can gain pardon without repentance*."[1]

Repentance does not mean a once and for all act of repentance and faith in the Savior in the Catholic system. No, the word "repentance" is viewed as an ongoing penance for sins committed. The *Catholic Almanac* is helpful in crystallizing the Romish concept of presumption:

> "Presumption: A violation of the theological virtue of hope, by which a person striving for salvation either relies too much on his own capabilities or expects God to do things which He cannot do, in keeping with his divine attributes, or does not will to do according to his divine plan."[2]

Keating goes on to say, "...to presume on one's salvation is to play fast and loose with one's soul. It is the most terminal form of Russian roulette."[3]

At the outset, we see that Christians presume the exact opposite understanding of assurance. The Christian dares not "presume" that he could add one single solitary thing to the death of Christ for his own salvation. The Catholic dares not "presume" that God could possibly be satisfied with Christ's death alone without exacting an extra pound of flesh from the sinner by way of penance. Which "presumption" betrays the gospel? They both cannot be right. Something has to go. We shall have more to say on penance in our section on the forgiveness of sin. However, for now, let us examine the underlying theology which prevents Catholics from having the assurance of forgiveness of sins in the death of Christ alone.

We begin with the Catholic understanding of man's relationship to Adam in the fall of mankind. Traditional Roman Catholic theology (Karl Rahner, *et al*, notwithstanding) understands that Adam's sin caused damage to his posterity, but did not do sufficient harm to the will of man to prevent man from reaching out to God. However, man did inherit a negative disposition

1 Keating, *Catholicism and Fundamentalism*, pg. 164. Emphasis added
2 *1990 Catholic Almanac*, (Huntington, IN: Our Sunday Visitor Publishing, ©1990) pg. 323
3 Keating, *Catholicism and Fundamentalism*, pg. 164

from Adam. This negative disposition is defined in terms of a deprivation of positive righteousness or simply, "original sin." In this condition, man cannot face God or go to Heaven. Roman Catholic "original sin" must be taken out of the way. This is done in the waters of their baptism. For Roman Catholic babies who die without the "sacrament" of baptism their destiny is Limbo, where they await the prayers and merits of loved ones to free them unto God. This Roman baptism of infants will be covered in an upcoming chapter more thoroughly but for now we need to understand that in Rome, baptism is the same as one's regeneration. In fact, all Roman Catholics understand their baptism to be the "born again" experience. At their baptism, Rome believes God transfuses grace into the heart of the baby to clean out the soul from the pollution of Adam's sin. It is precisely at this point where the Roman Catholic religion departs from Christianity. We cannot emphasize this enough.

The Catholic religion introduces the infusion of grace for the remission of original sin in the infant. The infant is then left with complete forgiveness of Adam's original sin but there remains in the baby a propensity toward sinning which also must be dealt with. The ball is now rolling for the Catholic religion's understanding of salvation. Just as the sin of Adam had to be purged in the waters of baptism through an infusion of grace to make alive the spiritually dead soul, so likewise, all post-baptismal sins have to be dealt with by infusion of grace! This grace is infused through the sacramental system developed by the Roman Catholic religion. The Romanist religion is actually a dispensary of grace from the Father through Christ to the Romanist priest and onto the practitioner. This is why the priest has so much authority. It is through the sacrament of penance that the priest is able to confer forgiveness of sin and the corresponding penalty to be paid for that sin by the penitent. The Catholic religion teaches the merit of Christ is applied through various sacraments to eliminate post-baptismal sins of each person baptized. With respect to baptism, Trent has this to say:

> "If anyone denies that by the grace of our Lord Jesus Christ which is conferred in baptism, the guilt of original sin is remitted, or says that the whole of that which belongs to the essence of sin is not taken away, but says that it is only canceled or not imputed, let him be *anathema*. For in those who are born again God hates nothing, because there is no condemnation to those who are truly buried together with Christ by baptism unto death, who walk not according to the flesh, but, putting off the old man and putting on the new one who is created according to God, are made innocent, immaculate, pure, guiltless and beloved of God, heirs indeed of God, joint heirs with Christ; so that there is nothing whatever to hinder their entrance into heaven. But this holy council perceives and confesses that in the one baptized there remains concupiscence or an inclination to sin, which, since it is left for us to wrestle with, cannot injure those who

do not acquiesce but resist manfully by the grace of Jesus Christ; indeed, he who shall have striven lawfully shall be crowned. This concupiscence, which the Apostle sometimes calls sin, the holy council declares the Catholic Church has never understood to be called sin in the sense that it is truly and properly sin in those born again, but in the sense that it is of sin and inclines to sin. But if anyone is of the contrary opinion, let him be *anathema*."[1]

It is impossible to understand the Catholic religion without first understanding their overall view of salvation. For the Catholic, salvation is not something one possesses. It is something to be attained through a system of grace-granting obediences. The Catholic is told that he or she is born in original sin and needs to be baptized for the forgiveness of that original sin. Next, the Catholic is told that there remains a propensity to sin which ultimately leads to sinning. These sins have to be washed away too. How? The answer is through the blood of Christ. But how can I appropriate the grace purchased through the blood of Christ? The answer is through the divinely ordained sacraments of the Church. So, for the Catholic, there is no salvation *per se*, only the constant and continual "getting dirty/getting cleaned" cycle. Sinning is dirty business which requires an infusion of grace which is obtained through the sacraments of Rome.

> "For Catholics, salvation depends on the state of the soul at death...
> He did his part, and now we have to cooperate by doing ours. If we
> are to pass through those gates, we have to be in the right spiritual
> state. We have to be spiritually alive. If a soul is merely in a natural
> state, without sanctifying grace, which is the grace that gives it
> supernatural life, then it is dead supernaturally and incapable of
> enjoying heaven. It will not be allowed through the gates. But if it
> has sanctifying grace, then heaven is guaranteed even if a detour
> through purgatorial purification is required first. The Church teaches
> that only souls that are objectively good and objectively pleasing to
> God merit heaven, and such souls are ones filled with sanctifying
> grace."[2]

The entirety of the Catholic religion stands or falls on this idea of "infusion-ary grace" for the cleaning up of one's soul. Let us read carefully the Catholic understanding of justification:

> "The Catholic Church, not surprisingly, understands justification
> differently. It sees a true eradication of sin and a true sanctification

---

[1] Schroeder, pg. 23. From the 5th Session of Trent, paragraph 5
[2] Keating, *Catholicism and Fundamentalism*, pg. 166

and renewal. The soul becomes objectively pleasing to God and so merits heaven. It merits heaven because it is now actually good."[1]

To the Catholic, God is in the business of granting grace by the merits of Christ, through the sacramental system, in order to make a person ethically righteous enough to perform works which in turn merit that person salvation. The sanctuary of purgatory is the safety net for those who are not quite ethically righteous enough to enter Heaven at death. The Catholic is bent on the notion that God actually removes the sin of the penitent and objects to the Christian idea of God covering the sinner's sin. Here we have a weird twist which bears further clarity. The Catholic position is that God eradicates sin and gives grace for holiness. The Catholic believes the Christian to be in error to think that God only covers sin. The irony is that the Christian believes that God eradicates all his or her sins *by covering them with the blood of Christ*. The further irony is that the Catholic does not have any comfort in the *real eradication of sin* since the sin removed is immediately replaced in his experience by myriads more. These sins too have to be eradicated and on and on it goes! There is never a true removal of sin in the Catholic system because the one taken out of the way through penance a minute ago is replaced by another one instantly. The second sin will send one to Hell or purgatory just as sure and as fast as the one that was just taken out of the way! The Romanist fails to grasp the solemnity of sin in the eyes of God. The Romanist plays the game of sin in a pious manner but fails to grasp the depth of sin. In so doing, the Romanist will fail to grasp the deepness of the death of Christ.

It is safe to say that, for the Catholic, salvation is a process of moving toward God by virtue of paying off sin resulting from one's inclination to sin. This payoff is aided by grace infused through the sacramental system. In all this the idea of security is preposterous to the Catholic. But there is more. There is the underlying assumption that the death of Christ on the cross only serves to make salvation attainable by the works of man. Christ's death opened the door so that God would be pleased with the sacrifices of man for salvation.

Catholic theology is based upon two pillars. The first is the absolute freedom of the will to choose to come to God through the Catholic system. These words are revealing:

> "Grace abounds and can always be grabbed if only reached for. God does everything short of getting down on his knees in front of us and begging us to repent."[2]

---

[1] Keating, *Catholicism and Fundamentalism*, pg. 167, 168

[2] Keating, *Catholicism and Fundamentalism*, pg. 167

[handwritten: freedom of the will / universal atonement / man's will is depraved.]

The second pillar is the universal atonement of Christ which has made salvation possible for everyone in the entire world.

Arminian[1] Evangelicals may not like to hear this but the fact is inescapable. The Catholic religion is able to build an *autosoteric* (self-salvation) system because it builds upon the unscriptural foundation that Adam's sin did not impair the will from choosing God. The Catholic also posits an unscriptural "given" that the death of Christ redeemed everyone in the world. Hopefully the reader will see that there is a razor edge difference between the Arminian contention of a general atonement and corresponding disassociation of Adam's sin to his posterity and the Roman Catholic foundation. Both are in grave error. The Catholic is perhaps even more consistent with building upon these false pillars than the modern evangelical Arminian.[2]

The Catholic, furthermore, sets forth a difference between "salvation" and "redemption." The Catholic thinks that all men are "redeemed" but only those who continue in the sacramental grace of the Catholic religion have a hope of salvation. Keating is direct in his comments:

> "The truth is that we are all redeemed—Christians, Jews, Moslems, animists in the darkest forests—but our salvation is conditional."[3]

The evangelical Arminian might use different words but say the same thing. The idea is that Christ died for everyone and salvation is conditionally dependent upon man exercising his free will to choose God. The reader needs to comprehend the Arminian as coming from a similar, though not exact, misunderstanding of Adam's sin. Regrettably this leads to similar errors in understanding of Christ's death. At this point the Romanist is amazed that the Arminian can start so well and ignore the rest of Scripture which (for them) logically leads to a Catholic system of salvation. The Arminian jettisons the Catholic system while retaining the same two pillars, i.e., freedom of the will and universal atonement of Catholic theology! Thus, in critically critiquing the Catholic religion, we are left with short-handled hoes and dull shovels if we try to correct the Catholic error with

---

[1] By Arminian we mean those "otherwise" Evangelicals who begin their theology by disconnecting Adam's sin and guilt from all babies born. This is done either by saying Christ's death on the cross eliminated it or by sheer declaration of it to be so. We are somewhat bewildered that modern evangelical writers cannot see how the utter misrepresentation of the link between Adam and mankind falls into the hands of Rome.

[2] In our opinion, the Roman Catholic scholar has a right to be stupefied at the "evangelical Arminian" resistance to his religion. He could rightly claim common ground when it comes to depravity, general atonement, freedom of the will, new covenant obedience and defining faith as at least a part of the *ground* of justification!

[3] Keating, *Catholicism and Fundamentalism*, pg. 169

something which is at base Catholic! The Catholic apologist is well aware of this and that is precisely why he picks on the evangelical Arminian. He knows the Arminian at heart believes in *autosoterism*.[1]

We urge the reader to come to grips with the scriptural determination on the issue of salvation.[2] Simply put, does God save or does man save himself? By saving himself, we mean the ability to choose God unaided by the work of God's Holy Spirit. The corollary teaching is the alleged right to resist God should God will to save a man. It should be sobering to the evangelical community as we contemplate the Catholic position. The Romanist thinks highly enough of the sin of Adam to believe that God *must* bring life to the soul while the baby is absolutely passive in the waters of baptism. This life giving act of God frees the will to accept or reject the Catholic road to salvation. How ironic that the average evangelical boasts too of his "free will" and ventures to say that God's gift of life to the soul is achieved and determined by the man. In the final analysis, Rome will chastise the evangelical Arminian for agreeing on the basics of Adam and free will but ignoring the biblically conditional Roman Catholic system of attaining salvation![3]

Yet, it is this conditional salvation which surely sets apart the Romanist religion from Christianity. We must understand, the Romanist draws his conclusions on salvation from a faulty understanding of both the effects and corruption of Adam's sin. This leads to an even greater misunderstanding of Christ's atonement. Only upon understanding Rome's theology of sin and Adam shall we be able to unravel the Roman religion.

At this juncture we are heartbroken by the confusion which exists not only among Catholics but among well-meaning Christians when it comes to

---

[1] This term "*autosoterism*" is best explained on pages 33-51 of B. B. Warfield's excellent little book entitled *The Plan of Salvation*, (Grand Rapids: Eerdmans Publishing Co., ©1980)

[2] We must insist that foggy theology is at the root of much that is wrong in evangelical circles. Either we check up Rome here or we reduce our struggle with the Vatican to Rosary beads, scapulars, intrigue of popes, Latin Mass and other issues which never get to the heart of the matter.

[3] Our focus of attention must remain on the Catholic system of salvation. We are, however, gravely concerned with the indefensible position of Evangelicals who mistakenly grant so much to Rome by way of agreement. This puts them in a position of not being able to resist the sheer logic of Rome! When Evangelicals eliminate condemnation for all in Adam, boast of a universal atonement and champion the absolute freedom of the will to choose or reject God, they cannot safeguard the *necessity* of a spiritual birth from Heaven *and* a corresponding justification based upon the imputation of Christ's righteousness.

understanding the sin of Adam and the death of Christ. Not only is it prudent to correct the Roman Catholic notion of salvation but also to rescue wayward evangelical Christian theology to some extent.

The writing of Kenneth Hagin and his book, *The New Birth* is easy pickings for Catholic apologists. A booklet written by Wilson Ewin entitled *There is Therefore Now No Condemnation* falls prey to Catholic criticism. Excerpts from a Keith Green's tract called *Salvation According to Rome* is easily overcome by Rome which cites all the intrinsic inconsistencies. The trouble with Roman Catholic conclusions is that they are based on what may be a half truth or an unguarded statement written by an "evangelical" writer. For instance, this is what one Catholic writer is able to come up with in summary of evangelical salvation.

> "They (fundamentalists) conclude from the Bible that Christ actually promised that heaven is theirs in exchange for a remarkably simple act. All they have to do, at just one point in their lives, is 'accept Christ as their personal Savior'. Then it is done. They may live exemplary lives thereafter, but living well is not crucial. It does not affect their salvation. No matter what happens later, no matter how evilly they might live the remainder of their days, their salvation is assured."[1]

The problem with this citation is that it leaves gaping holes and begs for a clarification. The writer, in this case Kenneth Hagin, needs to be corrected for his error in turning salvation into an act of man rather than an act of God. It is not true that salvation is effected by a simple act of man. While it is true that man is the one who believes, it is also true that no one can believe unless he is born from above. It appears that in Hagin's zeal to emphasize the responsibility of man to believe, he has put the cart before the horse. Faith does not bring about the new birth. The new birth brings about faith. Consider the words of John in 1 John 5:1, "Whoever believes that Jesus is the Christ is born of God."

Secondly, the terminology, 'accepting Christ as a personal Savior,' is regrettable. There is a receiving of Christ after one is born from above. But this receptivity is an acknowledgment of Christ as Lord and Savior. It is a trusting in His death as the total sufficiency for forgiveness of sins. We would submit such language by modern Evangelicals is popular but rather sterile and misleading when compared with the biblical terms of "repentance" and "faith" in the Lord Jesus Christ.

---

[1] Keating, *Catholicism and Fundamentalism*, pg. 165

Repentance toward God + Faith in Jesus Christ persons work
The Needs of His person + work

Thirdly, we reject the notion of any writer whether Catholic or one who feigns Christianity who would hold to the unbiblical position that salvation has no meaningful relation to good works. When viewed rightly, the Christian experience of salvation is through faith alone but never by a faith that is alone. Much confusion could be cleared away if we but once understand that God is the author of salvation. He gives it as a free gift upon the basis of faith. This faith is the first fruit of regeneration (a term which will be considered presently). The *ordo salutis* (order of salvation) is first regeneration by the sovereign Spirit followed by an expression of faith which apprehends the merit of Christ for salvation. This state of regeneration is a state of renewal whereby the Spirit of God is given as a pledge to guide and direct the believer into both truth and an ethical life. Good works are not, as the Catholic might say, the basis of salvation. Neither are they optional as the careless Christian might suggest. Neither are they dormant in the life of one regenerated unto God.

What the Catholics, and sadly many well-meaning professing Christians, do not understand is that the principle of life given in regeneration issues forth in a life which strives to please the Lord but is ever mindful of the flesh that remains which wars against the Spirit. The Christian will both bear fruit and sin. The remedy for sin is confession to Christ and a reaffirmation of the priceless treasure of salvation applied to the sinner on the basis of Christ's atoning work on the cross.

Roman Catholicism is dead wrong in its understanding of the Reformers when it comes to the grace of justification. It is true that the Reformers saw justification as a forensic act whereby God imputes the righteousness of Christ to the unworthy sinner. But Catholicism's contention that this legal declaration does not consist in "an inner renewal and a real sanctification, only an external application of Christ's justice,"[1] is palpably false. Paul Althaus gives us insight into Martin Luther's struggle with the doctrine of *simul justus et peccator* (justified, yet a sinner).

> "When Christ makes Himself one with man, this 'alien' righteousness becomes man's own and makes him righteous before God. ...Man, including the Christian man, remains a sinner his whole life long and cannot possibly live and have worth before God except through alien righteousness, the imputation of Christ's righteousness."[2]

---

[1] Keating, *Catholicism and Fundamentalism*, pg. 167
[2] Althaus, Paul, *The Theology of Martin Luther*, (Philadelphia: Fortress Press, ©1966) pp. 228-9

"Thus our heart itself becomes righteous, not only because it is accepted as such through the imputation of Christ's righteousness; but it also becomes righteous because God's Holy Spirit is poured into the heart and He brings love and new obedience with Him."[1]

One can see by these citations that Luther did not believe the grace of justification was alone. Luther wisely differentiated the act of God's justifying the guilty sinner by virtue of the imputed righteousness of Christ from the principle of life implanted for the ethical transformation of the sinner. The one he called justification and the other sanctification. With this Calvin concurs:

"Christ given to us by the kindness of God is apprehended and possessed by faith, by means of which we obtain in particular a twofold benefit: first, being reconciled by the righteousness of Christ, God becomes, instead of judge, an indulgent Father; and, secondly, being sanctified by his Spirit, we aspire to integrity and purity of life."[2]

The *Westminster Confession of Faith* specifically avoids the accusation of the Romanist apologist in its opening statement on justification.

"Those whom God effectually calleth he also freely justifieth; not by infusing righteousness into them, but by pardoning their sins, and by accounting and accepting their persons as righteous: not for any thing wrought in them, or done by them, but for Christ's sake alone: not by imputing faith itself, the act of believing, or any other evangelical obedience, to them as their righteousness; but by imputing the obedience and satisfaction of Christ unto them, they receiving and resting on him and his righteousness by faith: which faith they have not of themselves; it is the gift of God.

"Faith, thus receiving and resting on Christ and his righteousness, is the alone instrument of justification; yet is it not alone in the person justified, but is ever accompanied with all other saving graces, and is no dead faith, but worketh by love."[3]

Rome has always blurred the distinction between justification and sanctification since it is blinded to the righteousness of Christ as the sole ground of our forgiveness and right standing before God. It is this writer's

---

[1] Althaus, pg. 234

[2] John Calvin, *Institutes of the Christian Religion,* (Grand Rapids, MI: Eerdmans, ©1957) Book 3, Chapter 11, Paragraph 1

[3] Williamson, G. I., *Westminster Confession of Faith*, (Philadelphia: Presbyterian and Reformed, ©1978) pg. 103, chapter XI, paragraphs 1 and 2

plea that those who profess Christianity begin to realize that Romanism presents a system that is contrary to the basic underpinnings of salvation. Christian theology rests upon a substitutionary and penal satisfaction of the death of Christ. Christians understand that the death of Christ was demanded by the perfect holiness of God which demanded a perfect sacrifice for sin. Security is rendered by the judicial determination of God that His Son was both the propitiation and expiation of sin. Christ died in the place of sinners and took away the curse of the law. As all are condemned in Adam, so shall all those in Christ be made alive unto God. By substitutionary we mean "in the place of." By penal satisfaction we mean "bearing the punishment due sin." Christ did not come to die to set up a system of meriting salvation as though His death relaxed the divine requirements for payment of sins committed. Neither did He die in hopes that some one might believe through the exercise of their "self willed" will! No, He died to save an army of the lost. He died to guarantee the salvation of all those whom the Father would give to Him.

Roman Catholic writers believe it to be immoral that God should demand from one who is innocent to pay for the sins of the guilty. That is why Romanism is based upon a system of personal penance. Listen to the *New Catholic Encyclopedia* on the subject of redemption:

> "Catholic theology began to move away from the system of substitutional penal expiation with St. Thomas. Today there is a positive theological reaction against the theory itself and not simply against the distortions, exaggerations, and, possibly, the amorality that such a doctrine fostered in its development. Biblical studies have shown that the theory does not have a sound basis in Scripture.

> "At its best, this system proposes to the faithful the doctrine of the inexorability of punishment for sin and the necessity of satisfaction. It presents the cross of Christ as the great manifestation of the evil of sin. But when it affirms that Christ assumed the punishment so that man would not have to suffer it or that Christ offered satisfaction so that men need not make it, the theory is theologically unsound. When it affirms that God delivered Christ to His cross to manifest to the world not only the evil of sin but also how severely sin is punished, this is nothing less than terrorism."[1]

Some Roman Catholic writers are moving away from understanding Christ's death as a penal substitution on behalf of sinners. We find this sobering analysis from a credible Roman Catholic source:

---

[1] *New Catholic Encyclopedia*, pg. 157

"Sacrifice of Expiation: If the theory of the redemptive death is cast in the juridical order, the death of Christ will be understood as a sacrifice of expiation. Theologians who hold this theory see Christ's death in an analogy with the expiatory sacrifices of the Old Law in which (so these writers consider) an animal was symbolically loaded with the sins of the people and then ritually slain. The animal is substituted for sinful man, and man, seeing the death of the animal, may understand what his sins deserve and how severe are God's punishments. By means of this sacrifice, God's anger is appeased and His wrath averted.

"This theory has had many adherents among both Catholics and Protestants, especially among the reformers themselves. *But recently, Biblical research has questioned, indeed attacked, this understanding of the death of Christ in terms of such an expiatory sacrifice. It is affirmed in this theory that the sins of mankind are imputed to Christ. God permits, even wills, that Christ be slain both to appease His anger and to manifest to the world the evil of sin and the fact that God will not forgive without satisfaction being made either by the innocent or by the guilty. It does not matter. This is nothing short of amorality, even immorality. In such an understanding of the redemption, God does not keep His own command to man to forgive without demanding satisfaction* (Matthew 5:38-48)."[1]

The modern Catholic thinking is moving away from appeasement language when it comes to the death of Christ, and into a new language of "immolation" which is far removed from any Christian understanding of the substitutionary atonement of Christ. For a further discussion consider the *New Catholic Encyclopedia* under the subtopic 'Redemption.'

A Question of Security

We close this section by endeavoring to answer the question of security for the believer. For the Roman Catholic, as we have pointed out again and again, there is only a false man-made security and salvation is only something to be moving toward through the Catholic system of penance and works. But what about the Christian? Can one have the security of salvation during his lifetime? Was the great apostle Paul assured of a heavenly home? In answering this question, we must first ask what is the basis of eternal security? When this is answered, the corresponding question of whether

---

[1] *New Catholic Encyclopedia*, pg. 158. Emphasis added

one is secure can be answered. But, before we answer these questions we need to observe an ironic twist to Romanism.

The Catholic thinks having assurance of Heaven is presumption. Yet, who has offered more false assurance to its adherents than the Catholic religion? The Catholics are assured if they perform so many duties, (such as Mass or certain days of obligation), they will be forgiven their sins. If they pray, do penance, give to the offering basket and confess their sins to the priest etc., they will be assured of escaping Hell! It is no secret that the "good" Catholic can pretty much eliminate the fear of going to Hell simply because he or she is taught that his or her life is probably not that bad! To assist in this false assessment the Catholic religion gives its people purgatory. Most Catholics believe they are neither "bad" enough to go to Hell or "good" enough to go to Heaven. Thus, the rank and file are given modest comfort and security by the Roman system. They are assured of at least purgatory! As we shall see, purgatory fits nicely into the Catholic religion which believes it is one thing to have sins forgiven and quite another to have the *penalty* for that sin wiped out! The sad delusion of Catholicism on the question of security is summed up in the recognition that they too have their security. It is wrapped up right in the middle of an almost fanatic trust in priests, bishops, cardinals and their pope. It is a security in the untrustworthy judgment of man upon himself. It is wrapped up in the sadness of a Catholic confession that Jesus has forgiven me, but I must pay the penalty. In this confession, the depth of sin is minimized by the paltry offerings of the sinner. The depth of the love of Christ is minimized by a conditional salvation. The justice of God is reduced to being satisfied with human sufferings.

In the final analysis, the Catholic religion gives assurance based upon the absolute pride of man and what man is able to muster up to the Deity. This system is very appealing to man because it allows him to take pride in his own good works. It appeals to that part of man which wants to place God in his debt. But, such a fleshly view of salvation is renounced by Paul who uses Abraham as an example.

> "For if Abraham were justified by works, he hath [whereof] to glory; *but not before God*." (Romans 4:2, emphasis ours)

Any "system" of works will appeal to man because it allows him to measure his progress and stimulate his fleshly spirit and ego. The Catholic likes to think he is somewhere between Heaven and Hell at all times and thus feels a carnal security. He can always measure himself with a yardstick supplied by the magisterium. It is not that the Catholic disdains security. No, he has plenty. Yet, it is all based on a very odd mixture of Catholic rules and self concocted mysticism which barrels down to a false security rooted in the pride of man!

The Catholic theologian would seek to put Paul in the same prideful position as he finds himself. Void of real security, but bathed in the security of his own system, the Catholic suspects Paul was involved in a similar religious odyssey. But is this where we find Paul? Absolutely not! Paul understood, and left for all to contemplate, the security of God's people, a security not based upon the never-ending efforts of men to do good, but rather a security coming from the Godhead. God in eternity past determined to have a people for Himself despite their unbelief. It is the firm conviction of Paul that all those whom God had chosen to believe in His Son would not perish but have everlasting life. In light of this, Paul answers his own questions in Romans 8:

> "What shall we then say to these things? If God [be] for us, who [can be] against us? He that spared not his own Son, but delivered him up for us all, how shall he not with him also freely give us all things? Who shall lay any thing to the charge of God's elect?" (Romans 8:31-33a)

Paul answers these questions with the conviction :

> "For I am persuaded, that neither death, nor life, nor angels, nor principalities, nor powers, nor things present, nor things to come, Nor height, nor depth, nor any other creature, shall be able to separate us from the love of God, which is in Christ Jesus our Lord." (Romans 8:38,39)

The security of the believer does not rest on what the believer does but rather on the veracity of God's promise. All have sinned and fall short of the glory of God and are equally condemned. But those whom God has caused to believe in His Son become beneficiaries of God's promise to have a people called out unto Himself. This promise enables a Christian to have the assurance that Jesus will:

> "...never leave thee, nor forsake thee. So that we may boldly say, The Lord [is] my helper, and I will not fear what man shall do unto me." (Hebrews 13:5,6)

The promise of God to save a people for Himself is a carry-over from the Abrahamic Covenant. Paul explains this in Romans 4:

> "Therefore [it is] of faith, that [it might be] by grace; to the end the promise might be sure to all the seed; not to that only which is of the law, but to that also which is of the faith of Abraham; who is the father of us all..." (Romans 4:16)

The fulfillment of the Abrahamic Covenant finds its origin even deeper in the council of the Godhead. Paul informs us that God chose from eternity past a people to proclaim His name through His Son Jesus Christ.

> "According as he hath chosen us in him before the foundation of the world, that we should be holy and without blame before him in love: Having predestinated us unto the adoption of children by Jesus Christ to himself, according to the good pleasure of his will, To the praise of the glory of his grace, wherein he hath made us accepted in the beloved." (Ephesians 1:4-6)

The down payment toward His promise of security is given to the believer in the form of the Holy Spirit, Who

> "...is the earnest of our inheritance until the redemption of the purchased possession, unto the praise of his glory." (Ephesians 1:14)

Paul understands God to be calling out from among all the nations a people for Himself who formerly were dead in their transgressions and sins (Ephesians 2:1). These people were formerly blasphemers and were called "not a people" by God (1 Peter 2:9,10). But now, God in His mercy has promised life for all those who believe in His Son (John 14:1-3). The security of the believer is wrapped up in the promise of God to never let go of all those for whom His Son died (John 10:25-29). Christ Himself bore witness to the authority of the Father in establishing for Himself a people in John 6:

> "All that the Father giveth me shall come to me; and him that cometh to me I will in no wise cast out. For I came down from heaven, not to do mine own will, but the will of him that sent me. And this is the Father's will which hath sent me, that of all which he hath given me I should lose nothing, but should raise it up again at the last day." (John 6:37-39)

Early on in Paul's preaching ministry he was faced with rejection by the Jews to whom he had taken the gospel. After judging that the Jews were not going to listen to them, Paul and Barnabas turned their attention to the Gentiles. Luke records for us the response of the Gentiles with a pointed remark on the fulfillment of God's promise.

> "And when the Gentiles heard this, they were glad, and glorified the word of the Lord: and as many as were ordained to eternal life believed." (Acts 13:48)

We have said previously that the key to understanding the security of the believer is to understand the basis of that security. We find the basis of security in the promise of the Father to call a people unto Himself. This decision was made in the confines of His own will and counsel. The carrying out of this decision is attributed to His electing love which does not allow the unbelief of man to stultify it. God will save, and those whom He will save are secure because He will not let them go. The work of Christ is sufficient for the forgiveness of their sins and the Holy Spirit is given as a down payment for the heavenly city which awaits all of God's people.

This is why the apostle can say boldly:

> "For what if some did not believe? shall their unbelief make the faith
> of God without effect? God forbid..." (Romans 3:3,4a)

Again, the apostle speaks of a remnant according to God's gracious election (Romans 11:5,6). Elsewhere, Paul speaks of God who has mercy on whom He will have mercy, according to His choice (Romans 9:15).

Paul knew Whom he had believed in and was convinced that God was able to keep that which Paul had entrusted to Him until that day (2 Timothy 1:12). That day would be the time of Paul's arrival at the heavenly throne. Until then, Paul would be hard pressed as having the desire to depart and be with Christ or remain on and bear the fruit of his ministry (Philippians 1). Paul was confident for himself and for other Christians that God, Who began a good work in them, would complete it until the day of Christ Jesus (Philippians 1:6).

What then of the passages of Scripture marshalled by the Roman Catholic apologist to prove that eternal security is a fabrication? In the first place, the Romanist is not the only one who struggles with the notion of eternal security. It is sometimes found among sincere Christians who are fully orthodox to raise the eyebrow at eternal security. Furthermore, the Arminian and Semi-Pelagian evangelical, not to mention several prominent pseudo-Christian cults, have always sought to undermine the sure foundation of God's Word which proclaims the will of God that Jesus would lose,

> "...nothing, but should raise it up again at the last day. And this is
> the will of him that sent me, that every one which seeth the Son, and
> believeth on him, may have everlasting life: and I will raise him up
> at the last day." (John 6:39,40)

We shall begin by pointing out that there is no scriptural basis for turning a professed believer back to his own works of merit to keep him from losing his salvation. The reader is to understand that we do not believe the Bible eaches such a loss of election. But, for the sake of argument, if it did, the emedy is nowhere given for one to "do penance" or "try harder" or 'perform a sacrifice" or "buy a Mass" or "punish oneself" or "give up an otherwise perfectly acceptable earthly enjoyment" or "do community service" or "join the monks" or anything else the mind could imagine to stop from losing one's salvation! In fact, one of the most useful passages of Scripture used to prove the possibility of losing one's salvation is Galatians 5. However, a close inspection reveals the real problem lies with those who are trying to keep their salvation through good works! Notice Galatians 5:

> "Stand fast therefore in the liberty wherewith Christ hath made us free, and be not entangled again with the yoke of bondage. Behold, I Paul say unto you, that if ye be circumcised, Christ shall profit you nothing. For I testify again to every man that is circumcised, that he is a debtor to do the whole law. Christ is become of no effect unto you, whosoever of you are justified by the law; ye are fallen from grace. For we through the Spirit wait for the hope of righteousness by faith. (Galatians 5:1-5)

We can see here that if there is to be a loss of salvation the problem is not one of faith apart from the works of the law in the finished work of Christ. The ones who are in danger of being severed from Christ are those who are trying to perform an add-on to what Christ has already done. Paul is adamant that those who begin by the Spirit, i.e., faith alone, cannot possibly be perfected by the flesh (Galatians 3:1-5). It is ironic that the very danger of "losing one's salvation" is spoken of in terms of returning to a system of works!

What then shall we do with those who have a sincere but misled idea of losing their salvation? The answer is to send them back to Christ to hear the gospel all over again and hope they will be able to hear with ears divinely opened. If they reject the grace of salvation on the basis of Christ's death alone then we have no place else to put them since they put themselves among those who crucify Christ again unto themselves and put Him to open shame (Hebrews 6:6). We would encourage Christians to mark well the biblical pattern. There is no remedy for an alleged loss of salvation short of an examination of one's faith to see whether or not one passes this test (2 Corinthians 13:5f).

Let us now examine the passages which arouse an interest in the question of the believer's security.

> "I therefore so run, not as uncertainly; so fight I, not as one that beateth the air: But I keep under my body, and bring [it] into

subjection: lest that by any means, when I have preached to others, I myself should be a castaway." (1 Corinthians 9:26,27)

There is no mention of eternal life here. The apostle is concerned with bein. found a hypocrite and thus creating confusion, hurt and mistrust among hi hearers. Paul felt the extra burden to live out that which he preached t others. All Christians live under the same testimony. The fact that Paul i concerned for the way in which he lives out his life is a testimony of hi salvation.

Also, all of God's people are to examine their faith. We know of only on disqualification from Heaven. It is when one's faith, which confesses t trust Christ alone and believes in Him alone, is proven to be barren b virtue of bearing no fruit! Paul does not pound out good works in hopes o arriving in Heaven. He examines himself as to whether he has in fac believed! It all goes back to faith.

However, if we are to believe that God uses the *means* of warning an alarm to accomplish the goal of persevering, then it is not odd that th Christian would respond in such a way. Those who have not been know. by God cannot perceive this weight nor do they understand that the weigh itself is the *means* by which God sanctifies His own people. Christians ar called to a fight with the flesh and the world. Both pull strongly to destro the testimony of the believer. We find the exhortations of Scripture to b most serious and designed to sober the children of God. It will be thos who hear such warnings that will either pull out of Christianity or striv against sin as a mark of their high calling in Christ Jesus. The elect of Go are stung by these rebukes and endeavor to persevere throughout their live. Those who have not been truly saved (after the hearing of the Word) wil not persevere. Instead, they will rail against the expressed warnings an show forth their false profession. It is with the present tense that Scriptur shows us all that is possessed by those in Christ. The security of th believer is affirmed by the present tense of Scriptures. These promises ar sure in Christ Jesus. But also the desire to persevere is an indication o regeneration. These marks of election are joined by the testimony of th Spirit of God placed into the believer (Romans 8:16, "The Spirit itsel beareth witness with our spirit, that we are the children of God.") Howevei the imperatives (New Covenant commands of God through His Son) follo hot on the heels of the "present tense promises." The Scriptures spur on an warn those expressing faith in Christ to "hold fast" and "put to death th deeds of the body" and "put off" the old man, etc..

Those who fail to do so will be found out as the "false brethren" (Galatian 2:4) or the tares among the wheat (Matthew 13:30). Ultimately, God alon knows who are His. This is to say that one cannot give another th assurance of his or her salvation. The best one can do is keep pointing to Christ and showing the gospel truth that God will save on the basis of the finished work of Christ alone. All those who believe in Christ alone as the satisfaction for their sins will not be disappointed. The Scriptures are written so as to give security based on the finished work of Christ apart from works of any laws. But it is also written to warn the unbelieving heart. Is it possible for one to deceive himself into thinking he is a Christian? The answer is yes! Where then is the security? The security is in what a person is trusting and the result of that trust. As we have said before, the faith of justification brings with it a desire to persevere and a continuing desire to trust the righteousness of Christ for salvation. Christ promised that His sheep would hear His voice and follow Him (John 10:27). Part of following Him is the recognition of an obligation to buffet the flesh and make it a slave lest one be disqualified! From Heaven? Yes! Then what of security? We are indebted to Charles Hodge who in commenting on another verse of Scripture brings to the front the ways and means of God:

> "It belongs, therefore, to the same category as those numerous passages which make the same assumption with regard to the elect. If the latter are consistent with the certainty of the salvation of all the elect, then this passage is consistent with the certainty of the salvation of those for whom Christ specifically died. It was absolutely certain that none of Paul's companions in shipwreck was on that occasion to lose his life, because the salvation of the whole company had been predicted and promised; and yet the apostle said that if the sailors were allowed to take away the boats, those left on board could not be saved. This appeal secured the accomplishment of the promise. So God's telling the elect that if they apostatize they shall perish, prevents their apostasy. And in like manner, the Bible teaching that those for whom Christ died shall perish if they violate their conscience, prevents their transgression, or brings them to repentance. God's purposes embrace the means as well as the end. If the means fail, the end will fail. He secures the end by securing the means. It is just as certain that those for whom Christ died shall be saved, as that the elect shall be saved. Yet in both cases the event is spoken of as conditional. There is not only a possibility, but an absolute certainty of their perishing if they fall away. But this is precisely what God has promised to prevent. This passage, therefore, is perfectly consistent with those numerous passages which teach that Christ's death secures the salvation of all those who were given to him in the covenant of redemption."[1]

---

[1] Hodge, Charles, *A Commentary on 1 & 2 Corinthians*, (Edinburgh: Banner of Truth, ©1978) pg. 149

The next passage which has caused some consternation among Christians as well as non-Christians who use it to disprove the assurance of the believer is Philippians 2:12, which reads:

"Wherefore, my beloved, as ye have always obeyed, not as in my presence only, but now much more in my absence, work out your own salvation with fear and trembling."

What are we to make of such a strong exhortation? Did Paul really expect for Christians who started by the Spirit to continue by some sort of man-made law? Was this verse the precursor to a sacramental system of salvation by merit? We think not! Should this passage be interpreted as using *sozo* (deliverance) as a reference to "eternal salvation," then it is in line with other passages of Scripture which command those who believe the gospel to persevere in steadfastness. There is nothing unusual in the Scriptures exhorting those who believe to strive against sin and the enemy of our souls. The important thing to remember is that Philippians 2:13 balances this perspective by showing that the power and authority to fight the good fight comes from God alone:

"For it is God which worketh in you both to will and to do of [his] good pleasure."

Some have argued, not unconvincingly, that *sozo* here should be translated as "deliver" with the idea that the Philippians were to work out their domestic quarrels among them since God was among them stirring them up to take care of in-house troubles. If this is the case, the passage has nothing to do with "eternal salvation" but rather temporal deliverance as a body of Christ experiencing conflict among its members (Philippians 4:2,3).[1]

We may cover Romans 2:6 in conjunction with other passages which bring into the picture the works of men before God (cf., John 5:29, etc.). Initially, we must comment on the fact that these "works" passages have no bearing on the eternal security question *per se*. If anything, these passages could be claimed as a ground of security on the basis of man's good deeds. Thus, the fact of security is not dimmed by an appeal to these passages. Rather, the reason for security is thrust onto good deeds of men. Or so it is alleged. As Keating puts it directly with reference to Romans 2:6, 2 Corinthians 5:10, and Romans 11:22;

"These verses demonstrate that we indeed will be judged by what we do and not just by the one act of whether we accept Jesus as our

---

[1] We recommend Gerald F. Hawthorne, *Philippians,* Word Biblical Commentary (Waco, TX: Word Books, ©1983) pp. 96-97

personal Lord and Savior. Yet it is not to be thought that being do-gooders is sufficient. The Bible is quite clear that we are saved by faith. The Reformers were quite right in saying this, and to this extent they merely repeated the constant teaching of the Church. Where they erred was in saying that we are saved by faith alone. If it is true that we are judged by our acts (presuming first we have faith), then it is not enough to say that faith alone, in the traditional Protestant sense of fiduciary faith—trust in Christ's promises—can be enough. If it were, we would not have to worry about our other acts."[1]

We are at sharp variance with the Catholic religion at this juncture. The Romanist wishes to include the works of men in an admixture with faith to give a semblance of security. To do so he appeals to these texts as proof that works plus faith are the ground of security.

To begin with, the Romanist misses the thrust of the entire New Testament. It is the consistent message to the Jew and Gentile that no one will be justified before God by his or her works. The ground of justification will be a righteousness revealed apart from the law (Romans 3:21,22). Paul proclaims that he does not want to be found "having a righteousness of my own that comes from the law." Rather, Paul wants to be found "in Him," as having a righteousness which comes from God on the basis of faith (Philippians 3:9). Paul laments the sad status of Israel:

> "For they being ignorant of God's righteousness, and going about to establish their own righteousness, have not submitted themselves unto the righteousness of God." (Romans 10:3)

We would lament the same for the Catholic religion. In their zeal to protect God from the misuse of grace, which He has freely given, the Romanist builds a fence around free grace. He does so by mixing in works. And, as with the Pharisees of old, these works take on the flavor and approbation of Rome serving to enslave its adherents.

With respect to the question of works before the judgment throne of God, we must see that any approval of works is not for one's eternal salvation. Rather, Paul often uses the fruit of faith in the place of faith to show the close connection but always with one producing the other. Thus, the things produced in Romans 2 (i.e., "perseverance in doing good," "every man who does good," "the doer of the Law") are all a product of a new heart given previously. Those performing these "good works" are those who have been circumcised "of the heart, in the spirit" (Romans 2:29). As in James 2, the deeds show forth the character of the man's faith and the

---

[1] Keating, *Catholicism and Fundamentalism*, pp. 174, 175.

condition of his heart. It is not that God sits on his throne with a scale ready to deal out punishment to those who are weighed according to their good works. If that were the case, then Christ would not have had to die at all! (Galatians 2:21) As we have stated previously, God did not send His Son to die so that He could relax and reduce His standards by judging men on the basis of their good works. Glory and honor are promised to everyone who does good in Romans 2:10. But unless this is read in conjunction with Romans 2:16, the gospel is denigrated by expanding it to include not only faith in Christ but also individual works. This is an aberration rather than "Good News"!

We began this chapter with the firm conviction that Roman Catholicism is constantly and consistently contrary to Christianity. It has been seen from the outset that the Roman understanding of "presumption," along with Rome's view of Adam's sin, and our discussion of the Catholic view of salvation are at odds. In everything important pertaining to salvation and eternal security, we have said the opposite. This consistent contrast of two theologies continues as we discuss the believer at the judgment seat of Christ.

Given the Catholic understanding of justification by faith plus works, and the corresponding system of grace whereby post-baptismal sins are the responsibility of the sinner, it is no wonder what Catholic theologians do with 2 Corinthians 5:10 along with Romans 14:10. Paul tells us in both Romans 14 and 2 Corinthians 5 that all Christians must stand before the *bema* (judgment) seat of Christ. The purpose of this *phanerothenai* (manifestation) is for the Christian to experience a probing search to receive for himself that which is due him for what deeds (good or evil) he has done in (with) his body. Paul is more succinct in Romans where he says that the Christian will give an account of himself before the *bema* of God. Catholic theologians see in these passages more than enough to substantiate their religion of "merit" salvation.

We see these passages with the backdrop of God's justifying grace. We know that "...by him all that believe are justified from all things, from which ye could not be justified by the law of Moses" (Acts 13:39). And, "[There is] therefore now no condemnation to them which are in Christ Jesus" (Romans 8:1). We further understand that David himself "also describeth the blessedness of the man, unto whom God imputeth righteousness without works" (Romans 4:6). Christians are comforted with God's grace whereby we are made heirs of God. Such sonship cannot be earned by works on this or the last day. As Paul writes to Titus,

> "Not by works of righteousness which we have done, but according to his mercy he saved us, by the washing of regeneration, and

renewing of the Holy Ghost; Which he shed on us abundantly through Jesus Christ our Saviour; That being justified by his grace, we should be made heirs according to the hope of eternal life." (Titus 3:5-7)

And again, Paul affirms that God has granted the adoption as sons of His own, having redeemed them out of the curse of the law.

"But when the fulness of the time was come, God sent forth his Son, made of a woman, made under the law, To redeem them that were under the law, that we might receive the adoption of sons. And because ye are sons, God hath sent forth the Spirit of his Son into your hearts, crying, Abba, Father. Wherefore thou art no more a servant, but a son; and if a son, then an heir of God through Christ." (Galatians 4:4-7)

What then of the *bema* seat? Is this where God takes into consideration our good works for the final determination of our eternal dwelling place? Is the judgment here spoken a consignment to punishment? We answer a resounding *No!* The *bema* seat of Christ is that moment in the Christian's life where all of his thoughts and motives are laid bare by the stare of the Lord. Paul alludes to this in 1 Corinthians 4:5, where we are told that the coming of the Lord will bring to light things hidden and disclose the motives of men's hearts, and then each man's praise will come from the Lord. Again in Colossians 3:4, the apostle informs us that all believers will be revealed in Christ. It is at this time where the Lord gives out rewards to those who have performed good works. This is in accordance with the grace and mercy of God more than to the "merit" of the works done. God has graciously promised to not forget.

"For God [is] not unrighteous to forget your work and labour of love, which ye have shewed toward his name, in that ye have ministered to the saints, and do minister." (Hebrews 6:10)

Likewise, we are reminded to, "be ye stedfast, unmoveable, always abounding in the work of the Lord, forasmuch as ye know that your labour is not in vain in the Lord" (1 Corinthians 15:58).

It is unclear to this writer as to whether the Christian is to expect "rewards" for service that are attendant to salvation as the gratuitous gift of God, or the reward is to consist in the inheritance (cf., Colossians 3:24). If the former, then the Christian is to be the recipient of certain rewards based upon faithful service to Christ. If the latter, then the Christian is to be viewed in the wholeness of his character as one who has been gratuitously justified and now receives the reward of the fruit of that justification, i.e., eternal salvation. Calvin understands God as rewarding the blessing previously given. By this he means that God first makes the blessing secure through absolute grace, but then rewards the blessing through the obedience wrought by the sure knowledge of the original blessing promised. Thus, Abraham is said to have been awarded the blessing after his act of obedience in offering up his son. This is so despite the absolute certainty of the blessing through the promise given many years earlier on the basis of gratuitous grace alone. Calvin comments,

> "Here assuredly we see without ambiguity that God rewards the works of believers with blessings which he had given them before the works were thought of, there still being no cause for the blessings which he bestows but his own mercy."[1]

With respect to these verses, the justification of the sinner is not in mind. That has been secured to the sinner by virtue of the imputation of the righteousness of Christ. One writer who holds to the view that the *bema* seat is for the Christian to receive rewards for faithful service gives us a helpful summary of this viewpoint.

> "It is important to see that the purpose of this tribunal is not positively penal, but properly retributive, involving the disclosure not only of what has been worthless but also of what has been good and valuable in this life. The judgment pronounced is not a declaration of doom, but an assessment of worth, with the assignment of rewards to those who because of their faithfulness deserve them, and the loss or withholding of rewards in the case of those who do not deserve them."[2]

In concluding this section, we observe that there exists a great chasm between God favoring His own with kindness in the New Heaven and New Earth, and God being obligated as a debtor conditioned upon the "merits" of His children. On one side of the chasm is the testimony of Christianity and on the other side that of Catholicism. All hope is gone if God should judge us on the basis of our own merit. Not so for the Catholic who confidently asserts,

> "We hope for heaven, however well disposed we might be spiritually, because we know we still have a chance to lose it."[3]

---

[1] Calvin, *Institutes*, Book 2, Chapter 18
[2] Hughes, Philip E., *Second Epistle to Corinthians*, NIC, (Grand Rapids, Eerdmans, ©1962) pp. 181, 182
[3] Keating, *Catholicism and Fundamentalism*, pg. 175

In concluding this, the Romanist fails to comprehend that the Christian has the assurance of Heaven because he hopes in the Lord Jesus Christ. The Christian believes the promises of God in Christ. The Roman Catholic cannot comprehend that, for the Christian, hope is in that which is seen although not in a physical sense. For Abraham saw the city of God in Hebrews 11. Also, Paul affirms that hope does not disappoint in Romans 5:5. It will do no good to say that confidence is contra to the Scriptures because to have such confidence is to eliminate hope via Romans 8:24. Hope in the Scriptures is not doubt. It is rather the settled assurance of things to come. The author of hope is God. Paul's prayer for the Christians at Rome was that the God of hope would fill them with all joy and peace in believing, "that ye may abound in hope, through the power of the Holy Ghost" (Romans 15:13). Abounding in hope is hardly characterized in Scripture as always wondering whether the good works I can muster will qualify me for a place in God's eternal kingdom! It is a matter of record, that one character trait of those who have not the gospel of Christ is that they have "no hope" (cf., Ephesians 2:12).

Chapter 7

Baptism

PREVIOUSLY, we have alluded to the Catholic sacrament of baptism. In this section we will examine Romanist claims as they pertain to baptism. But before we do that we need to correct the Roman Catholic understanding of election. Catholics think that we think one becomes elect at the instant of accepting Christ. While it is true that one is aware of his determination to follow Christ at the time of belief, one's election unto God is not determined by such a decision. Election is in the hands of God. It is God who has an elect according to His grace. The decision to elect was made by God in eternity past. It is not that we effectuate our own election by believing. Rather, we believe having been elected! (cf., Romans 11:5; Ephesians 1:4-11; 2 Thessalonians 2:13). Election is out of the hands of man. Neither faith nor any act of man brings about election. Therefore, baptism cannot turn someone into a Christian or into a member of the Body of Christ.

The Catholic religion is absolutely contrary to Biblical Christianity when it comes to both the meaning of and candidates for baptism. Christians view baptism as a symbol of an inward reality. We believe that the Bible teaches a "Believer's Baptism" for those who profess faith in Jesus Christ for their salvation. It is an ordinance of the Church which pictures an inward spiritual reality. The Catholic religion sees it altogether differently as can be seen from the following assertion:

> "The Catholic Church has always understood baptism differently, of course, understanding it as a sacrament that accomplishes several things, the first of which is the remission of sin, both original sin and actual sin: in the case of infants and young children, only original sin, since they are incapable of actual sin; in the case of older persons, both. 'Repent, Peter said to them, and be baptized, every one of you, in the name of Jesus Christ, to have your sins forgiven; then you will receive the gift of the Holy Spirit. This promise is for you and your children, and for all those, however far away, whom the Lord our God calls to himself' (Acts 2:38-39). We also read: 'Rise up, and receive baptism, washing away your sins at the invocation of his name' (Acts 22:16). These commands are universal, not restricted to adults.

"Along with this forgiveness of sins comes an infusion of grace. It is this grace that makes the soul spiritually alive and capable of enjoying heaven. There are other benefits, too, such as the elimination of punishment due for sins and the right to special graces necessary to enable the baptized to fulfill his baptismal promises."[1]

We shall sort out the Catholic position by first giving some theological markers. We have to deal with two issues here. The first is the meaning of baptism and the second is the candidate for baptism. Catholics assign a particular meaning to baptism and assign the giving of baptism to babies as well as adults. The picture becomes more complex because many earnest Protestant denominations assign baptism to babies as well. We must admit to a powerful stream out of the Protestant Reformation which does assign baptism to babies as well as adults. However, we do not know of a single Protestant community that gives the same meaning to infant or adult baptism as the Romanist. A Presbyterian or a Lutheran may indeed baptize babies but they do so with a completely different understanding of what they are doing. We recognize the efforts of many Christians who wish to maintain a bridge of continuity between circumcision in the Old Testament and baptism of the New Testament. Even so, the Protestant paedo-baptists are not Roman Catholic sacramentalists and the two poles of meaning must be kept separate though the candidates are the same in each case.

It is fair to say that some Protestant denominations practice infant baptism but for entirely different reasons than Rome. In saying this, we must emphasize that the Protestant insistence on paedo-baptism by some is distinguished as an effort to maintain some sort of covenant continuity. This does not discount the Christian formula of having to personally believe in Christ and trust Him as Savior in any way. There is no eternal salvation begun in Protestant baptized babies. Neither is justification language a part of the Protestant paedo-baptist formula.[2]

---

[1] Keating, *Catholicism and Fundamentalism*, pp. 177, 178

[2] There are two issues involved here. The first is the practice itself of infant baptism. The second is the meaning of the practice! Several Reformers and precursors to many modern denominations continued the practice of infant baptism while eliminating the Roman Catholic meaning of baptism. This explains why so many sincere Christians continue the practice of infant baptism. Essentially, these Reformers emptied infant baptism of Catholic meaning and kept the practice while substituting their own new meaning. We do not wish to denigrate the sincerity of modern day covenant theologians who still champion infant baptism within the framework of their understanding of the two Covenants. Yet we can hardly pass by this issue by merely making mention of the error that Rome imposes on the meaning of baptism. We believe that both the meaning assigned by Rome to their infant baptism, and the practice of it, regardless of any attached meaning, serves to confuse the biblical data available as to the proper candidates for a biblical baptism.
continued on following page

Protestant views aside, the Roman Catholic religion is confident that both their practice and their meaning of baptism can be defended from Scripture. When we break down the Catholic arguments from Scripture, we find them relying basically on one passage to give meaning to their infant baptism (i.e., regeneration).

As to meaning, Catholics are convinced that one is "born from above" or "born again" in the waters of their baptism. Romanists think their baptism is the teaching of John 3:5. "Jesus said that no one can enter heaven unless he has been born again of water and the Holy Spirit (John 3:5)."[1] It is the universal teaching of Rome that the water in John 3:5 is the water of Baptism. It is almost an *a priori* assumption! We ask, "Why?" Baptism is nowhere mentioned in this context. Nicodemus, to whom this pronouncement was made, was chided for not knowing this teaching (cf., John 3:10). Why would our Lord chide Nicodemus for not knowing about Christian baptism? It had not even been introduced yet! Furthermore, the entire passage speaks of being born of the Spirit. Water is introduced, but the text does not say water *and the* Spirit. It reads literally, *water and Spirit*. The two could very well be taken together as different aspects of the work of the Spirit. Nicodemus should have understood how many times the Spirit is referred to in terms of washing or water in Israel's past. There are fully four different meanings which could be assigned to the term water as it is used here in conjunction with the Holy Spirit:

- 1. Water and Spirit are contrasted: You must be born (not only) of water but the Spirit. Water equals Old Testament ritual cleansing. Thus, one must be born of the water (ceremonially clean, but of

---

In refuting the Roman Catholic practice of infant baptism we are forced into a dilemma. For in so doing, we find ourselves refuting the exact same arguments for the practice of infant baptism called forth by our Protestant covenantal friends. We trust the reader will understand that it would be unwise to only attempt to topple the scaffold of meaning without addressing the scaffold of practice whether it be in the Romanist or Christian camp. We are equally aware that many would disagree with our exegesis within the Christian community. They would want to retain what appears to them a perfectly biblical practice only chasing out the Catholic meaning. We can only hope the reader is aware how fervently this difference must be maintained and protected by Protestants of the covenantal persuasion. We are wary of the Protestant community being able to maintain this critical distinction in light of Vatican II's pronouncement on Christian baptism and the non-Catholic religions which we shall get to presently.

For our part, we see it important to question not only the meaning but also the practice regardless of what meaning is considered in the practice. Nevertheless, our argument in this book is not nearly so much with the practice of infant baptism as with the absolutely heretical meaning ascribed to it by the Roman Catholic religion.

[1] Keating, *Catholicism and Fundamentalism*, pg. 178

the Spirit, too). Christ was granting that Nicodemus was born of the "water," i.e., clean.

- 2. Water and are Spirit contrasted: You must be born of water (figure for cleansing due to repentance) and the regeneration of the Holy Spirit.

- 3. Water and Spirit are the same, only two aspects: You must be born of water (cleansing work of the Holy Spirit) as well as the regeneration of the Holy Spirit.

- 4. Water and Spirit are contrasted: You must be born of water (John's baptism) and the Spirit (cf., 1:26,31; Matthew 3:11; Mark 1:8; Luke 3:16).

The Old Testament seems to use water as a symbol of the cleansing work of the Holy Spirit (cf., Psalm 51:2,3; Isaiah 1:16 and Jeremiah 33:8). But, the water in Ezekiel 36:25,26 is closely associated with the Spirit's work in regeneration. This has led some to translate John 3:5 as, "You must be born of the water, (even) the Spirit," the idea being that water and Spirit refer to the same thing (purification), with water representing cleansing and Spirit signifying regeneration (see 3, above).

In all of this, if the new birth could be called down by baptism, which is not even mentioned in the context, what should we do with John 3:8, which states clearly that the Spirit is free?

> "The wind bloweth where it listeth, and thou hearest the sound thereof, but canst not tell whence it cometh, and whither it goeth: so is every one that is born of the Spirit." (John 3:8)

One thing is for certain. Water and Spirit are not inseparable in the New Testament. Throughout the book of Acts and the rest of the New Testament we find that the Spirit is free to fall as He will. He is not called down by a priest as part of a sacramental ritual. As it is in the context of John 3:1-8, the Spirit is free and comes from above under the jurisdiction of God, not man. We ask the reader to compare the coming of the Holy Spirit as it is given throughout the New Testament to find out if John 3:5 must mean water baptism as Rome insists (cf., Acts 2:4,17,33; 8; 10:44-48; and 19:1-7).

We point out that in addition to Rome's insistence on John 3:5 meaning water baptism, there is an equal reluctance (defiance?) to see a distinction between baptism in/with/by the Holy Spirit and water baptism. We understand that the Spirit is about the business of baptizing believers into Christ (Romans 6:3), baptizing believers into the body of Christ (1 Corinthians 12:13), and indwelling the believer (baptism with the Spirit) at the time of conversion (Ephesians 1:13). In all this there may be a close association with water in the New Testament, but the Spirit is not dependent upon water and comes quite apart from it to those who believe. The Romanist must prove that John 3:5 means water baptism. It cannot be done.

Furthermore, the Romanist must prove that their water baptism calls down the Spirit of God and washes away sin. It cannot be done. Also, the Romanist must prove that infants should be the recipients of this so-called sacrament of grace. It cannot be done.

Aside from John 3:5, two verses are mustered to prove that baptism will wash away sins. They are Acts 2:38 and 22:16. Let us turn our attention to these passages before concentrating on the Catholic arguments for infant candidates.

In his inaugural sermon to his countrymen at Pentecost, Peter responds to those who have been "smitten in conscience" when they ask him what they should do (Acts 2:37). He tells them,

> "Repent [*metanoia*, not do penance], and be baptized every one of you in the name of Jesus Christ for the remission of sins, and ye shall receive the gift of the Holy Ghost." (Acts 2:38)

From this the Romanists conclude that baptism calls down the Holy Spirit. They also see water as the physical agent involved in the granting of forgiveness of sins. What Roman Catholicism fails to consider is that water and Spirit are not inseparable in the outworking of salvation. In Acts 1:5 we have a distinction between the two. Notice that in Acts 11:16 we see the same distinction. Acts 2:4 gives us Spirit but no water. Acts 8:16 gives us water but no Spirit. Acts 10:44 gives us the Spirit first, and then water! Furthermore, Luke never uses baptism alone as the prerequisite for sin forgiveness. Baptism is always used in conjunction with the heart's attitude, such as repent (6 times), turn (11 times) and believe (39 times). While each of these terms stands alone in Scripture as the heart's attitude for salvation, baptism is never used alone. Here in Acts 2:38 the answer for those smitten by the preaching of the Word is to repent and then be baptized for (*eis*) the forgiveness of sins. It is uncertain whether the *eis* here should be translated as "because of" or "for" or "unto" or "so that." Grammarians are divided on its usage. Roman Catholicism naturally takes the meaning of *eis* to mean, "to have your sins forgiven." But either way, the text proves only that those who first repent and then are baptized will receive the Holy Spirit and have forgiveness of sins they have committed. Acts 2:38 is clearly a case of already repentant believers being baptized.

The case of Acts 22:16 is very similar to that of Acts 2:38. In Acts 22 Paul is recounting his experience at the house of Ananias as part of his defense of the gospel in front of the crowds in Jerusalem before being sent to Rome. He was in effect giving testimony of his regeneration experience. This is part and parcel of the normal Christian experience of those who have come to Christ. Paul tells his audience what Ananias told him to do after having received back his eyesight. Ananias informed Paul that he had been chosen by God to know His will, to see the Righteous One, and to hear a message from His mouth. After telling Paul further that Paul would be a messenger of the gospel, Ananias told Paul to "...arise, and be baptized, and wash away thy sins, calling on the name of the Lord" (Acts 22:16). From this the Romanists conclude that baptism forgives sins. It is lost entirely on this type of exegesis that Paul had already been touched by God. Paul was a broken and smitten man who had already seen the risen Lord as no other man had done before. It remained for this "Jew of Jews" to now identify through baptism with the Lord Jesus Christ. The normal formula for this is to arise and be baptized, calling on the name of the Lord. It is for believers to do this. The forgiveness of sin comes with the repentant heart. The water pictures the death, burial and resurrection of the Lord. Dunn summarizes:

> "Luke never mentions water-baptism by itself as the condition of or means to receiving forgiveness; he mentions it only in connection with some other attitude (repentance—Luke 3:3; Acts 2:38) or act (calling on his name—Acts 22:16). But whereas water-baptism is never spoken of as the sole prerequisite to receiving forgiveness, Luke on a number of occasions speaks of repentance or faith as the sole prerequisite (Luke 5:20; 24:47; Acts 3:19; 5:31; 10:43; 13:38; 26:18; c.f.; 4:4; 9:35, 42; 11:21; 13:48; 14:1; 16:31; 17:12,34). In other words, water-baptism is neither the sole preliminary nor in itself an essential preliminary to receiving forgiveness...

> "Finally we may note that in Acts Christians are called 'those who call upon the name of the Lord,' but never 'the baptized.' The essential characteristic of the Christian and that which matters on the human side is in the last analysis faith and not water-baptism."[1]

As we have stated, the baptism issue must be discussed on two fronts. We have tested the meaning of baptism as given to us by Rome and found their exegesis wanting in the two most familiar passages. A more complete analysis of Roman baptism would require a book of its own. Let it suffice for now to be alerted that Rome uses John 3:5 in connection with Acts 2:38 and 22:16 to try to prove that baptism removes sin. Along with these

---

[1] Dunn, James, *Baptism in the Holy Spirit*, (Philadelphia: Westminster Press, ©1970) pp. 96-98

verses, Rome appeals to 1 Peter 3:21, Galatians 3:27, Titus 3:5, 1 Corinthians 12:13 and Ephesians 4:5 with Romans 6.

The second front is the recipients of baptism. Rome not only concludes that baptism washes away sins for adults, but also for infants. This is the heart of Rome! Convinced by their own exegesis that baptism washes sin away, Rome now lines up infants born to Catholic families and washes away what they call the original sin of Adam in the waters of baptism. What shall we say to this? Rome compounds the error! Rome is wrong to assert that water baptism washes away sins, and doubly wrong to administer this to infants.

The proof of their insistence on baptizing babies is found in a number of conclusions and deductions which qualify more for wishful thinking than clear-headed biblical interpretation. Catholic exegesis runs quickly through this section and hopes to be convincing by quoting a few verses. They begin with Matthew 19:14, "...Suffer little children, and forbid them not, to come unto me: for of such is the kingdom of heaven." Catholics think Christians want to make these children only older children so as to avoid what they think is the obvious, i.e., infant baptism. This is not true. We recognize a number of things about this passage and the parallels in Mark 10:14 and Luke 18:16. For the record, Luke does use *brephe* which is the Greek term for babies. But he is the only one to do so. One might ask if Luke might not be using this term synonymously with *paidion* the normal word for child. Also, the children were "brought" to Jesus. The term used here is a dedication term, not a baptismal term. Also, there is no water or baptism mentioned here. What is mentioned is that Jesus laid His hands on these children and prayed. Furthermore, the entire context of all three gospels is to show that the kingdom of Heaven belongs to this kind [*toiouton*] or this sort of person, i.e., children! The teaching here is the same as that in Matthew 18:2-6, "Except ye be converted, and become as little children [*hos paidion*]." Again, the teaching is the same in Mark 10:13-16, which parallels Matthew 19:14—the point being that anyone wishing to enter the kingdom of God must be "as a child."

Perhaps this refers to the childlike faith of the Christian who believes that Jesus will save him based upon faith in Jesus alone apart from works of the law, including religious sacramental systems! There is neither water here nor baptism, and we might ask of the text as interpreted by the Romanist: "How is a baby being baptized an example of an adult entering into the kingdom of Heaven?"

Before discussing the household baptisms, which are cited by both Protestants and Romanists as proof of infant baptism, we must direct our attention to a rather glib and unsubstantiated statement by one Romanist concerning circumcision. It is asserted simply "...Paul notes that baptism has replaced circumcision (Colossians 2:11-12)."[1] Really? What are we to do with such *de facto* statements given without a shred of proof or even discussion? Catholicism makes the crossover from circumcision in the Old Testament to Roman Catholic baptism in the New by fiat. We notice that there is no proof of this crossover in the Bible. Perhaps Catholicism senses it would be futile to try to construct a solid biblical argument for such an unwarranted assumption. Catholics tend to mesh together the Old Covenant ritual of circumcision with Roman Catholic baptism. This is done on the sole ground that infants were circumcised in the Old Covenant. Thus, Catholicism builds an imaginary bridge from Old Testament circumcision to their New Testament baptism.

If New Covenant baptism is nothing more than the replacement of Old Covenant circumcism, then it could be argued that the meaning of baptism and the candidates for baptism should be determined by the meaning of circumcision. But does Colossians 2:11,12 teach this? We answer, "No." Neither Colossians 2 nor any other passage in the New Testament teaches us that baptism takes the place of circumcision. Baptism does not replace circumcision as though one is the same as the other! Circumcision was given to both the spiritual and physical seed of Abraham, including the sons of Keturah and Ishmael. Baptism is reserved for all those who call upon the name of the Lord. Circumcision marked out a national identity of the nation of Israel. All males born into the nation were circumcised. Baptism is reserved for those born again into the New Covenant. There was no necessity of faith in order for circumcision in the Old Covenant. Faith is the prerequisite for the waters of New Testament baptism. Circumcision was given automatically in Israel to identify a people under local, earthly national promises which are a shadow of the heavenly ones to come. Not all of Israel are true Israelites (cf., Romans 9:7,8). Thus, circumcision has no reference to the New Covenant in Christ's blood. In the case of Abraham, circumcision was a seal of the faith of Abraham, faith which he possessed prior to circumcision (cf., Romans 4:11). Contra Romanists, the function of the seal of circumcision in the life of Abraham was to ratify that which was present—not to bring it about! There is not a shred of evidence that circumcision removed the stain of original sin in any of Israel. It is nonsense to say that baptism removes sin while at the same time saying it takes the place of circumcision. When did circumcision ever do this?

What about Colossians 2:11,12? Paul tells the Colossians that:

"In whom (Christ) also ye are circumcised with the circumcision made without hands, in putting off the body of the sins of the flesh by the circumcision of Christ: Buried with him in baptism, wherein

---

[1] Keating, *Catholicism and Fundamentalism*, pg. 178

also ye are risen with [him] through the faith of the operation of
God, who hath raised him from the dead."

From this the Romanist concludes that baptism takes the place of circumcision.[1]

In the first place, verse 11 specifies that the work here is done by the Lord
without hands. It is a work on the heart which cannot be performed through
religious formulas. It is the Spirit's work. This circumcision is that of the
heart (cf., Romans 2:28,29). It is not the national circumcision of the Old
Testament which is in view here. Secondly, the removal of the body of
flesh is figurative language which references the cleansing work of the Holy
Spirit very similar to 1 Peter 3:21 along with Galatians 3:27 and Romans
2:28,29. The clause, "Buried with him in baptism," refers in a figurative
way to our death, burial, and resurrection with Christ in the same sense that
Romans 6:1-5f is used by Paul to convey the same reality. The baptism here
has nothing to do with a physical circumcision or a physical baptism. The
baptism here may have the water ritual for confessing believers in the
backdrop, but the emphasis is on the spiritual reality of the believer being
baptized into Christ as well as being raised with Him! All believers are
baptized into His death and raised with Him to newness of life while
awaiting their final resurrection.

Our final expositional argument with the Romanists on the meaning and
candidates of baptism centers around the contention that infants *must* have
been part of the so-called household baptisms of the New Testament. There
are five passages normally cited as proof that infants were baptized. Four
are in the book of Acts. They are Acts 11:14; 16:15, 33; and 18:8. There is
not a mention of an infant or a child being baptized in any of these passages!
Also, in each passage there is at least the indication, if not outright statement, that the ones being baptized had believed! When Peter recounts the
conversions at the house of Cornelius in Acts 11:14, he tells how Cornelius
was first impressed by God that Peter would come and speak words by
which the household of Cornelius would be saved. All we have to do is go
back to Acts 10:44ff to relive the experience. The Holy Spirit fell and they
began speaking in tongues and Peter wanted to baptize those who had re-

---

[1] It is at this juncture that some of the finest Reformation exegetes have done the
bulwark of their exposition on the relationship between circumcision as a sign and seal of
Old Covenant blessings and baptism to the New Covenant. We are fully aware that Dr.
Boettner was in sympathy, as a Presbyterian, with the covenantal scheme which included
baptizing infants into the household of God. We have already expressed our disagreement
with this particular interpretation of the scriptural data *but hasten to add that we stand
100% with Boettner* against what he calls the Romanistic "perversion of the meaning of
baptism." (*Roman Catholicism*, pg. 190)

ceived the Spirit just as he had! Where are the babies? Did the alleged babies receive the Holy Spirit apart from baptism? If so, then what of Rome's doctrine of infant baptism to call down the Spirit? If they did receive the Spirit, did they speak in tongues? This is argumentation from silence at its very worst! Household does not have to mean babies! In fact, it was very common in poor homes to house relatives which included uncles and cousins.

In Acts 16:14 Lydia had to have her heart opened by the Lord and then she believed and was baptized. She and her household were baptized but there is no mention of children or infants. The silence is deafening. In Acts 16:33 the Philippian jailer was baptized along with "all his." Catholics contend the "all his" here must mean babies of the household. We ask, "Why?" Roman Catholicism seems to have no answer other than if it were only his wife the text would have said so! This is typical Romanist exegesis. An entire argument is built from silence. Roman Catholics want us to believe that Luke would have reported *only the Philippian jailer and his wife* if that is all he meant by baptism. We will give you what remains of this critical passage: "...and (he) rejoiced, believing in God with all his house" (Acts 16:34). So much for non-believing infants being baptized.

Acts 18:8 says simply that Crispus believed in the Lord "...with all his house." The ones believing were being baptized. Notice the end of Acts 18:8, which reads, "...and many of the Corinthians hearing believed, and were baptized." This is the norm for the Christian experience. Believers are baptized! Catholicism pushes its point that Paul said he baptized the household of Stephanas in 1 Corinthians 1:16. What is left out is that 1 Corinthians 16:15 tells us the rest of the story of the household of Stephanas. It was the household of Stephanas which Paul singled out as the first fruit of Achaia who devoted themselves for the ministry of the saints. Where do we find non-believing infants being baptized?

In the final analysis, infants are alleged by the Catholic community to have been baptized in the New Testament to replace circumcision and eliminate original sin. Thus, the first and perhaps foremost pillar of the Romish sacramental system falls into a pile of dust and debris when examined by the Word of God. When the Catholic says,

> "At any rate, there is nothing in the New Testament that says infants and young children are unsuited to baptism,"[1]

we can readily see how much Romanists have fallen in love with their own contrivances. The Christian knows better and reserves the ordinance of baptism to the professing believer.

---

[1] Keating, *Catholicism and Fundamentalism*, pp. 179, 180

Baptism and History

Catholicism makes sweeping statements about early Christian practices when it comes to baptism. It asserts, "The present Catholic attitude accords perfectly with early Christian practices."[1]

But does it? We refer the reader to T. E. Watson's excellent little book entitled *Should Infants Be Baptized?* He could find no mention of infant baptism from Dionysius (95 A.D.), Epistle of Barnabas (125 A.D.), Shepherd of Hermas (150 A.D.), Ignatius of Antioch (107 A.D.), or Clement of Rome (100 A.D.). We add to these Melito, Polycarp, Theophilus and Athenagoras along with Clement of Alexandria (195 A.D.). We also recommend the historical section of Paul Jewett's book entitled *Infant Baptism and the Covenant of Grace* as an additional historical guide to the question of early infant baptism. The earliest writer to mention infant baptism was Tertullian about 200 A.D. His understanding is worth mentioning:

> "And so, according to the circumstances and disposition, and even age, of each individual, the delay of baptism is preferable; principally, however, in the case of little children... The Lord does indeed say, 'Forbid them not to come unto me.' Let them 'come,' then, while they are growing up; let them 'come' while they are learning; let them become Christians when they have become able to know Christ."[2]

This citation would be enough to answer the bewildering question asked by Catholics as to why, if the early Church opposed infant baptism, did not someone speak out against it? Tertullian at least did! Has it not occurred to Roman Catholicism that it was not an issue because the practice of it was non-existent in the early Church?

Certainly the reader has come to understand that there is a far reaching and deep chasm which separates what we are saying from the theology of Rome. Who could disagree that our differences go right to the heart of one's understanding of salvation itself? Furthermore, in our disagreements, we are held by biblical strictures whereas the Romanist is free to wander through the vineyard of his own traditions and philosophies eating the fruit thereof, a fruit forbidden to Christians!

---

[1] Keating, *Catholicism and Fundamentalism*, pg. 180
[2] Watson, T. E., *Should Infants Be Baptized?*, (Grand Rapids: Baker House, ©1976) pg. 60

Chapter 8

Penance

AS WE have seen in the previous section on baptism, Romanists believe baptism washes away sin. Original sin is washed away in the waters of infant baptism and pre-baptismal sins are washed away in✗ the waters of adult baptism. But what about post-baptismal sinning? How does a Catholic expect to have sins committed *after baptism* removed? The answer for the Romanist is the sacrament of penance. In the sacrament of penance, or reconciliation, the penitent confesses his sins to a Catholic priest, who then absolves the sin and prescribes some type of "penance" for the penitent to accomplish as a suitable penalty for his sins. The normally assigned penance is saying so many prayers on the Catholic Rosary or perhaps some other service to God. In contrast, the Christian position has been, and always will be, that each individual is a priest before God and has ✗ one high priest in Heaven, Jesus Christ, through whom we have access to ✗ God and forgiveness of sin in His name. There is no need of an earthly priest to confer forgiveness. The Christian can go directly to God and does not need a human priest to stand in the gap!

If the Roman priesthood can be shown to be a bogus tradition of men then the entire religion begins to fall. As infant baptism is the pillar of Rome's enslavement of infants, so is the sacrament of penance the enslavement of Rome's communicants.

There are a number of assumptions in Roman Catholic theology which tend to boggle the mind, but none more audacious than the one which undergirds the sacrament of penance. It is twofold. First, the Romanist insists that the death of Christ was not sufficient to forgive sins and that Christ left us with our own "satisfactions" to perform for forgiveness of sins. The second is that Jesus was acting in the capacity of a man when he forgave sins on earth. We will deal with the second assumption first.

It is alleged that Jesus Christ was acting as a mere man when He forgave the paralytic his sins in Mark 2, and the adulterous woman her sins in John 8. This is another one of those fiat statements without any discussion or proof. How can we split the nature of the Son of God incarnate as to man vs. God in His capacity as sin-forgiver? Rome is silent as to the reason for such a

95

distinction. Keating forgets that this was God incarnate forgiving sins and not only the man Jesus. At least the Pharisees of the first century understood what Jesus claimed to be doing and they were right in their assessment! "Why doth this [man] thus speak blasphemies? who can forgive sins but God only?" (Mark 2:7) Evidently the Catholic apologist would chide the Pharisees and say, "No, a man can *also* forgive sins. This one before you has come as an example to show you just how you, too, can learn to forgive sins!" We hear the echo of Acts 8:19, "Give me also this power…"!

By what line of logic the Catholic apologist declares that Christ forgave sins only as man we cannot venture a guess. We do know that the title "Son of Man" is a common ascription of Jesus Christ and stands for His substitutionary head. Jesus would bear the curse of the Law and penalty of sin for His fellow men. But to deduce that He spoke as a man when He forgave sins is a *non sequitur*.

Having begun this astounding intrigue, the Romanist plows on! His next step is to show proof that Jesus passed along His "man only ability" to forgive sins onto His disciples.

Romanists rest their entire doctrine of penance upon one passage of Scripture. It is alleged that in John 20:22-23 Jesus Christ passed along to His select disciples the authority to actually forgive sins. They were not, according to Catholic dogma, given authority to merely *announce* the forgiveness of sins in Christ. Neither were they only to *declare* that forgiveness was available in Christ Jesus. No, we are told by Catholic apologists that they were given the authority to *really* and *actually* forgive sins. Moreover, it is alleged that they were given charge to pass this authority along to others! Hopefully the reader can begin to appreciate the absolute power the Catholic religion has over its constituency.

We observe from the text of John 20:23 that Jesus says, "Whose soever sins ye [you, plural] remit, they are remitted unto them; [and] whose soever [sins] ye retain, they are retained." From this the Romanist insists that there is power resident within the disciples that allows them to render the verdict on forgiveness of sin. This is deduced on the strength of the sentence "Whose soever sins *ye* remit…" The emphasis is on the *ye*!

This is where the quarrel with Rome begins. We say Christ conferred onto His disciples the authority to *proclaim* that forgiveness of sin is available to those who believe in Christ (cf., Luke 24:47). He did not give his disciples the authority to forgive sins based upon their appraisal of a person's willingness to do personal penance! We deny Christ gave power to only a select group and that this resident power was and is as unique as that of Christ to forgive sins. Also, we deny the manner in which Rome conducts the outworking of this alleged power to forgive sins in the confines of a confessional box or a whispering in the ear of a priest. We learn from Matthew 18:18 that this binding and loosing was given to the Church on the whole for matters of order and cleansing. Further, we observe how forgiveness of sins would be understood by the apostles themselves as is illustrated to us in redemptive history. The model we see in the book of Acts is the preaching of a full and free salvation. Forgiveness of sins is *proclaimed* in the name of Jesus Christ and there is not a word about a confessional box, penance or personal power to forgive sins! We notice in Acts 8, for instance, that Peter tells Simon, "...and pray God, if perhaps the thought of thine heart may be forgiven thee" (Acts 8:22).

We ask, "Where do we find this nonsense of the Romanist confession in the rest of the writings of the New Testament if such was established?" Where do Paul or Peter hear the confession of others? Where do we find the apostolic command for the apostles to breathe upon their successors in order that they, too, might have this alleged power to forgive sins based upon personal penance? It is clear that the apostles were given authority to proclaim forgiveness of sins only in the free forgiveness offered in the gospel based upon the work of Jesus Christ. This conclusion suffers no harm to the apostolic authority established by Christ for the purpose of instituting the early Church (cf., Ephesians 2:20). But to say that the apostles were endowed as men with the inherent ability to forgive sins is going too far! No one argues that the apostles wielded great authority in the formation of the Church. One cannot read too far into the writings of Paul to detect the need for such influence. But even this authority had its limits! With the onset of the written word and the passing away of the original Twelve, the focus of supremacy was on the Word as written and there simply is no record of the apostles ever having this alleged authority or of them passing it along to others.

For the purposes of historical review, we are indebted to the work of Peter J. Doeswyck. Doeswyck in his four-volume work entitled *History of Dogma* has taken the time to quote extensively from the early Church fathers. We ask the reader to consider Ambrose, Cyprian, Jerome and Augustine, respectively, when considering the modern notion of penance in the Romanist religion:

> "Now let us see whether the Spirit forgives sins. But here there can be no doubt, since the Lord himself has said: 'Receive ye the Holy Ghost, whose sins you shall forgive, they shall be forgiven.' Behold that sins are forgiven through the Holy Spirit. But men exhibit their ministry for the forgiveness of sin, they do not exercise the right of some power. For not in their own name but in that of the Father and the Son and the Holy Spirit do they forgive sins. They

ask, the God-head forgives; the obedience is of man, but the munificence is of the Power above."[1]

"After this also we pray for our sins, saying: 'And forgive us our debts, as we also forgive our debtors.' After the subsistence of food the pardon of sin is also asked so that he who is fed by God may live in God, and so that not only the present and temporal life may be provided for but also the eternal, to which we may come if our sins are forgiven, which the Lord calls debts, as He says in His Gospel: 'I forgave thee all the debt because thou didst entreat me.' Moreover, how necessarily, how providently and salutarily are we admonished that we are sinners, who are compelled to plead for our sins, so that, while indulgence is sought from God, the soul is recalled to a consciousness of its guilt! Lest anyone be pleased with himself, as if innocent, and by exalting himself perish the more, he is instructed and taught that he sins daily, since he is ordered to pray daily for his sins. Thus finally John also in his epistle admonishes in these words:' If we say that we have no sin, we deceive ourselves, and the truth is not in us. But if we acknowledge our sins, the Lord is faithful and just to forgive us our sins.' In his epistle he has combined both, that we should both entreat for our sins and that we should obtain indulgence when we entreat. Therefore, he said that the Lord was faithful to forgive sins, preserving the faith of His promise, because He who taught us to pray for our debts and our sins promised that mercy and forgiveness would follow."[2]

"And I will give thee the keys of the kingdom of heaven: and whatsoever thou shalt bind on earth...' [Matthew 16:19]. This passage the bishops and elders have misinterpreted and have assumed the arrogance of the Pharisees by thinking that they can either condemn the innocent or release the guilty; but in the eyes of God not the sentence of the bishop but the life of the sinner is considered."[3]

"He has given, therefore, these keys to His church (the believers), that 'whatsoever it should loose on earth might be loosed in heaven, and whatever it should bind on earth might be bound in heaven' [Matthew 16:9]. This means what whosoever (*quisquis*: anyone) in

---

[1] Saint Ambrose, *Theological and Dogmatic Works*, from: *The Fathers Of The Church*, (Washington, DC: The Catholic University of America Press, ©1963) pg. 203, Book 3, paragraph 137

[2] Cyprian, *Treatises*, from: *The Fathers Of The Church*, (NY: The Fathers of the Church, Inc., ©1958) pg. 147, Chapter 22

[3] Doeswyck, Peter, *The Roman Way of Salvation*, Volume 3, (Long Beach, CA: Knights of Christ, Inc., ©1963) pp. 52-55

His church does not believe that his sins are remitted, they are not remitted unto him; but whosoever should believe and should repent and turn away from his sins, the same, being established in the bosom of the Church itself, shall be healed by his very *faith and repentance*. For whosoever does not believe that his sins can be pardoned, becomes worse by the despair that there is nothing better for him than to remain evil, since he has no faith in the fruits of his own conversion."[1]

Thus far we have examined the Romish idea of confession to a priest and the false notion that forgiveness of sin resides within the hierarchy of Romanism. A simple comparison of John 20:23 with other verses of Scripture gives us light on the meaning of what Christ was doing in John 20.

"Go ye therefore, and *teach* all nations, baptizing them in the name of the Father, and of the Son, and of the Holy Ghost." (Matthew 28:19)

"And that *repentance and remission* of sins should be preached in his name among all nations, beginning at Jerusalem." (Luke 24:47)

"For John truly baptized with water; but ye shall be baptized with the Holy Ghost not many days hence. When they therefore were come together, they asked of him, saying, Lord, wilt thou at this time restore again the kingdom to Israel? And he said unto them, It is not for you to know the times or the seasons, which the Father hath put in his own power. But ye shall receive power, after that the Holy Ghost is come upon you: and *ye shall be witnesses* unto me both in Jerusalem, and in all Judaea, and in Samaria, and unto the uttermost part of the earth." (Acts 1:5-8)

"Then Peter said unto them, Repent, and be baptized every one of you in the name of Jesus Christ *for the remission of sins*, and ye shall receive the gift of the Holy Ghost." (Acts 2:38)

Now, in light of these verses, consider what John wrote on the matter and see if Rome's isolated use of this verse to justify the confessional box can stand in the presence of the previous citations:

"*Whose soever sins ye remit*, they are remitted unto them; [and] whose soever [sins] ye retain, they are retained." John (20:23)

---

[1] Doeswyck, *The Roman Way of Salvation*, Volume 3, pp. 48-49. Emphasis in original

It is apparent that the commission to evangelize is tightly woven into the commission to *proclaim forgiveness of sin* through faith in Jesus Christ. We cannot detect in the book of Acts or in the Epistles one shred of evidence for a priestly class imbued with special powers to forgive sins. Christ sent His followers to the remotest corners of the earth to preach forgiveness of sins—not to hear confessions!

Let us now move to another aspect of Romish penance and their doctrine of satisfaction. It would be wrong enough for the Romanist to teach that a priest alone has the power to forgive sins. But they are not done! The priest has power to also prescribe suitable satisfactions for sin to the poor misguided sinner who seeks his hope in Rome. Adherents to Rome are taught that their satisfactions to God are part of their forgiveness. We ask, "Where in Scripture is our own atonement for sins the basis for forgiveness? Where is penance shackled onto the repentant sinner by either Christ or the apostles?"

At the heart of Rome's doctrine of repentance is a dreadful misunderstanding of the completed work of Jesus Christ on the cross. Christians believe that they can add nothing to the finished work of Christ. For this reason, the Christian takes his sins directly to Jesus and pleads His blood alone for forgiveness. The Christian enters into the Holy of Holies upon the blood of the Lamb and finds absolution from the Father. For the Christian 1 John 1:9 is a comfort: "If we confess our sins, he is faithful and just to forgive us [our] sins, and to cleanse us from all unrighteousness."

The Romanist scoffs at this personal access to God. The Romanist is only comfortable with the means his religion offers by which Christ allegedly forgives sins. The Romanist wishes to introduce the means of this *free* forgiveness as that of his own sacramental system. In so doing, he robs us of access to Christ and His finished glory by adding conditions of penance. He builds a wall preventing entrance to Christ, very much like the Pharisees who built a "wall of law" stifling any direct access to God! Over and over we see this same theme in the Catholic religion. Romanists are bent on delivering a system of salvation rather than the Person of Christ. If we could identify one overarching principle which separates Romanism from Christianity it would be this: Rome has concocted a religion designed to arrive at Jesus Christ, whereas Christianity is a *relationship* with the Person of Christ and not a *system* fashioned by man to get to Him! Rome says, "Christ has told us to do this and that and more of the same if you want to have a relationship with me." The Christian says, "Christ has told us to place all of our trust and confidence in His finished work and we shall be saved." For the Christian, Christ has not come to offer a sacramental system. On the contrary, He offers Himself. No system in the world can be substituted for the Person of Christ. It only intensifies the denial of Christ to insist that He gave to the world the Romanistic religion. Christianity shudders at the thought of giving one inch to the foolishness of Rome! The Roman Catholic religion is convinced that Christ has taught their way of getting to Heaven. Christians deny this to be true. It is that simple!

We close this section with the words of Scripture which for centuries have comforted those who have escaped the bondage of Romanistic priestcraft and have been found by a High Priest whose ministry has no end and is not conditioned upon the frail offerings of sinful men for its effectiveness.

"But Christ being come an high priest of good things to come, by a greater and more perfect tabernacle, not made with hands, that is to say, not of this building; Neither by the blood of goats and calves, but by his own blood he entered in once into the holy place, having obtained eternal redemption [for us]. For if the blood of bulls and of goats, and the ashes of an heifer sprinkling the unclean, sanctifieth to the purifying of the flesh: How much more shall the blood of Christ..." (Hebrews 9:11-14a)

"And they truly were many priests, because they were not suffered to continue by reason of death: But this [man], because he continueth ever, hath an unchangeable priesthood. Wherefore he is able also to save them to the uttermost that come unto God by him, seeing he ever liveth to make intercession for them." (Hebrews 7:23-25)

Chapter 9

Purgatory

W E TURN our attention now to the logical conclusion of Romish theology as it pertains to forgiveness of sin. Building upon their commitment of self-sacrificing for the forgiveness of sins, the Romanist grand finale is the doctrine of purgatory. What is purgatory? Allow Keating to explain:

> "Purgatory is a state of purification, where the soul that has fully repented of its sins but has not fully expiated them has removed from itself the last elements of uncleanliness."[1]

As in all Romanist dogmas there are underlying presuppositions which call for religious ritual to satisfy them. Purgatory is no exception. Purgatory really begins with a faulty understanding of the term "redemption." The Romanist has committed theological error. He falsely bifurcates (splits the meaning) of New Testament language. This splitting up of theological terminology robs it of its meaning and intent! Thus, redemption is said to be separate from salvation. Forgiveness is said to be separate from satisfaction. Covered is not the same as clean. To understand Roman Catholicism one must therefore come to grips with this bifurcation in terminology. Thus, the Romanist can be redeemed, but not saved. He can have his sins forgiven, but still must pay the penalty for his sins. He can be clothed with Christ and covered with the blood of the Lamb, but still be unclean. Christ's sacrifice on the cross can be complete, but is not closed![2] This goes back to our original discussion of salvation. The Romanist believes that Christ died on the cross to make it possible for man to save himself through the system of Romanism. Let us listen to the council of Trent.

> "The council teaches the liberality of Divine generosity is so great that we are able through Jesus Christ to make satisfaction to God the Father not only by punishments voluntarily undertaken by ourselves to atone for sins, or by those imposed by the judgment of the priest

---

[1] Keating, *Catholicism and Fundamentalism*, pg. 190

[2] John Paul II, Apostolic Letter *Salvifici Doloris* (On the Christian Meaning of Human Suffering), February 11, 1984, paragraph 24

according to the measure of our offense, but also, and this is the greatest proof of love, by the temporal afflictions imposed by God and borne patiently by us."[1]

Read and re-read that sentence. In it you will find the Romanist mindset. He thinks God to be loving and generous in allowing us, through Christ, to atone for our sins. The highlight of God's love to His own, in the Romanist system, is the enduring of priestly imposed punishments and temporal afflictions given by God Himself to atone for our sins. Is it any wonder they have concocted a purgatory of torment to chase their own, even after the grave, to suffer for sins?

Before examining the alleged biblical proof of this horrid doctrine, let us first get to the heart of the matter. Can one be redeemed and possibly miss salvation? Are we called upon to atone for our sins? Though forgiven sins, can we expect to be punished for them after death? Has God demanded that we be actually and totally clean in order to enter Heaven rather than declared clean on the basis of the blood of Christ?

The heart of the matter is found in the astounding (for the Christian) assertion that Christ has left behind works for us to do in order to either pay back His redemption or wipe out the punishment due our sins. On page 194 of Keating's book he responds to an article which claims demands of divine justice on the sinner have been completely fulfilled in Christ. Keating does not agree:

"This presumes there is a contradiction between the Redemption and our sufferings *in expiation for our sins*."[2]

Keating contends there is no contradiction between Christ suffering for our sins and us having to suffer (expiation) for our own sins. He adds that the two are compatible, "whether [the sufferings] are in this life or the next."[3] So that we do not miss this crucial point, we will listen to Keating again:

"Analogously, it is not contrary to the Redemption to say we must suffer for our sins; *it is a matter of justice*."[4]

"Having one's sins forgiven is not the same thing as having the punishment for them wiped out."[5]

---

[1] Schroeder, pp. 98, 98. From the 14th Session of Trent, chapter 9

[2] Keating, *Catholicism and Fundamentalism*, pg. 194. Emphasis added

[3] Keating, *Catholicism and Fundamentalism*, pg. 194

[4] Keating, *Catholicism and Fundamentalism*, pg. 195. Emphasis added

[5] Keating, *Catholicism and Fundamentalism*, pg. 195

"Purgatory makes sense only if there is a requirement that a soul not just be declared to be clean, but actually be clean."[1]

Let's back up a moment and look at the big picture. The best place to start with an answer is with the terminology of Scripture. Romanists believe one can be redeemed by what they call "the Redemption" and yet end up lost. In other words, "the Redemption" is the death of Christ on the cross which put the whole world under the category of redeemed. By this the Romanist means "ready to be forgiven, provided they do what God in Christ has given them to do." It is a universal and hypothetical redemption that the Catholics speak of. Redeemed to the Romanist means that God has now the freedom to take to Heaven those who do what Rome says! It is nothing for the Romanist to say the entire world is redeemed and reconciled to God through the death of Christ.

But this redemption does not materially affect anyone so long as they continue to resist the Romanist religion. To them, the world is redeemed, but may or may not be saved. Salvation is dependent on adherence to the Romanist religion. Why? Because Rome sincerely believes that this is what Christ came to establish. To Rome, penance and purgatory are two gifts given to the redeemed for personal punishment so that the penalty due sin can be satisfied!

Contrary to all this is the Christian position which believes Jesus Christ died to actually effect redemption for His own people, a redemption received by faith alone! Christians believe Jesus accomplished redemption for His own on the cross. The word "redemption" describes something that is bought or redeemed with a price (cf., 1 Co. 6:20). Scripture assures us that Jesus Christ bought with His own blood those for whom He died (cf., Revelation 5:9). The ultimate purchase price was the blood of Jesus and nothing can be added to it for redemption. The Bible nowhere teaches us to buy ourselves with our sufferings. Even the idea of contributing to the purchase price of redemption is unheard of in the pages of Scripture. Furthermore, there is no justification in supposing that those who have been redeemed by the blood of the cross will miss out on salvation. Redeemed is another way of describing the benefit of the finished work of Jesus on the cross. There is no danger of the redeemed missing salvation. Neither is there the possibility of those reconciled missing salvation. Reconciliation, like redemption, is another way of describing the result of the death of Christ for God's people. We should add that there is equally no danger of those who have trusted the satisfaction of Jesus Christ, through faith in His finished work alone, of missing salvation.

---

[1] Keating, *Catholicism and Fundamentalism*, pg. 195

Christians believe redemption (buy with a price), propitiation (satisfaction of God's justice), and reconciliation (brought into a proper relationship) are all terms used to describe the finished work of Christ. We cannot add to the work of the cross.

The redeemed are the forgiven. The redeemed are those who have been reconciled. The redeemed are those who have been saved and await their final salvation at the consummation of the ages.

How does Keating stack up against Scripture in his insistence that one can be forgiven but still have to pay the punishment of sin either now or in the life after?

"Blessed [is] the man to whom the Lord will not impute sin." (Romans 4:8)

"…Christ died for our sins according to the scriptures." (1 Corinthians 15:3)

"Who gave himself for our sins…" (Galatians 1:4)

"In whom we have redemption through his blood, [even] the forgiveness of sins." (Colossians 1:14)

"…when he had by himself purged our sins…" (Hebrews 1:3)

"And their sins and iniquities will I remember no more." (Hebrews 10:17)

"Who his own self bare our sins in his own body on the tree…" (1 Peter 2:24)

"Unto him that loved us, and washed us from our sins in his own blood…" (Revelation 1:5)

"And you, being dead in your sins and the uncircumcision of your flesh, hath he quickened together with him, having forgiven you all trespasses; Blotting out the handwriting of ordinances that was against us, which was contrary to us, and took it out of the way, nailing it to his cross." (Colossians 2:13)

The Romanist fails to see that the reason Christ came in the first place was that the punishment for sin was too big for any mere mortal to make atonement. God required a perfect sacrifice. This lamb without blemish is our Lord Jesus Christ. He died in the place of undeserving sinners so that they would not have to pay the price of sin. If God could have been satisfied with the sacrifices and punishments of men, then Christ would not have needed to die. As it is, His death ended the earthly tabernacle and put an end to the sacrifices of men. There is not one place in the Scriptures that even remotely suggests Christians are forgiven but must still pay the penalty and punishment for sin as the ground of salvation. While it is true that sin brings about pain and discomfort and even chastisement from a loving Father, these consequences of sin in our lives are never raised to the lofty heights of making God favorably inclined to save as though these consequences served as satisfactory penal sacrifices!

A Look at the Evidence

Purgatory comes from the Latin term *purgatio,* which means to cleanse or purify. The Romanist considers baptism, penance, and purgatory to be the means by which God accomplishes purgation of the sinner! We read this from the Council of Florence of 1438:

> "It (the Council) has likewise defined, that, if those truly penitent have departed in the love of God, before they have made satisfaction by worthy fruits of penance for sins of commission and omission, the souls of these are cleansed after death by purgatorial punishments; and so that they may be released from punishments of this kind, the suffrages of the living faithful are of advantage to them, namely, the sacrifices of Masses, prayers, and almsgiving, and other works of piety, which are customarily performed by the faithful for other faithful according to the institutions of the Church."[1]

The Roman Catholic argument for a place called purgatory begins with the same assumption that gave us the Roman penance. The death of Christ is not enough, hence, man has to undergo more penalties and sufferings. We ask the reader to compare Ephesians 1:7,14; 4:30 along with Hebrews 9:12-15 for further proof that redemption has been accomplished by Christ alone.

Roman Catholic scholars use two main sources for their doctrine of purgatory. The first is the Bible and the second, the Apocryphal writings, especially 2 Maccabees. Let us examine the Bible passages.

Catholic commentary has it that baptism in 1 Corinthians 15:29 is the same as the baptism in Mark 10:38 and thus refers to the suffering of those left

---

[1] Denzinger, Henry, *The Sources of Catholic Dogma*, (St. Louis, MO: B. Herder Book Co., ©1954) pg. 219, paragraph 693

behind on behalf of those gone on to purgatory. But, to our knowledge, Paul never uses baptism in such a metaphorical way. However enigmatic this passage may be, it is a stretch to make baptism here equal to suffering! Note Paul uses baptism 11 times in this letter and never does he use this term in such a manner. Even if he meant that some Corinthians were suffering for the dead, it does not follow that the dead were in purgatory in need of relief from suffering. Was Paul in danger every hour (cf., 1 Corinthians 15:30) so the dead in purgatory could be relieved?

Catholics appeal to 1 Corinthians 3:13-15 but the emphasis of this passage is the testing of *works*, not the burning of men! Notice that the *works* will become evident, the *works* will be tested. The Romanist wrongly assigns the burning to the man rather than to his works!

Catholics appeal to Matthew 5:25,26, but there is nothing here about purgatory. The idea here is to avoid the judge through an out-of-court settlement lest one be found guilty and sentenced to jail where he has to pay more than the disputed sum of money. It follows on reconciliation.

In Matthew 12:32, Catholic exegesis sees purgatory in the words, "neither in this world, neither in the [world] to come." The idea is that there will be forgiveness in the age to come because there is *no forgiveness in the age to come for those who blaspheme the Holy Spirit!* We discount this fantastic assumption with the parallel passage of Mark 3:29 which takes the sense of "...neither in the [world] to come" as meaning *never!* (cf. also, Luke 12:10) Besides, Romanism teaches purgatory as a place of suffering that will not be in the world to come. Furthermore, Roman Catholic teaching on purgatory is not forgiveness, but satisfaction!

An appeal is made to 1 Peter 3:18-20. The Catholic posits from this passage a third place which is not Heaven, since Heaven is not a prison, and not Hell, since Christ did not preach in Hell. But is this place purgatory? Why would Christ preach in purgatory? Scripture knows two compartments of Hades (Luke 16) in which believers, prior to the resurrection, are waiting and unbelievers, prior to the resurrection, are waiting. But there is no hope of one crossing over one to the other. Once again, an enigmatic Scripture is wrestled down to prove a fantastic doctrine which has to be imported to the text.

Insofar as Luke 23:42 is concerned, Catholic scholars consider the thief on the cross an exception to everything they teach about purgatory and penance! The thief, however, must be viewed as an ordinary Christian saved by simple faith in Christ.

We should mention two other passages, cited to prove purgatory, before moving on. The first is the Romanist interpretation of Colossians 1:24;

> "Who now rejoice in my sufferings for you, and fill up that which is behind of the afflictions of Christ in my flesh for his body's sake, which is the church." (Colossians 1:24)

Roman Catholic commentary on this verse finds Paul teaching a doctrine of personal suffering to fill up or complete that which is needed to be paid back to Christ. Keating quotes Ronald Knox here with language which is anything but clear!

> "Ronald Knox explained this passage by noting that 'the obvious meaning is that Christ's sufferings, although fully satisfactory on behalf of our sins, leave us under a debt of honour, as it were, to repay them by sufferings of our own.'"[1]

Here we have more Catholic doublespeak. Notice Knox says Christ's death is fully satisfactory on behalf of our sins (the Christian position), yet we need to somehow pay them back! Roman Catholics see this, "as it were," a "debt of honor." This of course is said to be the obvious meaning of the passage. We would like to know the obvious meaning of this interpretation of the passage! How can Christ's death be at once fully satisfactory on behalf of our sins and yet require of us a payback? What does this "repayment" mean anyway?

To understand the true meaning of this passage one need only look to the life of Paul and the history of the Body of Christ. That which is "lacking" in Christ's affliction has nothing to do with the insufficiency of His death on the cross. It has nothing to do with the complete satisfaction of His death in order to save forever those whom the Father gives to Him. Neither can the Romanist charge in here with his doublespeak and suggest that suffering by the believer somehow fills up the cup of our salvation. Christ has filled that cup to the brim for all of His own blood-bought sheep. What Paul references here is the history of suffering which continues in the Body of Christ long after the resurrection. That which is lacking refers to that which has not yet been completed. The sense is that the Body of Christ will undergo oppression until His return and this suffering completes that which is lacking, or wanting, or yet to be fulfilled in the suffering initiated by Jesus Christ.

The second passage of Scripture marshalled in support of purgatory is not really a specific passage at all but rather a life. The Romanist likes to use

---

[1] Keating, *Catholicism and Fundamentalism*, pg. 194

David as an example of one of God's own who expiated his sin by suffering the loss of his first born. Keating tells us that David needed to undergo expiation. He asks, "Can we expect less?"[1]

Let us set straight the record. Nowhere in the context of David's sin and corresponding punishment by God is the term "expiation" used. Also, David was not the one who offered up his son for an expiatory offering. God took David's son. David did not march himself off to a confessional box and receive the dreaded penance from a local priest: that he would have to offer his son as penance for his sin. In truth, David did repent of his sin, but in so doing realized that he could not possibly expiate the penalty due his sin. In Psalm 51 David overthrows the Romish notion of self expiation with these cherished words:

> "For thou desirest not sacrifice; else would I give [it]: thou delightest not in burnt offering. The sacrifices of God [are] a broken spirit: a broken and a contrite heart, O God, thou wilt not despise." (Psalms 51:16,17)

Furthermore, David is the Old Testament illustration used by Paul in Romans 4 when he seeks someone of authority from the Old Testament to prove a major point. Paul's point is that a man is justified by faith apart from the works of the law:

> "Blessed [is] the man to whom the Lord will not impute sin." (Romans 4:8, from Psalm 32:2)

David is hardly an illustration of the Romish doctrine of self-expiation. We realize that David received a severe chastisement from the Lord for his sins. But to link such an historical incident so as to prove the doctrines of penance and purgatory is beyond the realm of responsible biblical exegesis and speaks volumes of how Romanists arrive at their dogma.

Once again we have probed the heart of Rome. It is a religion not dissimilar to all pagan religions. It portrays God as being in expectation and need of countless human sacrifices in order to be expiated (satisfied). As we shall see, this pagan concept of God's revelation extends even to the death of Christ. To Rome, Christ's sacrifice must be repeated endlessly in a non-bloody manner in the Mass. Is it any wonder the Roman Catholic religion is able to imprison millions? Guilt, fear and self-expiation appeal so well to the fallen nature of man. Rome has mastered these deep feelings and manipulated her adherents into a maze of Roman ritual which feeds this absolutely erroneous concept of God. Rome says that we cannot expect the

---

[1] Keating, *Catholicism and Fundamentalism*, pg. 195

death of Christ to be put in our stead on the Day of Judgment. We must rather place before God our own sacrifices mixed in with that of Jesus. And since Christ can do no more, it is our sacrifices which really count! This is, simply put, another gospel.

Chapter 10

The Eucharist

THERE is perhaps no greater conflict between the Christian and the religion of Rome than that which centers around the Romish sacrament of the Mass and the Eucharist. We believe this to be true because, unlike other Catholic dogmas, the Romanist actually appeals to the Scripture for his support of this doctrine. In short, Catholics are taught that the wafer and wine used in the communion service is actually changed into the real flesh and blood of Jesus Christ by a priest. This transformation is called transubstantiation wherein the appearance of the bread and wine remain the same, but the substance changes into the body and blood of Christ. It is taken by faith that this actually happens. The words of Trent are clear:

"First of all, the holy council teaches and openly and plainly professes that after the consecration of bread and wine, our Lord Jesus Christ, true God and true man, is truly, really and substantially contained in the august sacrament of the Holy Eucharist under the appearance of those sensible things. For there is no repugnance in this that our Savior sits always at the right hand of the Father in heaven according to the natural mode of existing, and yet is in many other places sacramentally present to us in His own substance by a manner of existence which, though we can scarcely express in words, yet with our understanding illumined by faith, we can conceive and ought most firmly to believe is possible to God. For thus all our forefathers, as many as were in the true Church of Christ and who treated of this most holy sacrament, have most openly professed that our Redeemer instituted this wonderful sacrament at the last supper, when, after blessing the bread and wine, He testified in clear and definite words that He gives them His own body and His own blood. Since these words, recorded by the holy Evangelists and afterwards repeated by St. Paul, embody that proper and clearest meaning in which they were understood by the Fathers, it is a most contemptible action on the part of some contentious and wicked men to twist them into fictitious and imaginary tropes by which the truth of the flesh and blood of Christ is denied, contrary to the universal sense of the Church, which, as the pillar and ground of truth, recognizing with a mind ever grateful and unforgetting this most excellent favor of Christ, has detested as satanical these untruths devised by impious men."[1]

Like all Romanist dogma the Eucharist appears to be innocent enough at first glance. So what if some believe that they are actually eating and drinking the body and blood of Christ? What harm can there be in that? It is not until we unravel what is behind this teaching that we come to grips with the deep heresy of the Romanist religion. The real problem with transubstantiation (besides the fact that it is not taught in Scripture) is the priestcraft of Romanism. In order to change the simple elements of the bread and wine there had to have been instituted a priesthood with such magical powers. So before we go directly to the sword fight of John 6, we would like to focus attention on Rome's unwarranted assumption with regard to the establishment of a special class of priests which are said to have the power to call down Christ from Heaven and put Him sacramentally into the elements of communion!

We scour the New Testament and find nothing of a new priesthood other than the community of saints which includes the entirety of the Body of Christ. We read from the book of Hebrews that the priesthood of the Old Covenant has been abolished and that Christ is now the eternal high priest who lives forever in intercession for His people:

"But this [man], because he continueth ever, hath an unchangeable priesthood. Wherefore he is able also to save them to the uttermost that come unto God by him, seeing he ever liveth to make intercession for them. For such an high priest became us, [who is] holy, harmless, undefiled, separate from sinners, and made higher than the heavens; Who needeth not daily, as those high priests, to offer up sacrifice, first for his own sins, and then for the people's: for this he did once, when he offered up himself. For the law maketh men high priests which have infirmity; but the word of the oath, which was since the law, [maketh] the Son, who is consecrated for evermore." (Hebrews 7:24-28)

"By the which will we are sanctified through the offering of the body of Jesus Christ once [for all]. And every priest standeth daily ministering and offering oftentimes the same sacrifices, which can never take away sins: But this man, after he had offered one sacrifice for sins for ever, *sat down on the right hand of God; From henceforth expecting till his enemies be made his footstool*. For by

---

[1] Schroeder, pg. 73. From the 13th Session of Trent, chapter 1

one offering he hath perfected for ever them that are sanctified." (Hebrews 10:10-14)

In stark contrast to the above biblical data we read this from the 22nd and 23rd sessions of the Council of Trent as the heart of Rome speaks concerning the Catholic priesthood:

- Canon 1. "If anyone says that there is not in the New Testament a visible and external priesthood, or that there is no power of consecrating and offering the true body and blood of the Lord and of forgiving and retaining sins, but only the office and bare ministry of preaching the Gospel; or that those who do not preach are not priests at all, let him be *anathema*."[1]

- Canon 2. "If anyone says that by those words, 'Do this for a commemoration of me,' Christ did not institute the Apostles priests; or did not ordain that they and other priests should offer His own body and blood, let him be *anathema*."[2]

It appears if one eliminates the priestly caste from the Romanist system then the Eucharist crumbles. We are not hesitant to add that the Eucharist cannot stand alone from a careful exegesis of John 6. But we feel the dogma of the priesthood slipped in, to serve the Eucharist; is of equal error as the Eucharist itself. They rise and fall together!

We appreciate the insight given to us by William Webster in his excellent little book *Salvation: The Bible and Roman Catholicism*. Webster is accurate in his understanding of the error of the Romanist priesthood:

"Does the Bible teach that the Lord Jesus Christ instituted a special class of men in the church known as priests who would be given the authority to reconcile men with God through the Mass and through confession and penance? The answer to that question, as we shall see, is quite simply 'no.'

"First of all, as we noted in the previous chapter, the whole concept of continuing sacrifices is completely contradictory to the teaching of the Word of God. The Lord Jesus did not commission or institute a human priesthood, beginning with the apostles, who would continue the offering of sacrifices in a Mass. All sacrifices have now been abolished because the 'once for all' sacrifice of Jesus Christ is

---

[1] Schroeder, pp. 162-3. From the 23rd Session of Trent, Canon 1
[2] Schroeder, pg. 149. From the 22nd Session of Trent, Canon 2

complete. Since the sacrifices have been abolished (Hebrews 10) there is no longer any need for a priesthood. Whatever it was the Lord Jesus was commissioning his apostles to do, it was not to authorise them to become priests who would continue his sacrifice in the offering of a Mass."[1]

When it comes to the language of the New Testament we again cite Webster who has borrowed from Boettner:

"In several places Paul lists the different kinds of ministries and men who are specifically set apart and gifted by God to do a work within the church, such as apostles, prophets, evangelists, pastors and teachers (Ephesians 4:11, 1 Corinthians 12:28). Nowhere does Paul mention priests. Paul did appoint elders in the churches, but, as we have seen 'priest' is a different word altogether."

"In contradistinction to a select class of men set apart for the special ministry of priesthood, the New Testament teaches that all Christians are priests. But the only sacrifices they offer are spiritual in that they have access to the throne of God in prayer and can plead before him on behalf of men.

"But you are a chosen race, a royal priesthood, a holy nation, a people for God's own possession, that you may proclaim the excellencies of Him who has called you out of darkness into His marvelous light. (1 Peter 2:9)

"To Him who loves us, and released us from our sins by His blood, and He has made us to be a kingdom, priests to His God and Father. (Revelation 1:5-6)

"Under the New Testament economy, there is but one priest, in the strict meaning of that word as defined by the Apostle Paul: 'One taken from among men, ordained for men in things pertaining to God, that he may offer both gifts and sacrifices for sins' (Hebrews 5:1). Our great High Priest, of whom all the priests under the Mosaic dispensation were but figures, is 'the one Mediator between God and man' (1 Timothy 2:5). He presents the only effectual atoning sacrifice. He, on the ground of that sacrifice, makes intercession for those who come to God through him, and obtains accep-

---

[1] Webster, William, *Salvation: The Bible And Roman Catholicism*, (Edinburgh: Banner of Truth, ©1990) pp. 29-30

tance both for them and their services, and authoritatively blesses his people…"[1]

The Christian recognizes only one priest, who is Jesus Christ. The Christian cannot tolerate for a moment a so-called "priestly" caste over him blocking access to Heaven through the contrivances of both the Eucharist and the sacrament of penance.

But there are yet two other aspects touching upon the Eucharist that we need to address. The first is something we have grown used to by now in Catholic dogmatism. We refer to the "implications" of a dogma, or as we will address later in our section on popery, the "leaps." Having concluded that the wafer is in fact the actual body of Christ through transubstantiation, the Romanist concludes that it is worthy of worship as well. Trent explains:

> "There is, therefore, no room for doubt that all the faithful of Christ may, in accordance with a custom always received in the Catholic Church, give to this most holy sacrament in veneration the worship of *latria*, which is due to the true God. Neither is it to be less adored for the reason that it was instituted by Christ the Lord in order to be received. For we believe that in it the same God is present of whom the eternal Father, when introducing Him into the world, says: 'And let all the angels of God adore him;' whom the Magi, falling down, adored; who, finally, as the Scriptures testify, was adored by the Apostles in Galilee."[2]

Perhaps the Catholic can better realize why a Christian knows better than to substitute Catholic rituals and esoteric dogmas for the simplicity of the gospel. The Christian sees the adoration of a piece of bread. To him, this is idolatry and superstition of the worst sort. Obviously, the Christian is not willing to buy into the whole system. One would have to accept the Romanistic priesthood first and then transubstantiation. It would then follow that the bread and wine must be worshipped. It also follows that one would then be schooled in more Catholic teaching as to the best way to dispose of leftover consecrated hosts or what should be done if the consecrated host is dropped. This leads into more questions such as, "Is it possible for the wafer to be changed by a priest who does not believe in transubstantiation?" These details and more could fill a separate volume, but we trust the reader gets the point! The Christian is aware at the outset that the entire system is built on the wrong foundation.

---

[1] Webster, pp. 35-36

[2] Schroeder, pg. 76. From the 13th Session of Trent, chapter 5

The second aspect touching on this entire dogma is the fact that Catholics are taught that the consecrated wafer is part of a non-bloody sacrifice of Jesus Christ. When eaten, this serves to protect the Catholic against sinning while acting as an antidote to sins previously committed. Trent explains:

> "Therefore, our Savior, when about to depart from this world to the Father, instituted this sacrament, in which He poured forth, as it were, the riches of His divine love towards men, making a remembrance of his wonderful works, and commanded us in the participation of it to reverence His memory and to show forth his death until he comes to judge the world. But He wished that this sacrament should be received as the spiritual food of souls, whereby they may be nourished and strengthened, living by the life of Him who said: 'He that eateth me, the same also shall live by me,' and as an antidote whereby we may be freed from daily faults and be preserved from mortal sins."[1]

We shall save an analysis of the sacrificial aspect of the wafer until the next section on the Mass. Let us turn our attention now to the battleground of John 6 and the Romish claims of transubstantiation.

We feel that we can resolve the issues of John 6, but not to the satisfaction of the Romanist. It is well-documented and articulated that Romanism teaches that Christ gave to His disciples a command to actually eat His flesh and actually drink His blood in John 6. The Romanist couples this passage with the narrative of the Last Supper and believes that the way in which John 6 was to be fulfilled was given by Christ when He said, "This is my body." Christians have argued that the Lord used a figure in both John 6 and in the synoptic narratives to the effect that bread refers to Himself as the sustainer of spiritual life. Much ink has been spilled over this issue. Neither side is willing to give an inch. We are not sure what we can add to the arguments already given by eminent scholars. We ask the reader to repine with the entirety of John 6 and meditate upon what the Lord was teaching His followers.

We shall begin our discussion by refuting the allegation that to take the bread and blood as a figure in John 6 is to abandon a literalist approach to Scripture. It is not literal to force a meaning when a metaphor is intended. All literalists allow for figures of speech as they are used by a writer. To discount the use of a figure is to depart from a literal interpretation of the text. All literalists strive to interpret the Bible in a normal sense, allowing figures where they are intended. We regret the Catholic claim that Christians

---

[1] Schroeder, pg. 74. From the 13th Session of Trent, chapter 2

depart from their literalist ways when it comes to John 6. We do nothing of the sort. We recognize the author's figure and use it literally!

We believe the controlling verse of John 6 is verse 35:

> "And Jesus said unto them, I am the bread of life: he that cometh to me shall never hunger; and he that believeth on me shall never thirst." (John 6:35)

Notice the problem Jesus encountered is given to us in verse 36:

> "But I said unto you, That ye also have seen me, and believe not." (John 6:36)

We observe that our Lord uses the word "believe" both in verse 35 and in verse 36. In the first, He shows that "to believe" in Himself is to never hunger or thirst. In the second, He shows that some of those present did not believe and this was the problem!

In verse 40 we notice the promise of eternal life is to those who believe:

> "...every one which seeth the Son, and believeth on him, may have everlasting life..." (John 6:40)

Again in verse 47 we observe:

> "Verily, verily, I say unto you, He that believeth on me hath everlasting life." (John 6:47)

At this point Jesus says simply:

> "I am that bread of life." (John 6:48)

He is not saying that He is literal bread. He is contrasting the sustenance which He gives to His own with that of the manna given to the Jews in the wilderness. They ate and died. But the one who eats of Christ will not die! Now here is the rub! Romanists believe that Jesus was telling people to literally eat Him! We say He masterfully uses the figure of bread, as it was the common sustenance of the day, representing Himself as the fulfillment of the manna (type) given to the Jews in the wilderness. Christ Himself is the antitype of that manna.

The much disputed passage is John 6:51:

> "I am the living bread which came down from heaven: if any man
> eat of this bread, he shall live for ever: and the bread that I will give
> is my flesh, which I will give for the life of the world."

The Lord goes on to repeat the same essential thought only adding to it the
drinking of His blood in verse 53. The entire pericope ends in verse 59. The
Romanist thinks the astonishment of the Jews upon hearing this was due to
the fact that they understood Him clearly and simply could not grasp how
they could literally eat Jesus and drink His blood. With this we agree. But
the key is that Rome thinks the Jews had a *right* understanding of Jesus; that
He really did want to be eaten in some physical way! We say they did not
have a right understanding of Jesus' words. The Jews of John 6:52, like
Rome, took Jesus as though He wanted them to be cannibalistic. They, like
Rome, were wrong. When they were disgusted and cried out in verse 52,
"How can this man give us [his] flesh to eat?", Rome thinks they were on
track, but left Jesus before He would show them *how* to eat Him (at the
Last Supper). Rome thinks that because Jesus did not pause and correct
their understanding of literally eating Jesus, they must have heard Him
right!

> "There is no attempt to soften what was said, no attempt to correct
> 'misunderstandings,' for there were none. His listeners understood
> Him quite well. No one any longer thought he was speaking
> metaphorically. If they had, why no correction? On other occasions,
> whenever there was confusion, Christ explained what he meant."[1]

We are reminded that when our Lord said, "Destroy this temple, and in
three days I will raise it up," (John 2:19) the Jews were quite sure that He
was referring to the Temple and took Him quite literally and were disgusted!
To our knowledge, the Lord did not correct their crass literalism. Those
who thought Jesus was teaching a physical eating of Him were missing the
entire point! But there was no misunderstanding by those who had ears to
hear. They knew that Jesus had set Himself up as one greater than Moses
and now greater than the manna. They knew that the hard thing to swallow
was not a future Catholic transubstantiated wafer, but rather absolute trust
and faith that He was the antitype to manna given by God alone.

The Jews, on the other hand, were repulsed at the very thought of eating
Jesus and what that meant in light of clean and unclean. There are actually
three ways to see this episode. First, are those who are disgusted with the
thought that they have to somehow eat Jesus (crass literalists). Second, are
those who think they can in some way eat Jesus physically (Roman

---

[1] Keating, *Catholicism and Fundamentalism*, pg. 233

Catholic). Third, there are those who understand eating Him means believing in Him and seek no other way of literally digesting Jesus.

The trouble with those who grumbled was a lack of faith masked in the crassly literal interpretation of eating the flesh of Jesus. Thus, of the three groups, the Romanist is with the first century Pharisee in 'hearing' Jesus say that He must be eaten somehow. The only difference is that the Romanist is actually trying to eat Jesus! It is interesting that the Jews who bellowed at the thought of it were never quite so ingenious as to try to find a way to do it. They evidently were disgusted enough by what they thought they understood to be repulsed by the thought! Those who were given of the Father did not have to try to figure a way to eat Jesus. They knew Jesus was talking about something more than Romanistic voodoo here. But the Romanist is the hybrid. Like the Christian, he believes that Jesus was saying something hard and marvelous. But like the Jew, the Romanist thinks Jesus meant literally to eat Him. The result? An entire religion built around faulty exegesis which alleges that a priesthood can actually turn a wafer into the body of Jesus Christ.

We began this section with the claim that verse 35 actually controls the chapter. It is not surprising, then, to find that Jesus returns to the same word "unbelief" in characterizing those who left Him. "But there are some of you that believe not" (John 6:64). Their unbelief was deeply rooted in a failure to grasp the Person and mission of Jesus Christ. They were not in unbelief due to their failure to understand that Jesus would provide a way literally to eat His flesh and drink His blood.

Roman Catholics also hold to what they consider some airtight logic between the words of the apostle Paul and Nicholas Cardinal Wiseman. Copying the logic of Wiseman, Catholics put forth the argument that Paul is warning those in Corinth about eating the bread or drinking the blood in an unworthy manner proves that Paul believed in transubstantiation. How? Because one cannot eat the bread or drink the blood in a worthy manner unless he believes there is real presence in the wafer and wine! Catholics also think the only way one can drink and eat from the Lord's table in an unworthy manner is to have the actual body and blood present in the elements. To the Romanist, one cannot eat in an unworthy manner unless the bread is actually the body and the wine the actual blood of Jesus Christ.

Romanists must think trampling the flag is not treating the nation in an unworthy manner since the nation it represents is not in the flag! Or having a drunken orgy at a baptism is not unworthily participating in that ordinance since Christ is not in the water! Any first-year seminary student can point out that the manner *and* demeanor of the Corinthians was severely criticized by Paul. To say that the Corinthians could not have participated in the

Lord's table in an unworthy manner (adverb modifying the demeanor and disrespect for others in the body) unless they believed the bread and wine had become Christ is ludicrous. The Romanist is dead wrong! We ask the reader to examine for himself 1 Corinthians 11:17-34 and witness for himself the nature of "unworthily" participating in the Lord's table at Corinth.

A final note to this passage is the meaning of 1 Corinthians 11:29,

> "For he that eateth and drinketh unworthily, eateth and drinketh damnation to himself, not discerning the Lord's body."

The *Douay-Rheims* translates the last clause of 1 Corinthians 11:29 as not discerning "the body of the Lord." The oldest Greek manuscripts do not have the words, "of the Lord." They simply say, "not discerning the body," omitting the words, "of the Lord." But even if we take the later reading, "body of the Lord," to what is Paul referring? The Romanist takes Paul to mean that the bread is now the actual body of the Lord. They say, to not discern the "body of the Lord" means to not recognize their doctrine of transubstantiation. Those who do not believe in transubstantiation are guilty of not discerning "the *body* (transubstantiated) of the Lord." Those who do this, therefore, eat and drink condemnation unto themselves! We say "No way!" We are not certain if Paul is referencing the crucifixion of the Lord when he says, "the body of the Lord." If this were true, then Paul would be chastising the Corinthians for not meditating appropriately on the death of Christ and all that comes to mind in His death. We think Paul is probably referencing *the Church or community of saints* with his use of "the body of the Lord." In which case Paul is disappointed in the demeanor of the "body of the Lord" (i.e., the local body of believers) toward one another as they come to the communion table. Either way, there is no room for the Roman Catholic false doctrine of transubstantiation in this context. It is foundational to see here the tireless effort in Romanism to scour the Scriptures for a possible support of fabricated dogma. Here they boldly proclaim, "St. Paul's words are meaningless without the dogma of the Real Presence."[1] We might say that the dogma of Rome is meaningless without the clear-cut teaching of Scripture to support it.

---

[1] Keating, *Catholicism and Fundamentalism*, pg. 245

The Mass

CATHOLIC scholars go on the offensive when it comes to their Mass. They are generally convinced that non-Catholics have not the foggiest idea of the real meaning of the Mass and therefore reject it without understanding it! For example:

"Fundamentalists do not like the Mass, and they like it even less than they otherwise might because they misunderstand what it is."

"One comfortably may assume these men never read an official Catholic explanation of the Mass—or if they did, that they did not understand it."[1]

We seek to eliminate any future misunderstanding of the meaning of the Mass by this citation from Vatican II, *Sacrosanctum Concilium 47*:

"At the Last Supper, on the night He was betrayed, our Savior instituted the Eucharistic Sacrifice of His Body and Blood. He did this in order to perpetuate the sacrifice of the Cross throughout the centuries until He should come again, and so to entrust to His beloved spouse, the Church, a memorial of His death and resurrection: a sacrament of love, a sign of unity, a bond of charity, a paschal banquet in which Christ is consumed, the mind is filled with grace, and a pledge of future glory is given to us."[2]

The Catholic wants us to understand that he believes Jesus Christ instituted a "Eucharistic Sacrifice of His Body and Blood" at the Last Supper. What irritates Catholic scholars is the enlistment of "re-crucifixion" language that opponents of Romanism might use in describing the Mass. Instead, they want one and all to get it straight. Catholics want us to understand that Jesus "transubstantiated" the bread and wine *while* He was with His disciples! Thus, they say, He was present in actual flesh and blood as well as

---

[1] Keating, *Catholicism and Fundamentalism*, pg. 246
[2] Keating, *Catholicism and Fundamentalism*, pg. 246

sacramentally present in the bread and wine. The Catholic position is that the Last Supper was the institution of an unbloody sacrifice which would carry the same weight as the real one to come the next day. The assumption is threefold: 1) Jesus turned the Last Supper into an unbloody commemorative sacrifice of His impending death replete with sin-forgiving power; 2) Jesus wanted this to be continued until His return; and 3) Jesus turned His disciples into priests with power to transform the bread and wine into His body and blood.

As we have said before, the Mass is only as good as the priesthood. Take away the priesthood and there goes the Mass.

We think we have it right so far as we can decipher the Catholic mindset. Most Catholic scholars think Christians have an undeveloped sense of the mysterious and the supernatural. One is told this if he questions the validity of the Mass.

So as not to be accused of whipping a dead horse, we will defer to the Catholic understanding of their Mass. We must, however, add what has been left out to give the complete picture of the Mass. For the time being, let us all agree that the Roman Catholic Mass is not a re-crucifixion of Christ. He does not die again on the Catholic altar. He does not suffer and die again.

Having said this let us look at the whole story. Christians have never believed that Jesus Christ is killed again by Catholic priests at their altar. What we do believe is that Romanists cannot get around the fact that their Mass is a *sacrifice*. Catholics can say all they want about not re-crucifying Jesus but when it comes right down to it, the Mass is a sacrifice! They may say it is the *same* sacrifice as Calvary. They may say it is a sacramental sacrifice instituted by Jesus. They may say it is a sacrifice after the order of Melchizedek. But nonetheless, it is a sacrifice. This fact and its ramifications constitute what is abhorrent to the Christian. Listen to Trent:

> "For, appeased by *this sacrifice*, the Lord grants the grace and gift of penitence and pardons even the gravest crimes and sins. For *the victim* is one and the same, the same now *offering* (referring to Christ) by the ministry of priests who then offered Himself on the cross, *the manner alone being different*."[1]

What Rome is boldly saying is that the Mass is a sacrifice which takes away sins and appeases God. They try to soften this by saying, "All the efficacy

---

[1] Schroeder, pg. 146. From the 22nd Session of Trent, chapter 2. Emphasis and parentheses added

of the Mass is derived, therefore, from the sacrifice of Calvary."[1] Catholics
like to say that the Mass is a re-presentation of the once and for all original
sacrifice. At issue is Catholic doublespeak! The Mass is said to be at once
the re-presenting of Christ's sacrifice while at the same time something quite
different! It is a sacrifice but not a re-crucifixion. There is an appeasement
toward God but no real blood. Is it any wonder that Christians are unable to
grasp all of this?

What then is the Mass? The *Catholic Almanac* explains for us, quoting from
Vatican II:

"The Second Vatican Council made the following declarations,
among others, with respect to the Mass.

"'...As often as the Sacrifice of the Cross in which 'Christ, our
Passover, has been sacrificed' (1 Corinthians 5:7) is celebrated on
an altar, the work of our redemption is carried on. At the same time,
in the sacrament of the Eucharistic bread the unity of all believers
who form one body in Christ (c.f.; 1 Corinthians 10:17) is both
expressed and brought about. All men are called to this union with
Christ...' (Dogmatic Constitution on the Church, No. 3).

"'...The ministerial priest, by the sacred power he enjoys, molds
and rules the priestly people. Acting in the person of Christ, he
brings about the Eucharistic Sacrifice, and offers it to God in the
name of all the people. For their part, the faithful join in the offering
of the Eucharist by virtue of their royal priesthood...' (Ibid., No.
10)"[2]

Notice the language. There is an *altar*, a *sacrifice* and an *offering*.

"Among its decrees on the Holy Eucharist, the Council of Trent has
stated the following points of doctrine on the Mass:

"There is in the Catholic Church a true Sacrifice, the Mass instituted
by Jesus Christ. It is the Sacrifice of his Body and Blood, Soul and
Divinity, himself, under the appearances of bread and wine.

"This Sacrifice is identical with the Sacrifice of the Cross, inasmuch
as Christ is the Priest and Victim in both. A difference lies in the
manner of offering, which was bloody upon the Cross and is
bloodless on the altar.

---

[1] Keating, *Catholicism and Fundamentalism*, pg. 248
[2] *1990 Catholic Almanac*, pg. 212

"The Mass is a propitiatory Sacrifice, atoning for sins of the living and dead for whom it is offered.

"The efficacy of the Mass is derived from the Sacrifice of the Cross, whose superabundant merits it applies to men.

"Although the Mass is offered to God alone, it may be celebrated in honor and memory of the saints.

"Christ instituted the Mass at the Last Supper.

"Christ ordained the Apostles priests, giving them power and the command to consecrate his Body and Blood to perpetuate and renew the Sacrifice."[1]

It seems to us that Rome spends a lot of energy uselessly defending against the idea of a re-crucifixion of Christ. Christians have perhaps been guilty of using language which admits to an analysis of the Mass leading to such a conclusion. But clearly this is not the issue. The issue is the *sacrificial nature* and meaning of the Mass, not whether it is to be perceived as a re-crucifixion of Jesus or an "eternal now" of the moment of Christ's death, or whatever other esoteric camouflage Romanist word-purveyors might spin on this issue.

To unravel all this we must go back and ask the text of Scripture if Christ did in fact introduce the Catholic Mass at the Last Supper. Also, did He ordain a priestly class to perform this alleged re-presentation of His death?

The Last Supper of our Lord is recorded for us in Luke 22, Matthew 26 and Mark 14. Luke's account is as follows:

"And he took bread, and gave thanks, and brake [it], and gave unto them, saying, This is (*estin*) my body which is given for you: this do in remembrance (*anamnesis*) of me." (Luke 22:19)

The Romanists insist that Christ was transubstantiating the bread the moment He said, "This is My body." They think it is wrong to see here a figure of speech. They think the word "is" means that the bread *is* Jesus. They claim that to see these words in any other way does violence to the text. What are we to say to such exegesis?

In the first place, the word "is" would do too much if it did what the Catholics think it must do for them. This *is* My body would have to make

[1] *1990 Catholic Almanac*, pg. 212

the bread the actual body of Jesus and it would no longer have the properties of bread. It would be His body. The Romanist skirts this issue by saying the bread is Christ in its essence but retains the characteristics of bread in its outward appearance. We ask how any serious Greek exegete can swallow this use of the Greek *estin* (is)! Where is the Greek language ever used in this manner? When does "is" equal "outward appearance" as being one thing of the subject, but inward "reality or essence" something totally different?

Secondly, the word "is" is used by Jesus to define the New Covenant in His blood. "This cup [is] (*estin* supplied) the new testament in my blood, which is shed for you" (Luke 19:20). No one in the Romanist community wants to say the cup *is* actually the New Covenant. Obviously it is a figure for the New Covenant. Likewise, Paul in 1 Corinthians says, "This cup is the new testament in my blood" (1 Corinthians 11:25). Here, too, the "is" *estin* is used in a figure representing the spiritual truth of a New Covenant having been inaugurated.

Thirdly, our Lord uses the word *anamnesis* (remember) in His directions to His disciples. Paul uses the same word twice in 1 Corinthians 11:24,25. We are to *remember* and "do shew the Lord's death till he come" (1 Corinthians 11:26). There is not a word about instituting a priesthood to transubstantiate the bread and wine. There is not a word about this memorial being a new sacrifice of Jesus. There is not a word about this alleged new sacrifice being able to effect the forgiveness of sins. There is not a word about grace being channeled through this memorial. There is not a word about adoring the bread or worshipping the wine. In short there is not a word about the Roman Catholic Mass!

What then about Paul's declaration that whoever eats the bread and drinks the cup unworthily shall be guilty of *the body and blood of the Lord*? Are we to believe that Paul means one cannot be really guilty of the body and blood of the Lord unless the wine and bread are transubstantiated? Hardly! We ask the reader to consider just how guilty one can become of the body and blood of Christ by believing in a system that seeks to perpetuate in the Mass a sacrifice for sins in light of the testimony of the Scripture. This testimony proclaims that believing in the original sacrifice once for all guarantees an end to the necessity of its perpetuation on any altar for forgiveness of sins:

> "By the which will we are sanctified through the offering of the body of Jesus Christ once [for all]. And every priest standeth daily ministering and offering oftentimes the same sacrifices, which can never take away sins: But this man, after he had offered one sacrifice for sins for ever, sat down on the right hand of God; From

henceforth expecting till his enemies be made his footstool. For by one offering he hath perfected for ever them that are sanctified." (Hebrews 10:10-14)

There are yet two other passages mustered in defense of the Mass by the Romanists. The first is found in Genesis 14:18. Genesis 14 recounts for us the victory of Abraham over Chedorlaomer and his confederation of kings. Upon returning victorious, Abraham is greeted by Melchizedek, king of Salem. This Melchizedek is identified as a priest of God Most High. Genesis 14:18 tells us that Melchizedek brought out bread and wine. The text does not say he sacrificed under the form of bread and wine. It says nothing of the sort. The bread and wine were part of the cordial of greeting and did not serve as part of any ritual or sacrifice to Abraham. However, the Romanist upon seeing bread and wine immediately forces a connection between it and what Christ is alleged to have instituted at the Last Supper. This is done by way of a faulty and loose connection between Christ and Melchizedek. All Bible students know that Melchizedek serves as a type of Christ who was to come. Psalm 110:4 informs us that the Christ will be a priest after the order of Melchizedek. Hebrews 7 clarifies for us as to the manner in which this will be. It is at this juncture where the Romanist errs. He thinks that Christ will be like Melchizedek in that He will do that which they allege Melchizedek did. But as we have seen, Melchizedek did not transubstantiate anything. Neither did he offer up a sacrifice to God under the form of bread and wine. The manner in which Christ is after the order of Melchizedek has nothing to do with the Catholic Mass! Hebrews 7 settles the issue. Christ is the fulfillment of Melchizedek in that He was not from the tribe of Levi, and also in the manner in which Melchizedek came on the scene, as it were, without heritage on earth.

> "For this Melchisedec, king of Salem, priest of the most high God, who met Abraham returning from the slaughter of the kings, and blessed him; To whom also Abraham gave a tenth part of all; first being by interpretation King of righteousness, and after that also King of Salem, which is, King of peace; Without father, without mother, without descent, having neither beginning of days, nor end of life; but made like unto the Son of God; abideth a priest continually. Now consider how great this man [was], unto whom even the patriarch Abraham gave the tenth of the spoils. And verily they that are of the sons of Levi, who receive the office of the priesthood, have a commandment to take tithes of the people according to the law, that is, of their brethren, though they come out of the loins of Abraham: But he whose descent is not counted from them received tithes of Abraham, and blessed him that had the promises. And without all contradiction the less is blessed of the better. And here men that die receive tithes; but there he [receiveth

them], of whom it is witnessed that he liveth. And as I may so say, Levi also, who receiveth tithes, payed tithes in Abraham. For he was yet in the loins of his father, when Melchisedec met him." (Hebrews 7:1-10)

The comparison is obvious and says nothing about the Roman Mass. Once again, as in the case of other dogmas, Rome continues to be a religion in search of biblical proof.

The second passage appealed to by Rome is somewhat surprising, but it serves to show the reach Rome is willing to make to substantiate a dogma. The passage under consideration is Malachi 1:11;

"For from the rising of the sun even unto the going down of the same my name [shall be] great among the Gentiles; and in every place incense [shall be] offered unto my name, and a pure offering: for my name [shall be] great among the heathen, saith the LORD of hosts."

The Romanist deduces that the Mass must be the fulfillment of this since it is performed on every continent by the Gentiles. Notice with us that the word "sacrifice" is not used in this verse. The Hebrew word *minchah* means offering. Here it is used of a grain or food offering to the Lord. In context, the Lord, through the prophet, is chastising Israel for profaning the table of the Lord! The Israelites were presenting to the Lord defiled sacrifices. In so doing, not unlike modern Romanism, they were uselessly kindling a fire on the altar of the Lord. Why? Their hearts were not right with God. They supposed they could please Him with a deformed manner of worship which was void of the heart that God required. In response to this the Lord says through Malachi that there would come a day when there would be a pure offering to the Lord. We assure you that the Roman Mass was not in the mind of the Lord! If this prophecy has been fulfilled (and we cannot be sure) then it is fulfilled in the words of the apostle Paul:

"Now thanks [be] unto God, which always causeth us to triumph in Christ, and maketh manifest the savour of his knowledge by us in every place. For we are unto God a sweet savour of Christ, in them that are saved, and in them that perish: To the one [we are] the savour of death unto death; and to the other the savour of life unto life. And who [is] sufficient for these things? For we are not as many, which corrupt the word of God: but as of sincerity, but as of God, in the sight of God speak we in Christ." (2 Corinthians 2:14-17)

"I beseech you therefore, brethren, by the mercies of God, that ye present your bodies a living sacrifice, holy, acceptable unto God, [which is] your reasonable service. And be not conformed to this world: but be ye transformed by the renewing of your mind, that ye may prove what [is] that good, and acceptable, and perfect, will of God." (Romans 12:1,2)

In the final analysis, the idea of perpetuating the actual sacrifice of Jesus Christ through the Mass is absolutely inimical to the scriptural accounts of the Lord's table. What Romanists cannot fathom is that there is no need to do such a thing! Even if Romanism did not attach a propitiatory meaning to this constant re-presentation there would still be no need for it in the Christian life. Christians know full well the importance of remembering the death of Jesus Christ! For in it we find absolute and complete forgiveness of sins from now and forever. We do not need to re-present it to make sure our sins are covered. To do so would detract from the purpose of the blood in the first place.

All of this goes back to the Catholic idea of salvation. Romanists need this re-presentation of the death of Christ because they do not fully believe a "once for all" sacrifice can in fact remove all sin. They believe that Christ's death, for it to effective, must be conjured up in the Mass over and over again. This is repulsive to the Christian. The Christian sees Romanism for what it is—a charade of manipulation which enslaves Catholics to their priests. These priests are said to be doing the right thing in continually offering the blood of Christ to the Father. How utterly incredible that a priest should think that He could offer Christ to the Father even once let alone continually! Let the reader take heart in the fact that Christ alone could offer Himself to the Father. When He did, it was once and enough. It is finished!

"[It was] therefore necessary that the patterns of things in the heavens should be purified with these; but the heavenly things themselves with better sacrifices than these. For Christ is not entered into the holy places made with hands, [which are] the figures of the true; but into heaven itself, now to appear in the presence of God for us: Nor yet that he should offer himself often, as the high priest entereth into the holy place every year with blood of others; For then must he often have suffered since the foundation of the world: but now once in the end of the world hath he appeared to put away sin by the sacrifice of himself. And as it is appointed unto men once to die, but after this the judgment: So Christ was once offered to bear the sins of many; and unto them that look for him shall he appear the second time without sin unto salvation." (Hebrews 9:23-28)

Chapter 12

The "Place" of Peter

WE MIGHT have entitled this section on the role of Peter in the Catholic religion as "Quantum Leaps." Everywhere we look the Roman position thrives on crossing imaginary bridges and building their castles on sinking sand. We will attempt to organize our thoughts from the lesser to the greater in attempting to show the reader the leaps.

In the first place we do not deny that Peter was a prominent apostle. One might even say that he was prominent among the apostles. Certainly the life laid out for him by God included many impressive assignments. However, one of them was not to start up the Roman Catholic office of pope! We find Peter in the Gospels as especially chosen by our Lord to have a prominent position in the unfolding of the preaching of the gospel. The book of Acts presents the prominence of Peter early on, but never suggests or hints that he has some sort of papal authority.

In Acts 1:15 Peter gives direction to the early band of believers in obedience to the prophetic Scriptures. He is conspicuous in Acts 2, but not alone! Again in Acts 3:1 he is prominent, but not alone! In the defense of the gospel, in Acts 4:8 and 5:29, Peter is the spokesman, but certainly not alone! In Acts 8 Peter goes down to Samaria, but not alone. He is fulfilling his commission to preach the Word in Acts 9 and 10, but no hint of popery can be detected from any of these historical incidents.

Roman Catholic scholars like to build a case for the "papalness" of Peter by citing accurately that Peter is at the top of the list of apostles. But what is to be proven here? We agree to the special and pronounced role of Peter. Where we part ways with Rome is in the "meaning" of the prominence of Peter. Romanists do not like to point out that James led the Church at Jerusalem and presided over the other apostles at the council of Jerusalem in Acts 15. Should James have papal authority attributed to him? Romanists do not like to talk about Peter's hypocrisy and compromise of the gospel in Galatians 2:12 where he had to be rebuked in a matter of faith and morals by Paul! The leap from Peter's name being first on the list of apostles to the modern invention of popery is further short-circuited by the apostle Paul in

2 Corinthians 12:11, where he states boldly, "...for in nothing am I behind the very chiefest apostles, though I be nothing."

It is fair to say that Rome's overemphasis upon Peter has had the reverse effect among Christians. It may be likened to the fact that all Christians are technically witnesses of YHWH yet, due to the cult of Jehovah's Witnesses, dare not use this terminology to describe Christian evangelism. Likewise, the success in converts to the religion known as the "Church of Christ" (Campbellism) prevents Christians from saying too hastily that they are members of the "Church of Christ" though it is absolutely true. In our zeal to protect the Body of Christ from Romish abuses of Peter's true role in God's redemptive program, we have perhaps de-emphasized the glorious role Peter played.

But the fact of prominence leads to popery only when you are in Rome. In this case, we cannot do as the Romans do! We remind the reader that Peter referred to himself as an apostle. But he was also a fellow elder with others in his role within the Body of Christ (cf., 1 Peter 5:1). He gives way to the apostle Paul in the book of Acts as the apostle of significance. He acquiesces to the writings of Paul in his own epistle (cf., 2 Peter 3:15,16). He is presented everywhere as a wonderfully spontaneous and zealous follower of Jesus Christ, but never as having papal authority.

Despite this portrait of Peter in the New Testament, leaps are made in Catholicism to subdue the simplicity of the record. For instance, Keating quotes Luke 22:31-32 and concludes:

> "Christ prayed that Peter would have faith that would never fail, that he would be a guide for others, and Christ's prayer, being perfectly efficacious, was sure to be fulfilled. Here *we see the roots of papal infallibility and the primacy that is the Bishop of Rome's*."[1]

Can we not see the leaps here? Why is this the root of papal infallibility? What does Christ's prayer have to do with the bishop at Rome? This is typical Romanist exegesis. Keating has taken a straightforward text that has nothing to do with popes or Rome and somehow found a bridge for Romanism to be imported into the first century.

Peter is a fellow elder among the saints. From this we are asked to leap into the one-man office of bishop (a term used interchangeably with elder) and see a dominant role in the office. We are asked to ignore the fact that the New Testament Church was run by a plurality of elders (bishops). From this alleged dominant one-man bishopric, we are asked to leap to Peter as

---

[1] Keating, *Catholicism and Fundamentalism*, pg. 208. Emphasis added

the Bishop at Rome. We might concede that Peter was at Rome, but why should he be accused of forsaking being "a fellow-elder" (1 Peter 5:1) among others to being a dominant bishop at Rome? Was Paul the dominant bishop at Ephesus? Was not the apostle Paul at Rome also? The Romanists leap to the conclusion that Peter exercised his apostolic authority as a one-man show! They view Peter as using *their* understanding of the office of bishop to command authority. But the Scripture presents Peter as having authority based upon being called an apostle among other apostles. Peter's role in the Church is "fellow-elder."

There are more leaps. Peter is said to be the dominant bishop in the Church at Rome as well as establishing Rome as the seat of all future influence. Peter is said to have been imbued with infallibility in matters of faith and morals. The next leap is Peter's authority to confer this infallibility onto succeeding generations in the form of apostolic succession. From humble beginnings, as an apostle chosen to preach the gospel among other apostles, we have leaped into the modern-day super-Peter of the Catholic religion! The religion of Rome has recast Peter's role! From fellow elder, prone to making mistakes, he becomes super-Peter, the first pope of the See at Rome, controlling all of the Church through the office of the Bishopric of Rome! And their proof? Simple! Peter used to be called Simon, and the Lord prayed that he would be an encouragement to his fellow believers. We can hear the exasperated huff of the Roman Catholic as he moans, "Wait just a minute, have you never read Matthew 16?" "Does that not settle the issue once for all?" Indeed we have, and it does—but not in favor of the see at Rome!

Matthew 16

At the outset the reader should be aware that Matthew 16:18 has been a battleground among Bible expositors for centuries. This fact should give caution regarding any interpretation of the text at which we arrive. Naturally, the Romanist wants to see in this passage the ground work for modern popery. And likewise, Christian scholars labor hard to avoid the Romanist implication as well as interpretation of this passage.

In Matthew 16:18 our Lord turns to Peter and says, "thou art Peter, (*petros*, masculine for stone), and upon this (*taute*) rock (*petra*, Greek feminine for rock), I will build my church." Expositors have been divided as to whom or to what Jesus was referring when He said, "this rock." Romanists say it is Peter. Thus, Peter is the rock upon which the Church will be built. Others say it is not Peter, but Peter's confession, i.e. "Thou art the Christ, the Son of the living God." Thus, the Church would be built upon that confession.

Others say that Jesus was referring to Himself: "...thou art Peter, and upon *this rock* (Jesus) I will build my church." The use of the "this" is said to allow for a differentiation between Christ and Peter. Can anyone say for sure? We do not think so. There has been much written concerning the Greek used in this one small verse. The arguments counterbalance each other. Some note that *petra* is feminine so "this rock" could not have referred to Peter since Peter is *petros*. This is countered by those who point out that *petra* is the natural word for large stone and it is a figure anyway. They turn it back and ask if Christ would have used the feminine *petra* to refer to Himself. The Romanists, in defending the antecedent as Peter, think they have a find in the fact that the Aramaic spoken by the Lord uses the same form for both masculine and feminine. So they say that Jesus was really saying, "thou art Peter (Aramaic, *kepha*), and upon this *kepha* I will build my church," the second *kepha* being the same as the first. This is countered by the fact that the New Testament was written under inspiration in Greek—not Aramaic. Matthew was inspired to recount the episode using the distinctives of the Greek language. Besides, there is absolutely no consensus that Matthew was originally written in Aramaic. One cannot build a case on suspected Aramaic originals!

It appears to this writer that all the bickering that has followed this verse throughout the ages has tended to obscure the real issue. The real issue is whether a reference here to Peter as "this rock" establishes the Roman papacy! Notice how clever Keating is in trying to convince us that to admit Peter is "this rock" is to admit the papacy:

> "The play on words seems obvious, but commentators wishing to avoid what follows from this—*the establishment of the papacy*— have suggested that the word rock could not refer to Peter but must refer to his profession of faith or to Christ."[1]

Let me reiterate that no one can be sure to whom or to what Christ was referring when He said "this rock." We need not give ground to Rome on the matter. It is inconclusive. However, suppose that we were convinced it was Peter to whom Christ was referring. Does this lead to the inevitable conclusion of Roman popery? The answer is a resounding no! Regardless of the confidence of Romish writers, establishing that Peter was the "this rock" does not lead to popery. We have already noted the initial prominence of Peter as the first to preach the gospel to the Jews, Samaritans and finally to the Gentiles. This prominence is not lost to Christian scholarship. But what does this have to do with the pope of Rome? It is a quantum leap of the worst order to say that Peter's prominent role in the early Church leads to Roman popery. Keating breaks a sweat in railing at Christian commen-

---

[1] Keating, *Catholicism and Fundamentalism*, pg. 208. Emphasis added

tators who engage Romanists on the issue of who the "this rock" might be. He thinks if he can squash the opponent by use of antecedents and fictitious Aramaic originals then he has saved the day for the Roman pontiff. Had he only researched a little he would have found a number of Christian scholars who would have agreed with him that maybe Jesus was referring to Peter. But he would have been sorely frustrated to see that this does not prove popery in the least.[1]

We continue this section by mentioning that normally, Catholic scholars are fairly eager to find support for their dogmas from ancient literature. Such is the case of Keating who rambles on about Peter being in Rome through citation after citation of early writers. What of course is missing is a citation that affords Peter the Romish authority that they say he always had. Also conspicuously absent from Keating's work are any citations of antiquity which support his exegesis of Matthew 16:18. A cursory review of ancient exegesis on Matthew 16:18 finds a broad range of interpretation. For instance, Augustine thought "this rock" referred to either Christ Himself or to Peter's confession that Jesus was the Son of the living God:

> "...but when it was said to him, 'I will give unto thee the keys of the kingdom of heaven, and whatsoever thou shalt bind on earth, shall be bound in heaven; and whatsoever thou shalt loose on earth, shall be loosed in heaven,' he represented the universal Church, which in this world is shaken by divers temptations, that come upon it like torrents of rain, floods and tempests, and falleth not, because it is founded upon a rock (petra), from which Peter received his name. For petra (rock) is not derived from Peter, but Peter from petra; just as Christ is not called so from the Christian, but the Christian from Christ. For on this very account the Lord said, 'On this rock will I build my Church,' because Peter had said, 'thou art the Christ, the Son of the living God.' On this rock, therefore, He said, which thou hast confessed, I will build my church. For the Rock (Petra) was Christ; and on this foundation was Peter himself also built. For other foundation can no man lay than that is laid, which is Christ Jesus. The Church, therefore, which is founded in Christ received from Him the keys of the kingdom of heaven in the person of Peter, that is to say, the power of binding and loosing sins."[2]

---

[1] We highly recommend William Hendricksen's excellent commentary on Matthew for a thorough discussion of this issue. Hendricksen believes Peter is the antecedent to "this rock" but refuses to let it lead to Romanism. *New Testament Commentary*, (Grand Rapids, MI: Baker Book House, ©1973) pp. 644-650

[2] Augustine, *Homilies on the Gospel of John*, from *Nicene and Post-Nicene Fathers of the Christian Church*, (Grand Rapids: Eerdmans, ©1978) pg. 450

"Origen (d. 254) was the first Father to write a complete commentary on the Bible. He was from Alexandria, Egypt, and explained Matthew 16:18 as follows: 'If you suppose that on this Peter alone the whole church is built by God, what would you say about John, the son of Thunder, or about any other of the apostles? Is it at all possible to say that against Peter in particular the gates of Hell shall not prevail, but that they shall prevail against the other apostles and against the elect? ...Let us consider in what sense it is said to Peter and to every 'peter' (believer): 'I will give unto thee the keys of the Kingdom' ...Consider how great a power the Rock has... and how great a power every one has who says: 'Thou art the Christ, the son of the living God...'

"Chrysostom explains: 'Thou art Peter, and upon this Rock I will build my church,' which means, upon the faith of his confession' (Migne, P.G. 58, 534). 'Upon this Rock (petram)': He did not say 'upon Peter (petrum),' nor upon a man, but upon his faith (fidem) He has built his Church' (Migne, P.G. 52,806).

St. Ambrose (d. 397), an independent Italian bishop, followed Origen's interpretation of the Rock: 'Peter is an everlasting door against whom the gates of Hell shall not prevail; John and James, the sons of Thunder, are everlasting doors; everlasting are the doors of the church (all believers)' (Migne, P.L. 16,647). 'They do not possess the inheritance of Peter, who do not possess the faith of Peter' (Migne, P.L. 16, 496).

"St. Jerome (d. 420), official Bible translator and interpreter of the Church of Rome, writes in his commentary on Matthew: 'Thou art Peter (Petrus) and upon this Rock (Petram) I will build my church' ...To Simon, who believed in the Rock (Petra), that is, Christ, the name of Peter (Petrus) was given' (Migne, P.L. 26, 121). 'The Rock is Christ, who granted to His apostles that they too should be called 'rocks'; (Migne, P.L. 25, 1066). The Church is founded ...upon all the apostles ...and the strength of the Church is established upon them all equally (et ex aequo super eos Ecclesiae fortitudo solidetur) (Migne, P.L. 23, 258.)"[1]

Hopefully the reader can begin to see the leaps which are taken to get the apostle Peter from 'equal among many' to the so-called vicar of Christ at Rome. Aside from Matthew 16, Romanists sometimes resort to other less

---

[1] Doeswyck, Peter, *Ecumenicalism and Romanism*, (Long Beach CA: Knights of Christ, Inc., ©1961) pg. 81f, from: Migne P.G. 13, pp. 99, 1011-1015

significant arguments to bolster their position. We turn our attention to a sample of these.

Catholics often call upon Isaiah 22:22 as a support that the keys given to Peter are a trust given to one Prime Minister to whom all others are in obedience. The idea is that Isaiah speaks prophetically at least in principle to the concept of keys which are used to open and shut. The keys of David are taken away from Shebna, the wicked steward, and given to Eliakim. From this passage the Catholics argue that Peter outbinds and outlooses all the other apostles. We say, 1) the passage in Isaiah is quoted in Revelation 3:7 and the keys of David are with Jesus Christ; 2) Isaiah 22 refers to the keeping in or putting out as based on obedience to God's Word, not on the obedience to God's servant; 3) Christ does not have Isaiah 22 in mind in Matthew 16. Isaiah 22 is fulfilled by David's son, yet by *David's Lord*; and 4) the raising up of Eliakim is only temporary. Isaiah 22:24,25 tells us of the end to this arrangement. It appears that the office ended in history as it came to be used for wicked nepotism much like Rome uses the papacy!

With this in mind let us now turn our focus to the greatest leap of all. The Romanist not only claims Peter to have been the vicar of Christ on earth with corresponding apostolic succession but also that the Bishop of Rome is infallible in matters of faith and morals. Such an outrageous claim is not unexpected within Romanism. It becomes a handy vehicle for power, control, and corruption. Rome sets the standard for idolatry with her dogma of papal infallibility. Let us see if there is any possible proof from Holy Writ to substantiate their claims.

Infallibility of the Pope

The Roman Catholic Church teaches its adherents that the pope is the vicar of Christ and infallible in matters pertaining to faith and morals. The Romanist religion furthermore contends that the Bible implicitly teaches that Peter was infallible in this way and such an anointing by God was passed along to Peter's successors.

The first difficulty is arriving at a precise definition of this alleged infallibility. Even using Rome's own definition of infallibility leaves one with an empty uneasiness about what they are trying to say. Trying to understand the dogma is like drinking coffee with a fork. It appears that every time a Christian thinks he has a grasp on papal infallibility, he has missed it! The definition keeps changing or, "undergoing refinement," as the Romanist teachers are apt to say!

We should begin by confessing that we claim no infallibility in trying to understand exactly what papal infallibility means. It was not a part of the specified decrees and dogma of the Romanist religion until the first Vatican council of 1870. Despite the objections of many bishops and the silence of historical verification from the first thousand years of history, the first Vatican Council hammered out a definition of papal infallibility.

> "Infallibility belongs in a special way to the Pope as the head of the bishops (Matthew 16:17-19; John 21:15-17) and is something he... 'enjoys in virtue of his office, when, as the supreme shepherd and teacher of all the faithful, who confirms his brethren in their faith (cf., Luke 22:32), he proclaims by a definitive act some doctrine of faith or morals. Therefore his definitions, of themselves, and not from the consent of the Church, are justly held irreformable, for they are pronounced with the assistance of the Holy Spirit, an assistance promised to him in blessed Peter.'"[1]

This is the official teaching of the Roman religion on this matter. But like all teaching it is left to the theologians to explain. We wish to be fair and only interact with what they say is the meaning of the above statement.

In the first place we are told that infallibility means only that a pope (or council) is protected from teaching error or promulgating error when he speaks in matters pertaining to faith and morals *ex cathedra* (out of the chair of Peter). A pope may himself be immoral (and many were), but that does not invalidate him from teaching properly on morals. Also, a pope is not to be considered infallible if he gives only his teaching or opinion on a matter. Though weighty, it may be wrong without violating the doctrine of infallibility. Also, infallibility does not extend to timing. It does not guarantee that popes will speak *when* they should. Neither is infallibility to be understood apart from studying and preparation. A pope still must study. Popes are not infallible when they speak on matters of discipline and customs. They are probably right, but not necessarily right. We join those of you who are beginning to become a little anxious as to what this doctrine means in the positive sense. Thus far we have defined it by analyzing what it is not. This is a little like describing an elephant by saying it is something that has no stripes or cloven hoofs or wings. The "what it is not" definition continues with this enigmatic statement from Keating:

> "Boettner does not quite grasp what infallibility covers. He does not understand that it is a *negative protection* and that a Pope too lazy to do his homework would not *be able* to make an infallible decision

---

[1] Keating, *Catholicism and Fundamentalism*, pg. 216

on *anything.* The charism of infallibility does not *help a pope know what is true, nor does it 'inspire' him to teach what is true.*"[1]

One might ask, if infallibility is a "negative protection," then why should it matter if the pope studies or not? If he is really guaranteed protection from teaching doctrinal or moral error, then why study? How does this alleged doctrine really work anyway? Evidently, the pope studies hard and then teaches something. But wait, is it *ex cathedra* or not? Who says so? We presume the pope makes the decision as to whether he is speaking *ex cathedra.* But how does he know when to speak or if he is speaking *ex cathedra* if, as Keating says, "infallibility does not help a pope know what is true"? We are left with the conclusion that a pope does not infallibly *know* when he is speaking infallibly. Neither does anyone else. This is why the doctrine is spoken in terms of what it is not.

Consider this bit of amazing logic as Keating thinks he has found a safe harbor among the logic of former radio priests Rumble and Carty.

"Before the definition of infallibility in 1870, the Popes did not know they were infallible with the same full certainty of faith as that possessed by later Popes. But they were infallible in fact. The gift of papal infallibility was essential to the church, not the definition of the gift."[2]

We are asked to believe that something was essential to the Church yet unknown and undefined while it was essential. If you can believe this you can believe anything. The Romanist further insults our intelligence by saying the reason it was left undefined for 1,850 years was because it was never disputed! In our opinion it is very difficult to dispute something unknown! Could it be that it was never "known" or "disputed" because it was never a fact of the Body of Christ or, embarrassingly enough, of the Romanist religion either!

What is infallibility? How are we to understand what Keating calls the "niceties of infallibility"? Evidently these niceties enable the Romanist scholars to determine for themselves just exactly when or where a pope was actually speaking *ex cathedra.* If we strive to point out an error of judgment or inconsistency, we are put in our place by the quick assertion that this pope or that pope was merely expressing his opinion. Or perhaps a particular pope was wrong, but he was not speaking *ex cathedra* at the time. So history is reoriented by the Romanist, in effect, to nullify the mistakes of

---

[1] Keating, *Catholicism and Fundamentalism,* pg. 224. Emphasis added

[2] Keating, *Catholicism and Fundamentalism,* pg. 217

the popes and protect the alleged doctrine of infallibility. The practical effect
of this is that if everyone agrees that a given pope has spoken something
which is credible in the eyes of historians then perhaps it was infallible.
Catholics pride themselves by noting that no pope has ever officially
contradicted what an earlier pope officially taught about faith and morals.
This becomes an empty boast when the Catholic historian is able to declare
that any differences can easily be reconciled by declaring that one or the
other in conflict did not in fact speak *ex cathedra*, or more simply, declare
the matter to not involve morals or doctrine. This is precisely what they do
with Paul's dispute with Peter. They maintain that what Peter was up to in
Galatians 2 had nothing to do with faith or morals. It is alleged that,
"Peter's conduct at Antioch was not an attempt by him to teach formally on
doctrine or morals."[1] The apostle Paul disagrees with this Catholic revision
of history. Notice the emphasis and importance Paul placed on the tremen-
dous moral and doctrinal error Peter was involved in at the time:

> "But when Peter was come to Antioch, I withstood him to the face,
> because he was to be blamed. ...And the other Jews dissembled
> likewise with him; insomuch that Barnabas also was carried away
> with their dissimulation." (Galatians 2:11,13)

There is yet another aspect of this Romanist dogma which defies reason as
well as the Scriptures. There are in the Christian Bible 66 books with a
myriad of complex teachings and wondrous webs of deep and enriching
concepts. Yet there remain some things hard to understand. We cannot help
but ask why the popes of Rome have failed to do their studying and call
upon this alleged power to protect them from error to explain to the waiting
world the "official" interpretation of Jesus Christ on all the passages of the
Bible. This would end the need for commentaries and theologians. This
would be of great benefit to the Church to have once and for all the meaning
of the Bible in all its breadth and depth. Why has this been withheld? The
answer is obvious. No one man or council has been given such extra-
ordinary power or insight. The pope is not by any elusive definition
infallible. In fact, the only thing "infallible" concerning the Romish doctrine
of papal infallibility is the biblical condemnation of it!

Biblical Claims for Infallibility

It should seem obvious to the reader that there is not much one can do if a
council convenes and declares a doctrine to always have been and now is
even more! Who or what checks the council? We answer, "The Word of

---

[1] Keating, *Catholicism and Fundamentalism*, pg. 225

God should!" The Romanist says, "No." For him, the Church sits over the Word—not vice versa. Nevertheless, Christians are bound by the Scriptures, not the whim of councils. Nothing has really changed since the Reformation! What scriptural endorsement is there for papal infallibility? Very simply, nothing! The Romanist marshals up the tired old argument that when Christ gave direction to the apostles he was really injecting them and their successors with infallibility. This subject has been covered in another section. But it is useful to note how often this basic distinction between Romanism and Christianity comes to the fore. Catholics cite John 21:15-17; Luke 22:32; Matthew 16:18; Matthew 28:19; John 16:13 and 1 Timothy 3:15 as proof that papal infallibility is "implicitly taught."[1] There is of course no shred of credibility in such an assertion. For instance, in 1 Timothy 3:15 Paul instructs Timothy on how to conduct himself in the household of God which is the Church of the living God, "the pillar and ground (*hedraioma*—meaning support) of the truth." Rome sees here a Church which writes the truth. The text says nothing of the sort. The Church upholds (supports) the truth already given, i.e., the gospel of Christ and the inspired writings of His apostles. It is the duty of the Body of Christ to adhere to and protect the Word once delivered. The Church has no authority to declare a man to be infallible and hold his teaching up as equal to the truth. Contrary to what Catholics read into the text, the Church is never given any guarantee of infallibility. For the Church is composed of individuals, all of whom are subject to the error of men. There is no such thing as an infallible man or some entity called infallible Church. The minute this claim is made then men stand above the Word. Who checks the men? In Rome, nobody!

We applaud Keating for his refreshing candor at the end of endless nonsense on the "niceties of infallibility." He hits the nail on the head when he says:

> "Fundamentalists' [his word for Christians] rejection of papal infallibility stems from their view of the church."[2]

But he goes too far in thinking that we think that Christ did not establish a visible Church. Christ most certainly did! We part ways with the Romish claim that Christ gave the Church the authority to invent things that bind the conscience of men. We reject the Romish assertion that the Church stands over the Word. We know full well what happens if men ever give up the right to interpret their Bibles to any religion, be it Rome or any other! It is too big a price to pay. Ultimately it will lead to control and dominion. In all

---

[1] Keating, *Catholicism and Fundamentalism*, pg. 216
[2] Keating, *Catholicism and Fundamentalism*, pg. 230

this there is the specter of a dictatorship. Sitting on top of all man-made religions is their one man. In the case of Rome it is their pope. Roman Catholics defend the Romish religion as having the right to invent the pope. They think they do not need to substantiate it from the Bible. For them the council is good enough! But who checks the council? Who checks the invention of the council? We say the Scriptures. The Christian receives the Spirit of God, Who prevents him from denying the true gospel or affirming a false gospel. The Christian stands in the long shadow of the apostle's pen—not on the passions of religionists throughout the centuries. This is why we take our cue from the apostle's rejoicing as he thanked the Thessalonians for receiving the Word:

> "For this cause also thank we God without ceasing, because, when ye received the word of God which ye heard of us, ye received [it] not [as] the word of men, but as it is in truth, the word of God, which effectually worketh also in you that believe."(1 Thessalonians 2:13)

We are again somewhat perplexed at the lack of corroborative evidence from antiquity regarding the infallibility of the pope. Why does Rome not parade out the early popes and Church Fathers in support of this modern Romish fantasy? In our estimation the evidence is so overwhelmingly against the superiority of one Bishop that it would be a fruitless exercise. Instead the Romanist finds cover with rhetoric:

> "As Christians got clearer and clearer notions of the teaching authority of the whole Church and of the primacy of the Pope, they got clearer notions of the Pope's own infallibility."[1]

Notions indeed! We offer some examples from early history to satisfy our suspicion that papal infallibility is not only late, but virtually rejected by early testimony. We are indebted to the research of James White in culling through the sources to provide us with this data from the early Church:

> "Cyprian (200-258), bishop of Carthage, was an impressive thinker and theologian, who died a martyr under Valerian. In a preface, written by him to the seventh council of Carthage, we read, 'For neither does any of us set himself up as a bishop of bishops, nor by tyrannical terror does any compel his colleague to the necessity of obedience; since every bishop, according to the allowance of his liberty and power, has his own proper right of judgment, and can no more be judged by another than he himself can judge another.'

[1] Keating, *Catholicism and Fundamentalism,* pg. 217

"Cyprian writes, 'Neither can it rescind an ordination rightly perfected, that Basilides, after the detection of his crimes, and the baring of his conscience even by his own confession, went to Rome and deceived Stephen our colleague, placed at a distance, and ignorant of what had been done, and of the truth, to canvass that he might be replaced unjustly in the episcopate from which he had been righteously deposed.'

"Another source of information in this regards comes from the 'Apostolic Canons.' These canons are appended to the 'Constitutions of the Holy Apostles.' Dating of the canons ranges from the early third to the fifth century. Canon 35 reads,

"'The bishops of every country ought to know who is the chief among them, and to esteem him as their head, and not to do any great thing without his consent; but every one to manage only the affairs that belong to his own parish, and the places subject to it. But let him not do anything without the consent of all; for it is by this means there will be unanimity, and God will be glorified by Christ, in the Holy Spirit.'

"When the council of Nicea met, one would think that the 'Vicar of Christ on earth,' the Roman Pope, would figure prominently in the proceedings. Instead, the bishop of Rome attended none of the proceedings, and was represented by but two presbyters. These representatives had little important part in the proceedings. The Council formed a very interesting canon, Canon 6. It is very important in that it gives us a clear understanding of the position of Rome at his time: 'Let the ancient customs in Egypt, Libya and Pentapolis prevail, that the Bishop of Alexandria have jurisdiction in all these, since the like is customary for the Bishop of Rome also. Likewise in Antioch and the other provinces, let the Churches retain their privileges. And this is to be universally understood, that if any one be made bishop without the consent of the Metropolitan, the great Synod has declared that such a man ought not to be a bishop.'

"The great scholar Jerome had written,

"'Wherever a bishop may be, whether at Rome or at Eugubium, at Constantinople or at Rhegium, at Alexandria or at Thanis, he is of the same worth, and of the same priesthood; the force of wealth and lowness of poverty do not render a bishop higher or lower; for all of them are the successors of the apostles.'

"One of the bishops of Rome itself, Gregory I (540-604), wrote,

"'Now I confidently say that whosoever calls himself, or desires to be called, Universal Priest, is in his elation the precursor of Antichrist, because he proudly puts himself above all others.'

"Such words would describe many of the medieval popes with great precision. But Gregory said more:

"'If then he shunned the subjecting of the members of Christ partially to certainheads, as if beside Christ, though this were to the apostles themselves, what wilt thou say to Christ, who is the Head of the universal Church, in the scrutiny of the last judgment, having attempted to put all his members under thyself by the appellation of Universal? Who, I ask, is proposed for imitation in this wrongful title but he who, despising the legions of angels constituted socially with himself, attempted to start up to an eminence of singularity, that he might seem to be under none and to be alone above all?'"[1]

---

[1] White, *Answers to Catholic Claims*, pp. 114-122

Chapter 13

Invoking the Dead

A S A prelude to our discussion on the Roman Catholic veneration of Mary, we respond to the general Catholic claim that it is perfectly within the bounds of God's revelation to pray to deceased people presumed to have gone to Heaven. Not only do Catholics have a fondness for praying to dead people, but also for erecting statues of the deceased in order to serve as motivational shrines and to give Catholics something to honor and venerate. All of this is sanctioned by the Roman Catholic magisterium. Trent explains:

"The holy council commands all bishops and others who hold the office of teaching and have charge of the *cura animarum*, that in accordance with the usage of the Catholic and Apostolic Church, received from the primitive times of the Christian religion, and with the unanimous teaching of the holy Fathers and the decrees of sacred councils, they above all instruct the faithful diligently in matters relating to intercession and *invocation of the saints*, the *veneration of relics*, and the legitimate use of images, teaching them that the saints who reign together with Christ offer up their prayers to God for men, *that it is good and beneficial suppliantly to invoke them and to have recourse to their prayers, assistance and support in order to obtain favors from God through his Son, Jesus Christ our Lord*, who alone is our redeemer and savior; and that they think impiously who deny that the saints who enjoy eternal happiness in heaven are to be invoked, or who assert that they do not pray for men, or that our invocation of them to pray for each of us individually is idolatry, or that it is opposed to the word of God and inconsistent with the honor of the *one mediator of God and men, Jesus Christ*, or that it is foolish to pray vocally or mentally to those who reign in heaven. Also, that the *holy bodies of the holy martyrs* and of others living with Christ, which were the living members of Christ and the temple of the Holy Ghost, to be awakened by Him to eternal life and to be glorified, *are to be venerated by the faithful*, through which many benefits are bestowed by God on men, so that those who maintain that *veneration and honor are not due to the relics of the saints, or that these and other memorials are honored by the faithful without profit, and that the places dedicated to the memory of the saints for the purpose of obtaining their aid* are visited in vain, are to be *utterly condemned*, as the Church has already long since condemned and now again condemns them."[1]

Joseph Zacchello gives us some more insight as he cites a typical prayer to Saint Joseph:

"We come to thee, O blessed Joseph, in our sore distress. Having sought the aid of thy most blessed spouse, we now confidently implore thy assistance also. We humbly beg that, mindful of the dutiful affection which bound thee to the immaculate virgin Mother of God, and of the fatherly love with which thou didst cherish the child Jesus, thou wilt lovingly watch over the heritage which Jesus Christ purchased with His blood, and by thy powerful intercession help us in our urgent need. Most provident guardian of the holy family, protect the chosen race of Jesus Christ; drive far from us, most loving father, every pest of error and corrupting sin. From thy place in heaven, most powerful protector, graciously come to our aid in this conflict with the powers of darkness, and as of old thou didst deliver the child Jesus from supreme peril of life, so now defend the holy Church of God from the snares of her enemies and from all adversity. Have each of us always in thy keeping, that, following thy example, and borne up by thy strength, we may be able to live holy, die happy, and so enter the everlasting bliss of heaven. Amen."[2]

Lest the reader accuse us of being in some way archaic in our research, we will follow the articulation of modern Rome as well in this section. Remember, this is modern Catholic apologetics. They wish to set the record straight for Romanism in these times.

Veneration

Contemporary Catholics begin to justify the veneration of relics by softening the word "worship" as it is understood in Catholic circles today. Sensing perhaps an avalanche of biblical protest, they back off on the idea of an earthly shrine or a deceased saint receiving what is reserved to God alone. So, the word "worship" gives way to "veneration." They think this is

---

[1] Schroeder, pg. 215. From the 25th Session of Trent
[2] Zacchello, Joseph, *Secrets of Romanism*, (Neptune, NJ.: Loizeaux Brothers, ©1948) pg. 143

acceptable since in their mind it is nothing more than giving honor to someone who deserves it! But this is not what Trent has said. Look closely at the excerpt from Trent above. Notice that (according to Trent) God *likes* it when we venerate saints and honor relics. In fact, anyone who thinks it might be inappropriate to think that God bestows profit on those who engage in relic veneration is to be condemned. In other words, this is not simply a gesture of good will in giving honor to whom honor is due. Modern Catholics need pay closer attention to Trent. To think that God does not give aid to those seeking it through veneration of relics and memorials is to be condemned. Catholics do not honor saints because they wish to remember those whom they suspect are in Heaven. No, they do so to get aid from God. We ask, "Where, in all the pages of God's Word, is this recommended?" We shall see presently that at least in the Old Testament it is soundly condemned.

But what about praying to the dead? This Catholic practice has been defended on the grounds that there is no difference between asking people alive on earth to pray for each other and asking people alive in Heaven to pray for us. Romanists mix the apples with the oranges here. We who are alive on earth ask others whom we know to be alive (and in the Body of Christ) to join us in our prayer requests to God in the name of Jesus Christ. Christians are committed to Jesus as the only mediator between us and God. The idea behind asking others to pray with us to God, through Jesus, is to make the earthly Body of Christ more aware of the need and to experience the power of God as He satisfies the needs of His earthly Body. Christians pray to God, through the mediatorial office of Jesus Christ, on behalf of each other. In all cases, it is the alive on earth, in the Body of Christ, praying on behalf of each other.

Now the Catholics want to throw a bunch of oranges into our order of apples. They wish to pray directly to an earthly dead person presumed to be in Heaven so that the dead saint can ask Christ for some favor on behalf of that person alive on earth. It is not denied that Catholics go straight to the source as well. But they are taught that there is greater power if the "presumed-to-be-saints" in Heaven are convoked as well. Trent says it is good and useful to use the dead to "obtain favors from God through His Son, Jesus Christ our Lord..."[1]

We cannot find a shred of evidence by way of example or command from the Bible for either the veneration of saints or prayer to the dead. Where does an apostle, for instance, invoke Moses or David to present his prayer requests to Jesus? It does not follow that commands to pray for one another on earth mean to convoke the prayers of those who might be in Heaven.

---

[1] Schroeder, pg. 215. From the 23rd Session of Trent

Furthermore, it cannot be explained just how the presumed saints can answer or hear the thousands of prayers in Heaven. Some Catholics think they solve the dilemma by saying that saints in Heaven have no limitations such as time or the ability to hear ten thousand prayers at once. But this is pure conjecture in order to support the dubious point in question. This speculative theology becomes dangerous. It is not hard to see how a primitive deduction based upon speculation can grow into outright heresy. Romanists come within a whisker of saying that deceased saints have at least some supernatural abilities normally reserved for God. This is done to protect the dogma of invoking the saints in Heaven.

Roman Catholics grasp at straws in their attempt to find something in the Scriptures to support their theories. They may quote Jeremiah 15:1 where God says, "Though Moses and Samuel stood before me, [yet] my mind [could] not [be] toward this people: cast [them] out of my sight, and let them go forth." They think this means that God is opening the door so that the dead Samuel and Moses might stand before Him. Moses and Samuel did not, and the point is well-taken that Israel had gone too far so that not even the presence of previous strong leaders could dissuade God's judgment. Catholicism looks in vain at Revelation 5:8 and 8:3 for help. In Revelation 5:8, the elders hold the bowl of the prayers of the saints which proves nothing to the point. This highly figurative, metaphorical language does not suggest that the elders are listening to and praying on behalf of the saints! In Revelation 8:3, incense is given to an angel that he might add it to the prayers of the saints. The prayers are still the prayers of the saints not those of the deceased or the angels. We are reminded of what the prophets of old had to say about this business of contacting the dead.

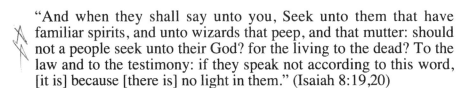

> "And when they shall say unto you, Seek unto them that have familiar spirits, and unto wizards that peep, and that mutter: should not a people seek unto their God? for the living to the dead? To the law and to the testimony: if they speak not according to this word, [it is] because [there is] no light in them." (Isaiah 8:19,20)

In the absence of any biblical example and with commands to the contrary we wonder why the Romanist persists in this error. We suggest that the core reason is the never-ending parade of speculations and dogmas encountered when Church councils are put above the Bible and religion takes the place of a living relationship with Jesus Christ. Ideas of men become more attractive for they hold esoteric promises, novelty and superstition all at once. The dark nature of man gravitates toward that which he cannot know. Without scriptural control, man's attempt to search the ways of the supernatural drives him to never-ending postulations and ideologies which he hopes will get him closer to his objective. But any fool knows the quagmire of despair that is conjured up by the mind of man and to where this can lead. Such is the case of the Romanist speculators who embark on dangerous journeys that serve to draw them away from the God of the Bible. Indeed, this drive toward the speculative knows no boundaries and direct disobedience to the Word is no obstacle to the Romanist!

We close this section with the sobering words of Moses taken from Deuteronomy:

> "There shall not be found among you [any one] that maketh his son or his daughter to pass through the fire, [or] that useth divination, [or] an observer of times, or an enchanter, or a witch, Or a charmer, or a consulter with familiar spirits, or a wizard, or a necromancer (one who calls up the dead). For all that do these things [are] an abomination unto the LORD: and because of these abominations the LORD thy God doth drive them out from before thee." (Deuteronomy 18:10-12)

Chapter 14

Mary

IF WE were to summarize the ingredients which serve to compose the Marian doctrines of the Roman Catholic Church, we would have in microcosm what is so wrong with this religion. A little misinterpretation by the *Vulgate*, a healthy dose of speculation, a few papal decrees, a liberal dosage of the meaning of a few choice Greek words and a totally gullible audience accustomed to feeding on the mysterious, and there you have it! The mighty Marian doctrines of the Romanist religion fit right into what we have already discovered to be true of Rome—absolute fantasy in religious garb.

Mary—the New Eve

We shall begin our investigation into the unprecedented role of Mary in the Romish religion by an examination of Genesis 3:15. Mary is said to be the "New Eve" by Catholic theologians. By this is meant that she is, in some new sense, the mother of mankind as Eve was the mother of all living (Genesis 3:20). Such lofty statements come about as the result of putting together a variety of thought strands and deductions. We believe the starting point in a small way is found in Genesis 3:15. The *Douay-Rheims Version* of the Bible translates 3:15 as follows:

> "I will put enmities between thee and the woman, and thy seed and her seed: *she* shall crush thy head, and thou shalt lie in wait for *her* heel." (emphasis ours)

This translation follows the *Latin Vulgate* of Jerome. However, Jerome had mistakenly translated the pronouns *ipsa* (feminine) instead of *ipse* (masculine). The mistake was never corrected! Both the original Hebrew and Greek Septuagint have them as masculine pronouns. The correct translation should be:

> "And I will put enmity between thee and the woman, and between thy seed and her seed; it (*ipse*, he, masculine) shall bruise thy head, and thou shalt bruise *his* heel."

148

The Latin translation leaves the impression that a woman would crush the seed of Satan and that in so doing she would come under severe Satanic attack. But is this what the inspired text says? This passage is a prophecy of Jesus Christ and *His* ultimate victory over Satan, even though He would have to suffer on the cross to do it.

This is the first thread in the tapestry of the devaluation of Jesus Christ and the elevation of Mary. Observe carefully the footnote found under Genesis 3:15 by the *Douay-Rheims*:

> "vs. 15. She shall crush. Ipsa, the woman; so divers fathers read this place, conformably to the Latin: others read ipsum, viz. the seed. The sense is the same: for it is by her seed, Jesus Christ, that the woman crushes the serpent's head."[1]

Notice that it is the woman who crushes the serpent's head. This is the beginning of Marian veneration. The Romanists have it wrong from the very beginning. From this error spills this doctrinal contribution from the *1990 Catholic Almanac*:

> "To the titles of Mary already familiar from the Gospels — 'the Virgin,' 'Favored One,' 'Mother of Jesus,' 'Mother of my Lord' (Elizabeth's greeting, meaning 'Mother of the Messianic King') — the early Church added other descriptions. By the mid-second century Mary was being compared to Eve. Eve was deceived by the word of the evil angel and by disobedience brought death; Mary, the obedient Virgin, heeded the message of the good angel and by her consent brought Life to the world. The title of 'New Eve' became common for Mary. By the time of St. Jerome (d. 419), it was proverbial to say, 'Death through Eve, life through Mary.'"[2]

From this humble beginning, the snowball of Marian superiority will roll down the slope of Catholic fantasy until she becomes, in their minds, immaculately conceived, sinless, assumed into Heaven and finally redemptress and co-redeemer with Jesus Christ. There are many planks in the platform of Marian demagoguery. Let us disassemble them one at a time.

Catholics champion the use of the term *theotokos*, which means God-bearer. They believe that Mary gave birth to God and thus she is to be elevated and worshipped. But the scriptural account of the birth of Jesus

---

[1] *Holy Bible, Douay-Rheims Version*, (Rockford, IL: TAN Books and Publishers, Inc., ©1971) pg. 8, Genesis 3:15
[2] *1990 Catholic Almanac*, pg. 261

Christ does not lead to such a conclusion. Mary was told that she would be with child *through the agency of the Holy Spirit*:

> "The Holy Ghost shall come upon thee, and the power of the Highest shall overshadow thee: therefore also that holy thing which shall be born of thee shall be called the Son of God." (Luke 1:35)

Mary did not conceive Christ on her own. The formation of the child in the womb of Mary was a supernatural event caused by God whereby the pre-existent Christ was made in the likeness of man. This holy creation was to be called the Son of God! Mary did not give to the child in her womb the God nature. His God nature pre-existed and was miraculously fashioned in the womb of Mary. This Hypostatic Union of human and divine nature was fashioned by God, and Mary gave birth to what God had fashioned. Mary was chosen to give birth to the God-man named Jesus. This is someone absolutely unique due to what God had done, not due to what Mary had done. However, there is some speculation as to whether Mary gave to Christ her human nature or whether Christ was fashioned in the womb with generic human nature. In either case, Mary did not give birth to God the Father, the Holy Spirit or the pre-existent Christ as the Third Person of the Trinity. The *kenosis* remains shrouded in mystery far beyond the comprehension of mere mortals. But with respect to Mary it can be observed from Scripture that she was the instrumental occasion for the miracle of Christ's birth and as such cannot be afforded an equal or higher honor. Mary's position before God is one of humility and wonder. She is not the receiver of praise or glory for being chosen to give birth to Jesus Christ. She is blessed, but not glorified. It is critical to see that flesh did not take on God, *but rather God took on flesh*. In this sense only can Mary be said to have been the God-bearer.

Though the Hypostatic Union is a mystery to us, it helps us to understand that man is both material and immaterial. The distinction between soul and body is real although incomprehensible. Likewise, Jesus Christ is both God and man in *one Person*—not two personalities, but one *Person*—with both *Human and Divine natures*. In this sense only can God be said to have been born. In this sense only can God be said to have died. We think the *Westminster Confession* summarizes this miracle accurately.

> "The Son of God, the second person in the Trinity, being very and eternal God, of one substance, and equal with the Father, did, when the fullness of time was come, take upon him man's nature, with all the essential properties and common infirmities thereof, yet without sin; being conceived by the power of the Holy Ghost, in the womb of the Virgin Mary, of her substance. So that two whole, perfect, and distinct natures, the Godhead and the manhood, were insepara-

bly joined together in one person, without conversion, composition, or confusion. Which person is very God and very man, yet one Christ, the only mediator between God and man."[1]

All Catholic railings about the one *Person* of Christ cannot be used to back the Bible into the unwarranted leap that Mary gave Christ His *divine* nature.

The Immaculate Conception

Romanists have taken up three positions on Mary concerning her status here on earth. They believe and teach their adherents that Mary was conceived without sin (Immaculate Conception), that she was a perpetual virgin, and that she was assumed into Heaven (Assumption of Mary). Let us examine them in order.

Catholics argue from Luke 1:28 that Mary was so full of grace that there must not have been any sin at any time in her:

> "And the angel came in unto her, and said, Hail, [thou that art] highly favoured, the Lord [is] with thee." (Later manuscripts add "blessed are you among women") (Luke 1:28)

Notice that this is the beginning of the Romish prayer to Mary, 'Hail Mary full of grace, the Lord is with you, blessed is the fruit of thy womb, Jesus, etc..' This prayer is normally a part of the Catholic Rosary bead prayers said in abundant repetition!

At any rate, the Roman exegete thinks he has found in the Greek word *kecharitomene*—which is translated 'favored one,' 'full of favor' or 'full of grace'—some reason to contrive the sinlessness of Mary. Hoping that nobody looks too closely, the Catholic scholar begins to inflate this Greek word with a meaning far beyond its semantic range, but never it seems, far enough for their wild fantasies. So incredible is the "logic" that we give it to you firsthand:

> "'*Charis*' means favor, disinterested benevolence, coming from God,' explains René Laurentin. 'Does this mean that *kecharitomene* means only the extrinsic favor of God? From two points of view it means much more.' Both theologically and philologically, he says, the word indicates 'a transformation of the subject'. The sense is not

---

[1] *The Westminster Confession of Faith*, Chapter VII: 2, pg. 72

just 'to look upon with favor, but to transform by this favor or
grace.' *Kecharitomene*, then, signifies a plenitude of favor or grace.

"The newer translations leave out something the Greek conveys,
something the older translation conveys, which is that this grace
(and the core of the word *kecharitomene* is *charis*, after all) is at
once permanent and of a singular kind. The Greek indicates a
perfection of grace. A perfection must be perfect not only
intensively, but extensively. The grace Mary enjoyed must not only
have been as 'full' or strong or complete as possible at any given
time, but it must have extended over the whole of her life, from
conception. That is, she must have been in a state of sanctifying
grace from the first moment of her existence to have been called 'full
of grace' or to have been filled with divine favor in a singular way.
This is just what the doctrine of the Immaculate Conception holds:
that Mary, 'in the first instant of her conception was, by a singular
grace and privilege of Almighty God in view of the merits of Jesus
Christ, the Savior of the human race, preserved exempt from all
stain of original sin.'"[1]

Our response may seem too simple for the reader but it is the best response.
The Greek term *charis* (grace) does not mean all that the Romanist wants it
to mean. It is simply not true. All this business about a "transformation" of
subject and "perfection intensively and extensively" is the height of
speculative nonsense for which Rome is ever prideful. Re-read the above
citation and listen to the leaps. Mary "must have been" this or Mary "must
have been" that! All this from one little Greek word that does not begin to
carry the weight that Rome piles on top of it.

Romanists evidently overlook that this word, *kecharitomene,* is used one
other time in the New Testament. We find this word used by Paul in
Ephesians 1, verse 6:

"To the praise of the glory of his grace, wherein he hath made [he
has favored, *echaritosen*, freely given] us accepted in the beloved."

The Catholic scholar cannot have it both ways. If the Greek is good for
Mary's Immaculate Conception (and it is not!), then it must be good for all
the saints since the same term is used with reference to all the saints and
spoken to us as well in Ephesians 1:6.

The Romanist theologians labor also under the burden of a misunderstanding of original sin. They think that "full of grace" means so full that Mary

[1] Keating, *Catholicism and Fundamentalism*, pp. 269, 270

neither had sin nor could she sin since her grace was full. We have already shown the fallacy of this logic above. But we do not want to leave this section without a remark on original sin. Catholics think original sin is nothing more than a deprivation or privation of sanctifying grace. Thus, if Mary was full of grace then she must not have partaken of original sin. Romanists leave out the solidarity of the "guilt" of Adam's sin when discussing original sin. Original sin consists not simply in the absence of grace but, more importantly, it is the actual polluted and corrupt nature and imputed guilt derived from Adam's fall. Modern Catholics retreat to the old Arminian argument that Adam's guilt is not constituted as a ground for condemnation. They think it is only the actual sinning of a person that Paul addresses in Romans 3:23. Catholics think only children who sin past the age of reason are guilty before God. This impoverished view of depravity opens the door for all manner of havoc when it comes to defining the grounds of our condemnation.

Having defined children "under the age of reason" as the exception to Romans 3:23, Romanists are at liberty to find other exceptions such as Mary:

> "Despite the phrasing, it (Romans 3:23) might be that it refers not to absolutely everyone, but just to the mass of mankind (which means young children and other special cases, such as Mary, would be excluded without being singled out)."[1]

We point out that Mary, if not Rome, seemed to know that she needed a Savior in Luke 1:47;

> "And my spirit hath rejoiced in God my Saviour."

Also, Romans 3 tells us that all have sinned and fallen short of the glory of God. Romans 5 puts all of humanity, including Mary, into a solidarity relationship with Adam. There are no scriptural exceptions to the subsequent guilt and pollution of Adam's fall. When faced with this, the Romanist does some fast maneuvering. The doctrine of "preservation redemption" is pulled out of the hat. The Catholic battle cry is, "Mary must have been saved by Jesus in a special pre-emptory manner at her conception." And where is the scriptural support for such outlandish speculation? There is none!

Catholics expect us to believe that Mary was *saved* by Jesus prior to her birth. In this way Jesus is said to be the *savior* of Mary despite the Catholic teaching that Mary was sinless! We ask, "Saved from what?" If Mary never inherited the Adamic nature, then in what sense was she in need of a savior? The Catholic answer is that she was *saved* from ever committing a sin!

---

[1] Keating, *Catholicism and Fundamentalism*, pg. 271

Obviously, this is a redefinition of the term "salvation." According to Rome, "salvation" can now refer to someone who is not in the least danger of perishing! Ironically, for Rome, Mary was *saved* from having to be saved! Evidently, to the Romanist, there is no difference between being saved from a fiery wreck by a rescue team and not being involved in the wreck in the first place. With this reasoning, Jesus Christ could be said to have been saved prior to His incarnation. This redefinition of the term "salvation" may be in the Catholic mind, but not in the Scriptures! The only salvation the Scriptures speak of, in the context of eternal life, is salvation from actual guilt and sin. Even when the word is used of general deliverance, it is deliverance from something. It never means informed avoidance of a difficult potential. Observe how Rome redefines terminology to fit their fantasy.

> "Mary, too, required a Savior. Like all other descendants of Adam, by her nature she was subject to the necessity of contracting original sin. But by *a special intervention of God, undertaken at the instant she was conceived, she was preserved from the stain of Original Sin and certain of its consequences. She was therefore redeemed by the grace of Christ, but in a special way, by anticipation.*"[1]

What can we say to this other than it is not in the least given to us by anything remotely scriptural. But as we have seen, the Romanist is not limited by the Bible. What is to stop Rome from declaring other dogmas and doctrines that have nothing to do with the revelation of God?

Perpetual Virginity

The subterfuge continues with the alleged perpetual virginity of Mary. Luke 1:34 says,

> "How shall this be, seeing I know not a man?"

Mindful of this, the Romanist goes to work. From these simple words of Mary in response to the angel Gabriel, Romanists leap to the conclusion that Mary was making a perpetual vow of virginity. Why? Because, in Romanist reasoning, Mary would have never asked, "How shall this be?", if she was planning to have sexual intercourse in the future:

> "If she anticipated having children and did not intend to maintain a vow of virginity, she would hardly have to ask "how" she was to

---

[1] Keating, *Catholicism and Fundamentalism*, pg. 270. Emphasis added

have a child, since having a child the normal way would be expected by a newlywed."[1]

But was Mary asking how she could go about having a baby since she had vowed never to have sex? Obviously not! Her question was not, "How do you expect this to happen in light of my vow?" Her question was "How can these things be since I have not known a man?" — the point being that she had not known a man sexually at the time of the announcement. There is no vow of virginity here. The Catholic wants us to think that Mary was astounded that she was going to have a baby because she had taken a vow of perpetual virginity even in marriage! The fly in the ointment is that we cannot find a hint of this alleged perpetual vow in all of Scripture! It is manufactured and brought to the text by Romanists!

Matthew 1:25 says:

> "And (Joseph) knew her not till she had brought forth her firstborn son: and he called his name JESUS."

The Romanist is undaunted. Catholic exegesis at this point wishes us to believe that Joseph neither had sex with Mary up to the point of Christ's birth *nor throughout their marriage!* Great lengths are gone to in order to prove that the word "until" does not imply that action happened later. They think that only the modern use of the word "until" anticipates action after the "until." For instance, "She waited until the car went by and crossed the street." So, the Romanist is content to affirm that Joseph had no relations with Mary "until" Jesus was born nor at any time after His birth. Catholics assert the ancient use of "until" does not even hint that the marriage was sexually consummated after the birth of Christ.

We readily admit that there are occasions where action or knowledge implied after the "until" does not make any sense. In such cases the "until" is better translated "up to." Thus, "Michal the daughter of Saul had no child unto (until) the day of her death" (2 Samuel 6:23). But the burden of proof on the Romanist is to prove that such is the case with Matthew 1:25. The word "until" is used some 30 times in Matthew alone. In most instances, unless context determines to the contrary, there is action implied after the "until." Usually it is a change of action. For instance, Jesus was taken into Egypt, "And was there *until* the death of Herod" (Matthew 2:15). Surely the implication is that Jesus returned after the death of Herod. Again we read in Matthew 18:30 that the debtor was thrown in jail "until" he should pay back what he owed. Surely the implication is that he would be released after the debt was paid. Again, when Noah entered the ark, they "knew not until the

---

[1] Keating, *Catholicism and Fundamentalism*, pg. 283

flood came, and took them all away" (Matthew 24:39). Surely our Lord is implying that those who drowned had some realization after the rise of the flood waters. Perhaps their realization came at the point of death that the teaching of Noah was accurate. Keating misleads his readers by saying, "In fact, if the modern sense is forced on the Bible, some ridiculous meanings result."[1] But there is no so-called modern sense to the Greek *heos*, i.e., "until." It simply is used differently in varying contexts. There is nothing in Matthew 1:25 which militates against action happening after the "until." It is perfectly within the bounds of good Greek grammar to say:

> "And he kept her a virgin until [only to the time] she gave birth to a Son; and he called Him Jesus."

If Matthew wanted to inform us that Mary and Joseph never had sex then he could have said:

> "And he kept her a virgin even after she gave birth to a Son and he called Him Jesus."

Matthew does not say this.

Mary's Other Children

Christians might try to appeal to the instances where the "brothers" and "sisters" of Christ are mentioned in Scripture to settle the issue of Mary's alleged perpetual virginity. But the Romanist is ever ready for an end run on these passages as well. They appeal to the wide semantical range of the word "brother" in Scripture. While it is true that *adelphoi* can be used to include uncles and cousins as well as non-blood related associates such as "brothers in Christ," only context can determine its usage. For it is *equally* true that the Greek word for brother or sister refers in fact to a bona fide blood brother or sister from the same mother!

Take for example, John 11:1 where we are told that Bethany was home to Mary and her *adelphee* (sister) Martha. Was she or was she not her blood sister? Why not a cousin? Why not a "sister in the Lord"? Luke 10:39 tells us that Martha had a "sister" named Mary. Real sister or cousin? The *Catholic Almanac* calls Martha the sister of Mary and Lazarus. Our point is that there is no reason to take *adelphee* here as anything but "sister" in the sense of a common mother and father. Now we ask the reader to consider Matthew 13:55-57:

---

[1] Keating, *Catholicism and Fundamentalism*, pg. 285

"Is not this the carpenter's son? is not his mother called Mary? and his brethren, James, and Joses, and Simon, and Judas? And his sisters, are they not all with us? Whence then hath this [man] all these things? And they were offended in him. But Jesus said unto them, A prophet is not without honour, save in his own country, and in his own house."

The Romanist has no problem with Martha being the "blood" sister of Mary and Lazarus. There is not a footnote of explanation in the *Douay-Rheims*. But notice what we find under Matthew 13:55;

"These were the children of Mary wife of Cleophas, sister to our Blessed Lady, (St. Matthew 27.56; St. John 19.25,) and therefore, according to the usual style of the Scripture, they were called brethren, that is, *near relations* to our Savior."[1] (emphasis ours)

Getting back to Matthew 13:55, we must ask if these *brothers* are near relations (cousins), as the Romanist says, or *bona fide* blood brothers from the womb of Jesus' mother, Mary. The *Douay-Rheims* takes for granted that Mary Clopas, mentioned as one of the women at the cross by John (cf., John 19:25), was in fact Mary's sister. This is taken for granted so that the children of Mary Clopas—James and Joses (cf., Mark 15:40)—can be identified as the James and Joses of Matthew 13:55, above. If this is true, then Matthew 13:55 would have to be interpreted as follows:

"Isn't this the carpenter's son? Isn't his mother's name Mary, and aren't his *brothers* (really cousins) James, Joseph, Simon and Judas (from His aunt, Mary Clopas)?"

The objection we have to such an explication is that Mary's parents would have had to name two of their daughters Mary. This is not likely. Secondly, we are not at all certain that Mary Clopas *was* the sister of Mary. She was at the cross, but it is unclear from John whether she was the sister of Mary or another Mary. The text reads,

"Near the cross of Jesus stood his mother, his mother's sister, Mary the wife of Clopas, and Mary Magdalene."

As we can see, we are hard pressed to know if Mary Clopas is meant by John as the sister of Mary, or another Mary. If another Mary, the Romanist argument falls in a heap since there would not be the alleged *cousin* relationship! Also, it is a leap to say that *the brothers* of Jesus in Matthew 13 are really the sons of Mary Clopas. Why should we say this? In Mark, the sons

---

[1] *Douay-Rheims*, pg. 19, Matthew 13:55

of Mary Clopas are called James *the Less* (*tou mikrou*) and Joses. No such designation is given of James in Matthew 13:55.

We ask the readers to consider Matthew 12:46,47; Luke 8:19,20; John 2:12 and John 7:3-5 in order to decide for themselves whether Jesus had any brothers or sisters from His mother. For our purposes we take exception to the accusation that Christians wish to give Jesus' family from Mary because we wish to demean celibacy and protect our level of devotion to Jesus alone. These accusations serve to betray the real Christian understanding of the Bible and it alone as our rule of authority. Christians deny all of Rome's fantasies because the Bible stands against them! Celibacy will stand or fall on its own merit as measured by the Word of God.

Assumption and Redemptress

Before moving away from this section we shall address two more aspects of Marian doctrines. Was Mary really assumed into Heaven by God so that she would not undergo physical decay? Also, are we to look to Mary as a Co-redemptrix of salvation?

We shall get to the heart of the matter with respect to the alleged assumption of Mary through a rather lengthy quote:

> "'But,' ask fundamentalists, 'if Mary was immaculately conceived, and if death was a consequence of original sin, why did she die?' Although she was wholly innocent and never committed a sin, she died in order to be in union with Jesus. Keep in mind that he did not have to die to effect our redemption; he could have just willed it, and that would have been sufficient. But he *chose* to die. Mary identified herself with God's plan of salvation, certainly from her saying, 'Let it be done to me according to thy word' (Luke 1:38), but really from the very start of her life. She accepted death as Jesus accepted death, and she suffered (Luke 2:35) in union with his suffering. Just as she shared in his work, she shared in his glorification. She shared in his Resurrection by having her glorified body taken into heaven, the way the glorified bodies of all the saved will be taken into heaven on the Last Day."[1]

We have selected this paragraph because it reveals the Catholic mindset when it comes to redemption. Earlier we showed that Romanism has a faulty view of redemption insofar as it relates to salvation. Here we see the

---

[1] Keating, *Catholicism and Fundamentalism*, pg. 275

error compounded as redemption relates to the will of God. Notice that elevating Mary as one who only chose to die, completely misses the necessity of the atonement of Christ. We are not convinced that Mary chose to die in order to identify with her son who chose to die as well. The whole idea centers around the Catholic contention that Mary shared in the plan of salvation while alive on earth, so why should she not undergo death in similar fashion as her Son before her? Their point is that Mary did not die because of sin like everyone else (cf., Romans 6:23 along with Romans 5:12f). She died only as *her choice* to participate fully with Christ and experience union with Him! This is bad enough theology! But it is the underlying root which is the real heresy of Rome. What Rome teaches as dogma, Christians know as heresy. Notice:

> "...he [Christ] did not have to die to effect our redemption; he could have just willed it, and that would have been sufficient."[1]

This is patently false. The death of Jesus Christ on the cross was absolutely necessary in that nothing else could satisfy the justice of God. For a theologian to say that God could have simply willed salvation apart from the blood of Christ is to deny the very nature of God. It also makes a mockery of the cross in that an innocent man (God incarnate, no less) died unnecessarily.

We cite only two passages, for the sake of brevity, although the entirety of the New Testament could be brought to bear in order to suffocate this reasoning of men.

> "Then he said unto them, O fools, and slow of heart to believe all that the prophets have spoken: Ought not Christ to have suffered these things, and to enter into his glory? And beginning at Moses and all the prophets, he expounded unto them in all the scriptures the things concerning himself." (Luke 24: 25-27)

> "For when Moses had spoken every precept to all the people according to the law, he took the blood of calves and of goats, with water, and scarlet wool, and hyssop, and sprinkled both the book, and all the people, Saying, *This [is] the blood of the testament which God hath enjoined unto you.* Moreover he sprinkled with blood both the tabernacle, and all the vessels of the ministry. And almost all things are by the law purged with blood; *and without shedding of blood is no remission.* [It was] therefore necessary that the patterns of things in the heavens should be purified with these; but the heavenly things themselves with better sacrifices than these." (Hebrews 9:19-23)

---

[1] Keating, *Catholicism and Fundamentalism*, pg. 275

The *necessity* of the death of Christ was never an option in the eternal plan of God. The nature of God demands, and all of Scripture designates, the blood shed before the foundations of the world as the absolute criteria for salvation.

Hopefully the reader can see that when the death of Christ is made optional by virtue of relegating it to the realm of choice rather than necessity for the redemption of man, the door is open for other heresies. In 1950, Pius XII declared that Mary did not undergo decay but was assumed into Heaven. Did she die? It is unclear to the Romanist. But to cover themselves and to protect the fiction of her perpetual sinlessness, they say, if she died, it was by her choice and not due to sin. Sensing the raised eyebrows of the Christian community, our objection is anticipated for us with their corresponding answer:

> "Still, fundamentalists ask, where is the proof from Scripture? Strictly, there is none. It was the Catholic Church that was commissioned by Christ to teach all nations and to teach them infallibly. The mere fact that the Church teaches the doctrine of the Assumption as something definitely true is a guarantee that it is true."[1]

The Christian will always ask for the proof in Scripture. Herein lies the difference between man-made religions, such as Romanism, and the Body of Jesus Christ here on earth.

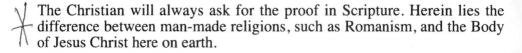

The latest addition of Romanistic idolatry is wrapped up in the highest insult to both Mary and Jesus Christ. As speculation knows no bounds, so Romanism has visited the realm of the unreal in its final verdict on the death of Christ and the person of Mary. Mary is said to "channel" all graces since she "gave the world its redeemer."[2] She is said to have "represented the whole of humanity at the annunciation,"[3] and as such she became the obedient second Eve in contrast to the disobedient first Eve.

> "Instead, through God's will, grace is not conferred on anyone without Mary's cooperation."[4]

And where is the scriptural proof, or at least a shadow of it, for such a high and lofty elevation of Mary? Catholic answers are consistent and revealing at the same time:

---

[1] Keating, *Catholicism and Fundamentalism*, pg. 275

[2] Keating, *Catholicism and Fundamentalism*, pg. 279

[3] Keating, *Catholicism and Fundamentalism*, pg. 279

[4] Keating, *Catholicism and Fundamentalism*, pg. 279

"True, scriptural proofs for this are lacking."[1] ⚡

Some Romanist theologians make a wave at John 19:26 where Christ commits Mary to the care of John. Their reasoning is that Mary (representing Jesus) is the spiritual caretaker of John (representing the entire world). This mystical exegesis leads to wherever one desires! In this case, Mary is given a boost into the heavenlies as the faithful, sinless carrier of mankind as the second Eve, the source of all grace as the mother of God, and finally, the giver of all graces as the Co-redemptrix of Jesus Christ.

From this fundamental error of speculative or mystical theology will emerge a devotion to Mary beyond the wildest imaginations of the Church. It is happening as this book is being written. Women say they are going to Mary since she can understand them better than the male Christ is able to. Mary is called upon to deliver whole nations. Alleged appearances of Mary with secret messages for the world are commonplace.

"Banneux, near Liege, Belgium: Mary appeared eight times between Jan. 15 and Mar. 2, 1933, to an 11-year-old peasant girl...

"Beauraing, Belgium: Mary appeared 33 times between Nov. 29, 1932, and Jan. 3, 1933, to five children in the garden of a convent school...

"Fatima, Portugal: Mary appeared six times between May 13 and Oct. 13, 1917, to three children in a field called Cova da Iria near Fatima, north of Lisbon...

"Guadalupe, Mexico: Mary appeared four times in 1531 to an Indian, Juan Diego, on Tepeyac hill outside of Mexico City...

"La Salette, France: Mary appeared as a sorrowing and weeping figure Sept. 19, 1846, to two peasant children...

"Lourdes, France: Mary, identifying herself as the Immaculate Conception, appeared 18 times between Feb. 11 and July 16, 1858, to 14-year-old Bernadette Soubirous at the grotto of Massabielle near Lourdes in southern France...

"Our Lady of the Miraculous Medal, France: Mary appeared three times in 1830 to Catherine Labouré in the chapel of the motherhouse

---

[1] Keating, *Catholicism and Fundamentalism*, pg. 279

of the daughters of Charity of St. Vincent de Paul, Rue de Bac, Paris."[1]

In the midst of this defection into the worship and adoration of a false deity, the Romanist theologian sits smugly, and calmly asserts concerning Christ:

"His (Christ) role as Mediator is not lessened because she has been allowed to assist him."[2]

We are at a loss to see how the role of the uniqueness of Christ as the only mediator of the New Covenant cannot be lessened when it is said that grace is not conferred on anyone without Mary's cooperation. Also, where in the Bible are we told that Mary assists Christ in the dispensing of grace? Who says so? There is not a word in Scripture to this effect! Also, what if Mary says "No." Then what? To assert that she never says "No" is to admit that she really has no part in it after all. To affirm that she might say "No" is to grant that "her say" could be different than Christ's. We are driving this point home because we are certain the relationship between Mary and the Godhead, in Rome's fantasy of the heavenly decision-making process, cannot be fully reconciled until it is explained in terms of Mary having joined the Trinity. We are waiting for this next in the madness of the Romanist religion! We would not be surprised if, in the minds of many Romanists, she has already arrived, as evidenced by the following citation:

"In his celebration of the Marian Year in Rome in 1950, Pope Pius XII accurately reflected the Church's view of the Virgin Mary in his pontifical prayer:

"'Enraptured by the splendor of your heavenly beauty and impelled by the anxieties of the world, we cast ourselves into your arms, Oh Immaculate Mother of Jesus and our Mother. Mary... we adore and praise the peerless richness of the sublime gifts with which God has filled you above every other mere creature, from the moment of conception until the day on which after your assumption into heaven. He crowned you Queen of the Universe. Oh crystal fountain of faith, bathe our hearts with your heavenly perfume. Oh Conqueress of evil and death, inspire in us a deep horror of sin which makes the soul detestable to God and the slave of hell. Oh well-beloved of God, hear the ardent cries which rise up from every heart in this year dedicated to you. Then tenderly, Oh Mary, cover our aching wound; convert the wicked, dry the tears of the afflicted

---

and the oppressed. Comfort the poor and humble. Quench hatred, sweeten harshness, safeguard the flower of purity and protect the Holy Church. In your name resounding harmoniously in heaven, may they recognize that all are brothers and that the nations are members of one family.. Receive, Oh sweet Mother our humble supplications and above all, obtain for us that on that day, happy with you, we may repeat before your throne that hymn which is sung today around your altars. You are beautiful Oh Mary. You are Glory Oh Mary. You are the joy, you are the Honor of our people.'"[1]

---

[1] Excerpt from *Forward* magazine, article written by the late Walter Martin entitled, "Charismatics and The Cult of Mary"

Chapter 15

Justification

"Therefore we conclude that a man is justified by faith
without the deeds of the law."
–*Romans 3:28*

THE Bible uses the term "justify" to identify and focus on God's act in declaring sinners to be acquitted of the punishment due their sin. Justification has relation to the law of God. Failure to obey God's law brings condemnation. The penalty which results from a failure to keep the law of God must be satisfied in order for God to acquit (justify) a sinner. Sin is lawlessness. The penalty of sin is death. Breaking God's law always brings the penalty of death. For the verdict of death to be overturned one must be justified. The Bible teaches that God has willed to save sinners through the death of His Son, our Lord Jesus Christ, on the cross. Christ came to seek and to save the lost. Salvation is the outcome of those who have been declared acquitted from the penalty due their sins. To be justified by God is to be declared free to enter Heaven. To be justified does not mean to be not guilty. It means to be declared not liable for the penalty of one's guilt! This is biblical justification: to be declared by God that there is no need for you to suffer personally for your sins. The basis of this justification is the finished work of Jesus Christ. He paid the penalty so others could go free. God, as the judge, has declared sinners to be justified or acquitted from the punishment due their sin. God does so on the basis of what Christ has done. The reason all men have a need of this justification is because all are sinners. We need only mention a few of the many biblical passages which speak to the guilt and condemnation of mankind.

"...for we have before proved both Jews and Gentiles, that they are all under sin; As it is written, There is none righteous, no, not one." (Romans 3:9b,10)

"For all have sinned, and come short of the glory of God." (Romans 3:23)

"Therefore as by the offence of one [judgment came] upon all men to condemnation..." (Romans 5:18a)

164

"And you [hath he quickened], who were dead in trespasses and sins." (Ephesians 2:1)

All are under sin, all are children of wrath and by nature constituted sinners in Adam's transgression.

The term "justification" centers around God's declaration to acquit man despite man's sinfulness. All stand condemned before God on the basis of our relationship to Adam and the subsequent sinning that inevitably overtakes us. We are left to contemplate the answer to the question posed in Psalm 130:3,

"If thou, LORD, shouldest mark iniquities, O Lord, who shall stand?"

The answer is that no one could stand if God punished us on the basis of our iniquity. However, God declares us to be free of the punishment due our sins. He justifies us. Justification describes our acquitted status before God. Though guilty, we are declared to be acquitted. To be justified is to be accepted without penalty due our person. When this term is used in relation to standing before God, it is always with a view of being declared acquitted in contrast to being declared condemned. Justification is a matter of acquittal in the eyes of God. We all stand condemned because of sin. The only remedy is to be justified. This acquittal, for the Christian, is based entirely on what Christ has already done. However, there is no declared acquittal, based *only* on what Christ has done, in the Roman Catholic religion. The final acquittal of the Romanist is based upon his own righteousness after having been purified through suffering.

The Roman Catholic religion and Christianity both agree that Jesus Christ came to die on the cross so that God could be just in the justifying of sinners. But, in the Romanist religion, the death of Christ has only cleared the way for God to justify poor lost sinners based upon their own righteousness gained through sufferings and obediences within the Roman system! The shed blood of Christ, for the Romanist, only enables God to be satisfied with personal sufferings and obediences (merit) for justification.

We are compelled to explain here Rome's understanding of justification. Rome affirms justification as an ongoing process, suspended on personal holiness, which ultimately earns a final verdict by God as to the sinners worthiness to enter Heaven. They do not submit to any other understanding of the term. They like to argue justification as an ongoing process of renewal in the sinner which starts at baptism. They argue justification is both the infusion of graces which makes one righteous and the corresponding declaration of acquittal based upon that person's righteousness. The

Romanist does not believe in a one time declarative acquittal based only on what Christ has done on behalf of the sinner. The Romanist does not believe that the righteousness of Jesus Christ stands in the place of sinners as their only ground of acquittal. Roman Catholics believe they can lose their justification because it is suspended on their personal merits, brought about by graces and given to them by God through a sacramental system. They cannot affirm that the death of Christ alone is the ground of justification. To say that would undermine their sacramental system.

So, when Scriptures say, "that a man is justified by faith without the deeds of the law" (Romans 3:28), Romanists understand this to mean an ongoing process of being made righteous until God finally acquits a sinner based upon a certain attainment of righteousness. Here is our first bone of contention. Romanists deny that justification is a one-time acquittal pronounced by God, at the moment of saving faith, which ensures safe passage into Heaven. They deny the righteousness of Christ as the sole ground for this acquittal. They believe man shares in the ground of his own justification through paying penalties due his sin or becoming righteous through the sacramental system. Christians could not disagree more. We affirm justification to be the declared acquittal by God of a sinner based upon the ground of Christ's righteousness alone. This acquittal is once and final for the Christian at the moment of saving faith. The Catholic religion reserves an ultimate acquittal for its adherents based on the righteousness attained by the sinner. This righteousness of obedience is said to satisfy God during one's stay on earth unless additional suffering is needed in purgatory.

The critical question is, "What does God take into account when He determines to declare the poor sinner justified?" Does God infuse grace into the sinner as an aid to enhance good works and then declare the sinner justified on the measure of those good works done in faith? Or, does God consider only the work of Christ and declare a sinner justified on the measure of Christ's work alone appropriated by faith apart from works of any law? This is the essence of the difference between the religion of Rome and Christianity.

Romanists believe that a sinner must *eventually* be "declared acquitted" before he or she can finally go to Heaven. They have their own declarative justification from God, in some sense, in light of the death of Christ. Romanists admit that God will *ultimately* declare a sinner to be justified on the basis of *something*! For the Romanist, that *something* is the combination of merit and Christ's death. We can see that Catholicism and Christianity will never come together on answering the *ground of justification*.

Is the ground of acquittal good works done in faith by the believer, or is the ground the finished work of Christ alone appropriated by faith? These two opposite representations of God's ground for the acquittal of guilty sinners will produce radically different gospel messages!

Romanism

Catholics believe that the ground of approval for acquittal is the improved sinner himself. God's justification consists in God making people righteous here on earth through the sacramental system, and in the life hereafter through the fires of purgatory. Through their system of temporal punishments, God acquits them on the basis of their righteousness. Romanism believes that God improves the sinner enough to declare him acquitted on the basis of that improvement. Their steps in the process of justification may be seen as follows:

Man is born in sin and is liable to pay the penalty for his actual sinning.

Man is made just through his faithful participation in the sacramental system. The sacramental system requires self-payment of sins in the form of penances and works.

Justification is a process which starts with baptism and is ongoing. However, most Romanists believe that they can only be purified enough to warrant acquittal after having suffered in purgatory for a season.

Christianity

Christians believe that the righteousness contemplated by God in the decision to acquit the sinner is only the righteousness of Jesus Christ which becomes ours through faith apart from works of any law or individual merit. This is translated into the battle cry of the Protestant Reformation as *Sola Fide* or justification by "faith alone."

What is Meant by "Alone" in the Expression "Faith Alone"?

When we say "faith alone" we mean faith as the instrument by which the righteousness of another becomes ours. By "alone" we mean without the good works of man, without the obediences of the Law and without the personal righteousness of the believer taken into account. It is a declaration of God based upon the work of Christ alone. In our analysis, we must not be derailed by terminology. Romanists eventually have a real or final justification. The question is the ground or basis of this acquittal, not the meaning of the term.

Christianity affirms the ground to be nothing other than the righteousness of Christ.

Christianity affirms that works are expressive of justification and not the cause of it.

The Romanist Position Restated and Clarified

So as to avoid the accusation that we have caricatured Rome, let us observe the decree of Trent on this vital question. Justification as taught by the Council of Trent is absolutely contrary to the Christian understanding:

> "Hence, to those who work well unto the end and trust in God, eternal life is to be offered, both as a grace mercifully promised to the sons of God through Christ Jesus, and as a reward promised by God himself, to be faithfully given to their good works and merits."[1]

> "If anyone says that the sinner is justified by faith alone, meaning that nothing else is required to cooperate in order to obtain the grace of justification, and that it is not in any way necessary that he be prepared and disposed by the action of his own will, let him be *anathema*.

> "If anyone says that men are justified either by the sole imputation of the justice of Christ or by the sole remission of sins, to the exclusion of the grace and the charity which is poured forth in their hearts by the Holy Ghost, and remains in them, or also that the grace by which we are justified is only the good will of God, let him be *anathema*.

> "If anyone says that justifying faith is nothing else than confidence in divine mercy, which remits sins for Christ's sake, or that it is this confidence alone that justifies us, let him be *anathema*.

> "If anyone says that the justice received is not preserved and also not increased before God through good works, but that those works are

---

[1] Schroeder, pg. 41. From the 6th Session of Trent, chapter 16

merely the fruits and signs of justification obtained, but not the cause of its increase, let him be *anathema*."[1]

Romans 3:28, as footnoted in the *Douay-Rheims Version*, has this to say:

"The faith to which the apostle here attributes man's justification, is not a presumptuous assurance of our being justified; but a firm and lively belief of all that God has revealed or promised."[2]

Keating adds:

"The soul becomes objectively pleasing to God and so merits heaven. It merits heaven because now it is actually good."[3]

Justification, for the Catholic, is the hope for acquittal after having trudged through the sacramental system of graces and obediences beginning with baptism. Catholic baptism is actually called the laver of regeneration! This is to signify the beginning of justification in the Romanist religion.

"In these words a description of the justification of a sinner is given as being a translation from that state in which man is born a child of the first Adam to the state of grace and of the 'adoption of the sons' (Romans 8:15) of God through the second Adam, Jesus Christ, our Savior; and this translation after the promulgation of the Gospel cannot be effected except through the laver of regeneration (can. 5 *de bapt*.), or a desire for it, as it is written: 'Unless a man be born again of water and the Holy Spirit, he cannot enter into the kingdom of God' (John 3:5)."[4]

In the Roman Catholic religion, there is never assurance on earth of a final justification from God. Justification, since it is based upon the obedience of the sinner, is always in jeopardy. To the Romanist, it consists in the renewal of the man but can be lost through sin and regained through the sacraments.

"For God 'does not forsake those who have once been justified by His grace, unless He be first forsaken by them.' And so no one should flatter himself because of faith alone (can. 9,19,20), thinking that by faith alone he is made an heir and will obtain the inheritance,

---

[1] Schroeder, pp. 43-5, Canons 9, 11, 12, 24

[2] *Douay-Rheims*, pg. 173, Romans 3:28

[3] Keating, *Catholicism and Fundamentalism*, pg. 168

[4] Denzinger, pg. 249, paragraph 796

even though he suffer not with Christ 'that he may be also glorified.'(Romans 8:17)"[1]

Catholic scholarship presents justification as an ongoing process based upon good works done in faith. These works, Catholic scholars insist, are "non-meritorious" since they originate with Christ, who works through the faithful. Thus, works for justification are all the good works worked inside a person as the Spirit of God produces them. Catholic theologians hold these works as the ground of justification while maintaining that they are not meritorious. We see this as untenable and contradictory. How can works be the ground of justification while at the same time non-meritorious? The Roman Catholic religion misses the mark. Good works are anticipated in the verdict of justification and hence an absolutely indispensable fruit of justification, but not the ground. Furthermore, good works done in faith are the necessary result of justification. Good works flow from justification. Justification is not suspended on good works. Also, good works *necessarily* flow from justification. God will produce fruit in His own. The Catholic position does not allow the absolute certainty of good works as stemming from justification. Instead, good works become the 'condition' and 'ground' of justification. There is no guarantee that the Catholic religious system will produce one good work. All is suspended on the righteousness of man. We are left with untenable and contradictory language. Good works, they say, are the ground of justification, yet non-meritorious. Good works, they say, are not *necessarily* produced by Christ, since they require the cooperation of man, yet these good works are absolutely essential to justification.

The unavoidable conclusion is that human effort must *cooperate* with the Spirit to produce such works. If one does not *cooperate* then one has missed being justified! So, in the final analysis, it is what the person *does* to allow Christ to produce good works. This "allowing" is then the bottom line work without which there would be no justification. Hence, we are where we started, the ultimate ground of Romanist justification is *cooperation unto good works*. This reasoning of Rome serves to undermine biblical justification and ruins the gospel of Jesus Christ!

The fallacy of this position is that it assumes justification can be grounded on good works done in faith. This suspends justification on obedience. However, it is the scriptural testimony that God justifies the ungodly:

> "But to him that worketh not, but believeth on him that justifieth the *ungodly*…" (Romans 4:5)

---

[1] Denzinger, pg. 254, paragraph 804

Even though (as we believe) good works are necessarily produced by the Spirit, they are not in themselves the ground of justification. Justification is a term reserved to describe that which is the status of a wretched sinner as he or she is acquitted before the judgment bar of God. This happens once for the sinner. This acquittal is the justification of God with the merits of Christ as the ground. It is Christ given to the sinner for his justification. The ground is not what we let Christ produce in us. We grant there will be good works produced by the Spirit of God but they are not the ground of our justification.

Roman Catholic theologians have two methods of dealing with verses which seem so obviously opposed to their notion of acquittal based upon improvement of the sinner. In the first place, good works done by the Catholic are incorrectly seen to fall outside of Paul's condemnation of a works justification by virtue of them being produced by Christ inside as a person permits.

In the second place, Catholics are taught that the New Testament differentiates between "works of law" which they call "Torah," and "good works done in faith," which they see as the ground of justification. Thus, every time the objection is raised that Paul disdains a works justification, the Catholic response is "Yes, but Paul refers only to 'works of law, and not works of love done in faith." This arbitrary dichotomy is a convenient way of eliminating the book of Galatians as a proof against a works justification. It also eliminates other Pauline passages since the Catholic is convinced that Paul is referring to only a "law works" justification when he condemns justification by works.

But while it is undeniable that Paul's burden was for the elimination of Jewish law righteousness (cf., Romans 2, 3 and 9 as well as Galatians and Colossians), it is a *non sequitur* that Paul wished to restrict only such "law righteousness" as found in Judaism. We would argue that "law righteousness" from any system, as well as "works righteousness" from any perspective, are adamantly opposed by the apostle as the grounds for justification. We can find no reason to restrict Paul's understanding of works justification to the Law of Moses alone. Even if the Law of Moses was the occasion for his writing and the centerpiece of his argument, it does not follow that religious laws of other systems are not excluded by the apostle. It is much more tenable that if Paul excluded the greatest law system given to man, as the ground of justification, then no lesser system, such as Romanism, shall be allowed to stand in its place!

Furthermore, Catholic theologians gore themselves on the horns of their own dilemma. They insist that sincere obedience to the commands of the New Covenant are the ground for justification. They do so by arguing that

Paul is only referencing the Mosaic Law when Paul thunders against sincere obedience for justification. Yet, if sincere obedience is the ground for justification then how could an Old Testament saint have been justified if this is precisely what Paul forbids? The only possible answer is that Old Testament saints were indeed justified by sincere obedience to the Mosaic Law but New Testament saints cannot be. But is this the argument of Paul? Not at all! It is wrong on two counts. First, it posits two different ways of justification. One is sincere obedience to the Mosaic Law and the other is sincere obedience to the New Testament law. But justification is never predicated on either Old or New Covenant obediences. Second, the Scriptures report that no one was saved or justified by works of sincere obedience in the Law of Moses.

> "Even as David also describeth the blessedness of the man, unto whom God imputeth righteousness without works..." (Romans 4:6)

> "For the promise, that he should be the heir of the world, [was] not to Abraham, or to his seed, through the law, but through the righteousness of faith." (Romans 4:13)

Roman Catholic scholars have a difficult time reconciling their false bifurcation with the text of Romans 4 and Titus 3:5. In the case of Romans 4, Abraham was justified through faith long before the Mosaic Law. Also, he was justified by faith alone while in the midst of performing good works done in faith, (cf., Hebrews 11). Neither "law righteousness" nor "good works done in faith" were taken into account by God for Abraham's justification. All works of any kind are eliminated by Romans 4. Also, Titus 3:5 tells us directly that "works of righteousness which we have done" are not the ground of justification. They are deliberately excluded!

Romanists often use the word "antecedent." This refers to those works done prior to faith in Christ. According to Rome, "antecedent" works are eliminated by Paul and Jesus as the ground of our justification. However, upon a hearty embracing of the gospel, good works, they say, begin to accumulate merit for justification. But this is the same thing as saying there is no justification. Everything is conditionally suspended upon sincere obedience for justification. This conditionalism is the heart of the matter. Strictly speaking, Rome teaches a conditional justification and hopes for the best. Such a conditional pardon is no pardon at all. It is difficult to see how this religion differs one iota from all pagan religions that predicate their eternal bliss on a conditional pleasing of their deities! All of Paul's thundering against a "works" justification are relegated to "antecedent" works or "Mosaic works" so that the Romanist can get on with the business of enslaving its adherents in its own system of works! These Roman works are proclaimed to be exempt from the apostle's denouncement of works salvation.

In the final analysis Romanism teaches that a sinner is acquitted on the basis of inward renewal through the sacramental system.

Christians believe that the sinner is acquitted on the basis of the righteousness of Christ through faith alone, and the renewal is from the acquittal.

Romanists teach justification on the basis of renewal. Christians teach renewal on the basis of justification. Both cannot represent the true teaching of the gospel of our salvation.

Biblical Analysis

The term "justify" does not mean to infuse with grace or to make someone righteous when used of standing before God in anticipation of acceptance.

To justify is to declare the sinner acquitted. It is in contrast to condemnation. We ask the reader to examine the biblical report when it comes to the use of this term.

1. Proverbs 17:15—Notice the term "justify" means to declare acquitted–not *make* righteous–in the following verse:

> "He that *justifieth* the wicked, and he that *condemneth* the just, even they both [are] abomination to the LORD."

Here we see a *declaration* of the wicked as *acquitted* without the law being satisfied. The teaching of the proverb is that this is an abomination! But we are interested in the terminology. To *justify* the wicked is not to *make* them just! It is to *declare* them to be *acquitted*. Also, to *condemn* the righteous is not to *make* them bad. It is to *declare* them to be bad. To do either is an abomination. However it is not an abomination to *justify* the wicked if the demands of the law are met. God *declares the wicked as acquitted* based upon Christ's satisfaction of His law on their behalf.

2. Isaiah 5:23—"Which justify the wicked for reward, and take away the righteousness of the righteous from him!"

Here we see the condemnation by Isaiah of those who would justify the wicked for a bribe. The word "justify" here means "to acquit." It does not mean "to make one righteous"!

3. Isaiah 43:9,26—"Let all the nations be gathered together, and let the people be assembled: who among them can declare this, and shew us

former things? let them bring forth their witnesses, that they may be justified: or let them hear, and say, [It is] truth. ...Put me in remembrance: let us plead together: declare thou, that thou mayest be justified."

Here, again, the use of the word "justify" is in the sense of acquittal. The idea is that there will be a declaration of justification after the witnesses have testified. For the Christian, there is need of only one witness. Our witness is Jesus Christ who will testify that He died to pay the price for our acquittal.

4. Deuteronomy 25:1 — "If there be a controversy between men, and they come unto judgment, that [the judges] may judge them; then they shall justify the righteous, and condemn the wicked."

The term "justify" is used here in the sense of declaration and not making people righteous.

We ask the reader of these and the following verses to ask the question, "How is the word 'justify' used?" Does it mean to make someone righteous? Or, is it used in the sense of acquitting someone? As we have said, the Romanist must *ultimately* agree with our use of justify. He cannot escape the fact that he, too, has a final declaration of God. But his is based upon the faulty notion of self punishment for sins and self-purgation through penances imposed by Rome.

Throughout this section we have argued two things. The first is that to justify does not mean to make one righteous. The second is that even in Rome there has to be a final determination by God to acquit the sinner based on something. For Rome there is no escape. They ultimately have a verdict and a declaration of justification.

Their fatal flaw is that this verdict and declaration of God is based upon obedience to their man-made religion. The Christian understands that God's final declaration of justification is based upon the work of Jesus Christ and Him alone apart from works of any law. This includes all laws.

5. Romans 3:19,20,28 — "Now we know that what things soever the law saith, it saith to them who are under the law: that every mouth may be stopped, and all the world may become guilty before God. Therefore by the deeds of the law there shall no flesh be justified in his sight: for by the law [is] the knowledge of sin. ...Therefore we conclude that a man is justified by faith without the deeds of the law."

When standing before a holy and righteous God, we believe He will accept us on the basis of Jesus Christ and *His work alone* imputed to us. We do not believe that anyone will be accepted on the basis of good works. We do not believe the Catholic contention that good works worked in us by God, with our consent, are the ground of our acceptance. What one believes constitutes the content of his faith. It also determines the content of the gospel message he is willing to proclaim. Both belief systems cannot be right. They are radically opposed to each other. The two streams of thought simply cannot tolerate each other.

Chapter 16

The Puzzle of James 2

THERE are many faiths in the world but only one true faith in the finished work of Christ for justification. This true faith is a gift of God (cf., Ephesians 2:89; Philippians 1:29) which contains within it the right comprehension of the gospel message. It is a faith that grasps the righteousness of Christ as a substitute for our own lack of righteousness for our salvation. It is a faith that perceives that Jesus has finished the work given to Him by the Father. It is faith that Jesus lives now and eternally on behalf of His blood-bought Church to rescue them and to intercede for them. It is a faith which understands that we can add nothing to what Christ has done on our behalf. It is a faith which constantly clings to the righteousness of Christ for our access to God (cf., Hebrews 10:19-23).

Christian faith unites us with Jesus Christ. By faith we are in Christ. Being in Christ gives us the benefits of Christ's active and passive obedience. Faith unites us to Christ. His righteousness is the ground of our justification.

We have concluded that the Romanist has not this faith nor does he have any desire to even dare presume this an appropriate way to discuss justification. The lines of distinction are clearly drawn between the Christian idea of justification and the Catholic idea. The two are absolutely incompatible. Both cannot be true.

At this time we would like to examine one passage of Scripture which is used by Catholic theologians to disprove the doctrine of justification by faith apart from works of law. We hold that the supernatural faith given by God to His elect people expresses itself in the appropriation of Christ's righteousness alone for justification. This righteousness of Christ is the ground or final cause of God's verdict to justify the sinner. It is the faithfulness of Christ in fulfilling the eternal plan of the Father which ever remains the sole ground of our justification before God. When God regenerates a heart unto faith, the sinner becomes alive in Christ and His righteousness. This union with Christ is vital to the safekeeping of the soul. To be in Christ is to have His righteousness for salvation (cf., Philippians 3:9). It is inconceivable to Paul or to the rest of Scripture that God may be empted to justify anyone on some other basis. Whether that basis is the .aw of Israel or New Covenant obediences binding on the professing)eliever, it is absolutely incomprehensible that God would be satisfied with ıny other standard than His Son's righteousness for the verdict of ustification. When it comes to a justification before the tribunal of God, for ins committed in the flesh, there can be no question that the New restament writers disdain obedience to the Law or any other works for the erdict of justification.

rhus, when the concept of justification before God is couched in antithesis vith any prevailing notions of justification, we can see that the burden of he apostle is to protect the righteousness of God by eliminating all other venues of justification except the righteousness of His Son. So, the voice)f the great apostle Paul echoes throughout the New Testament:

> "Therefore we conclude that a man is justified by faith without the deeds of the law." (Romans 3:28)

> "Therefore being justified by faith, we have peace with God through our Lord Jesus Christ." (Romans 5:1)

> "Knowing that a man is not justified by the works of the law, but by the faith of Jesus Christ, even we have believed in Jesus Christ, that we might be justified by the faith of Christ, and not by the works of the law: for by the works of the law shall no flesh be justified." (Galatians 2:16)

> "And be found in him, not having mine own righteousness, which is of the law, but that which is through the faith of Christ, the righteousness which is of God by faith." (Philippians 3:9)

rhe New Testament will simply not allow a foreign ground of justification o exert itself over the work once accomplished by Jesus Christ. The chief ıntagonist to Christ being the ground of justification in the early Church vas the Judaizer. The Judaizer tried to dilute the finished work of Christ by ıdding law-keeping formulas for justification. But Paul would have nothing o do with this idea and boldly proclaimed, "For Christ [is] the end of the aw for righteousness to every one that believeth" (Romans 10:4). Scriptures are replete with references describing what the Law can and cannot do. 3ut one would have to ignore the entire gospel message to miss the idea that he law cannot justify anybody,

> "...for if there had been a law given which could have given life, verily righteousness should have been by the law." (Galatians 3:21)

Why then do the Romanist and the Legalist insist on a righteousness befor
God which includes our own good works? The answer comes from thei
absolute commitment to separate "good works done in faith" from th
works of the Law. The Roman Catholic is taught that no one can be justifie
by keeping the Law of Moses. But, they say, Scriptures demand that ou
justification is based in part on the accumulation of good works done i
obedience as followers of Jesus. So, they reject the one burden only to loa
on another burden. This is part of the "Christ-came-to-give-us-a-system"
syndrome.

To buttress their position, the Roman Catholics like to appeal to the secon
chapter of James. They do so because it is precisely here where Jame
brings together the terms "justify" and "works" in a proximity which seem
to deny all that Paul is claiming for justification before God. Specificall
James says the following:

> "Ye see then how that by works a man is justified, and not by faith
> only." (James 2:24)

> "Likewise also was not Rahab the harlot justified by works, when
> she had received the messengers, and had sent [them] out another
> way?" (James 2:25)

> "Was not Abraham our father justified by works, when he had of-
> fered Isaac his son upon the altar?" (James 2:21)

Rome takes these passages and concludes that works constitute part of th
ground of justification. Forbidding works of law from the Mosaic system
Romanism forges ahead with a new set of obediences which, they say, ar
given to us by Christ for our justification. These works, they say, are bes
expressed in and through the Catholic sacramental system.

Christians over the centuries have fended off Rome on this point by appeal
ing to the context of James and pointing out that James is really writin
about demonstrating justification rather than achieving justification.[1] Th
argument is that James has Abraham showing forth justification. The teno
of James' theme is that Abraham was showing himself to have been justi
fied by offering up Isaac on the altar. Likewise, Rahab was showing hersel
to have been justified when she sent the messengers out by another way
Now it is true that there is a demonstrative sense to the word "justify." Suc

---

[1] For an in-depth discussion of Justification defended in this sense see: *Westminster
Theological Journal*, Vol. XLII, Spring 1980, Number 2. Articles written by O. Palmer
Robertson and Stanford Reid. There are numerous other writings and commentaries whic
defend Justification in varying ways centered around the "demonstrative" sense of *dikaio*.

passage is Matthew 11:19, where we are told that wisdom is justified by her children. This can only mean that wisdom is shown to be just by her children. The children of wisdom verify that wisdom is in fact wisdom. The children do not make wisdom wise, rather they show that there was wisdom in the first place. The argument for the demonstrative use of justify is common and may well be the answer to harmonize James and Paul.

However, there are some problems with this approach. It has yet to be proven to us that the word, "justify" can be used to show forth someone as having been justified. Even the illustration of wisdom being shown as just by her children is short of what most Christians want out of the word "justify" in James 2. There is a difference between saying that wisdom is justified (shown to be just) by her children and, wisdom is justified (shown *to have been justified*) by her children. It seems the best we can do with James 2 is to say that Abraham was "shown to be just" by offering Isaac up on the altar. It may be stretching things too far to say that Abraham was "shown to have been justified" when he offered Isaac.

One can do just things and be called righteous without being declared justified by God. Many just and righteous acts are performed by people who are not justified by God. If this be the case, then as wisdom was shown to be wise by the children she produced (Matthew 11:19), likewise Abraham and Rahab showed their righteousness in the work each one did. They did not, however, show that they *had been justified*.[1] It may be foreign to the context of James to introduce the idea of declared justification so prominent in the thinking of Paul. When Paul uses the term "justification," he couches it in contrast to any hope of being acquitted before God on the basis of individual merit. Paul's burden is to clean out the leaven of self-righteousness and look only to the finished work of Jesus on the cross for justification declared by God. James may be using the term "justification" in an altogether different manner. He might be pressing home the point that justification has an ordinary sense of approval for doing the right thing. It may be that James wishes to show that dead faith does not warrant justification of a person in a non-technical sense of the term. It may be that James is interested in the exhibition of faith by works for a justification readily apparent for all to see. One thing seems certain: for James to say that Abraham was declared to be justified before God on his merit would be a flat contradiction to what Paul says about Abraham in Romans 4. Rather, James might be using the term in a more common fashion to show that Abraham was shown to be a just person as well as openly justified by exhibition of his works in virtue of his faith. Yet, James is quick to point out

---

[1] For further reading on this question of the best way to use *dikaiöo* see my Masters thesis, *Professor Norman Shepherd On Justification: A Critique* (Dallas Theological Seminary, 1981)

that the Scripture was fulfilled which reckoned Abraham as righteous on th
basis of faith apart from any works (cf., James 2:23 and Romans 4:1-4).

The above conclusion may not satisfy some who are very concerned to kee
works away from justification even in a demonstrative sense. We, too, wan
to avoid anything which would take away from justification by faith alone
However, this does not warrant translating the two aorist passives and on
present passive verb form of *dikaiöo* (justify) as "shown to have beer
justified." It is absolutely clear from the context of James 2 that both
Abraham and Rahab were in some sense either shown to be just or justifiec
by their works. It must be pointed out that the word "shown" is not in the
passage. The passage says,

> "Ye see then how that by works a man is justified, and not by faith
> only." (James 2:24)

It does not say,

> "Ye see then how that by works a man *is shown to have been*
> justified, and not by faith only."

We are more comfortable with the idea of "shown to be just" by thei
works, from the verb justified. But, as it stands, it seems too far-fetched t
say Rahab and Abraham were *shown to have been justified* by their works
There seems to be simply too much of an emphasis on what these two di
for approval in the context to warrant this sense for the word "justify."

Certainly there is a demonstration exhibited here, but it is a demonstration o
faith rather than righteousness that permeates the entire chapter. What i
demonstrated in James 2 is the faith of Abraham and Rahab. The demon
stration is by works. These works are in turn approved by God as a demon
stration of faith.

What then of the word "justify" as used by James? Does he contradict Paul
How do we harmonize these two men chosen by God to write Hi
revelation to us? Perhaps another way of understanding James, withou
doing damage to either Paul or James, is to give up trying to make the wor
"justify" mean the same thing every time it is used in the Scriptures. W
might be better off allowing the context to determine the range of meaning
when trying to harmonize the various texts of the Bible. As an example
let's start with Paul.

It appears that Paul needs to be reconciled with himself before we can brin
James into the picture! In Romans 2:13 we read the following from the grea
apostle:

"For not the hearers of the law [are] just (*dikaios*, as an adjective) before God, but the doers of the law shall be justified (*dikaiothesontai*, future passive of verb)."

How shall we sort out the future tense of the word "justify" as well as the close connection it has with *poietai nomou* (doers of law)? How is it that the doers of law will be "justified" and one chapter later, in the same book written by the same author we read:

"Therefore we conclude that a man is justified by faith without the deeds of the law(*ergon nomou*)." (Romans 3:28)

Some have wanted to make Romans 2:13 hypothetical and realistic. In other words, if someone could do the law perfectly (and no one can) then they would be justified. The idea is that Paul is holding forth what it would take to be justified by the law if someone wanted to try it that way.

But it seems obvious that the context does not lend itself to a hypothetical law-keeping justification. Even if it did, would this not run counter to Scripture's overwhelming defense against works-based justification? Are we really to believe that Paul is introducing a possibility that if someone were to keep the whole law perfectly that he would be able to earn justification? The flow of the argument of Romans 2, along with Scripture's over-riding emphasis on the righteousness of Christ alone for our justification (cf., Galatians 3:21), help us to view the verse differently.

In light of the tension, could it be that Paul has in mind a future eschatological justification which is more of an approval of our good works as proof of our judicial justification? Could it be that Paul is using justification in Romans 2:13 as James uses it? This is no denial of the biblical teaching of a justification which is based entirely upon the work of Christ. We believe in His righteousness imputed to us for our justification before the law of God. We believe in a legal transaction whereby the condemned one is justified or acquitted based upon another paying the penalty. To this conclusion, Paul labors and we have believed with all of our hearts that Christ stands in the place of our condemnation and His righteousness alone is the ground of our justification. But, along with the constitutive aspect of justification there is a change, not only in the status of a sinner, but in the disposition of the sinner, as well. This dispositional change shows itself in righteous acts which we call good works. It appears that both James and Paul do not hesitate to apply the word "justification" when God approves a sinner on the basis of these good works. The doer of the law will be justified! Abraham was justified when he offered Isaac on the altar! Yet, both of these justification notifications stem from a previous judicial or forensic understanding. In the case of Abraham, he was already justified, by faith alone, in Genesis 15:6 when he is said to have believed God. The offering of his son in Genesis 22 served to, in effect, justify the justification. James picks up Genesis 22 as a true approval by God, but James' use of justification does not stand in the place of forensic justification. The blood of Christ still had to be applied to Abraham for his judicial justification despite both his faith and the completion of his faith by his good works.

It appears James uses justification in a way that does not speak directly of Christ's righteousness imputed for justification. Rather, it is a justification in fulfillment of what God had already declared for Abraham on the basis of faith.

Paul also uses Abraham, but he cites the same text (Genesis 15:6) to eliminate a law righteousness. It is Paul who uses the term "justification" in a judicial sense almost exclusively to rid the Church of works righteousness (cf., Romans 4). But Paul does not flinch from joining with James in concert to the testimony that judicial justification establishes the law (cf., Romans 3:31). Also, judicially justified sinners become doers of the law. The judicially justified are those who do not seek a justification by law, but instead live out their lives by faith working through love (cf., Galatians 5:1-6). This corresponds to the law of liberty (James 1:12), along with the royal law of James 2. In fact, the doers of the Word in James 1 are the doers of law in the context of Romans 2! In both cases these are sinners who have been redeemed and justified on the basis of the shed blood of Christ. The doers of the law are not forgetful hearers, but effectual doers! Does this dovetail with the remarkable words of Paul in Romans 8?

> "For what the law could not do, in that it was weak through the flesh, God sending his own Son in the likeness of sinful flesh, and for sin, condemned sin in the flesh: That the righteousness of the law might be fulfilled in us, who walk not after the flesh, but after the Spirit." (Romans 8:3,4)

The upshot of all this is that justification does refer to an acquitted status before God as Paul labors to prove in his never ending diatribe against works or law justification. In every context where this is the burden, the Scriptures shine through to protect the veracity of God in demanding the sacrifice of His Son so that God might be both justified and justifier of those having faith in Christ.

However, the term "justify" may have other uses when it comes to God's approval of good works accomplished in a state of judicial justification. This would be the way in which James uses this term. In addition, Paul is not afraid to speak of an eschatological justification centering around the doers of the law. These doers of the law are those circumcised of the heart who, being in Christ, are at the end of the law for righteousness; but nevertheless will be "justified" by God as the fruit of His Spirit manifests itself.

We then see justification as a declaration by God that a sinner is cleared of all charges against him on the basis of Christ's death (cf., Colossians 2:13,14). We see also that justify describes the approval of a sinner based on his good works which prove that faith is genuine. We again see that there will be a justification of those who are doers of the law by virtue of being in-lawed to Christ. The particular context will determine the nuance which the term must carry.

Roman Catholic scholars deny the judicial and forensic, declarative/constitutive definition of justification. The result is an entire religious system designed to keep people justified by their good works. To the Catholic, justify means to make righteous and then justify the sinner continuously on the basis of good works done in the state of righteousness. For them justification is ongoing and ultimately results in a final justification when one has accumulated enough good works or has been martyred.

The Romanist would do better to understand that the term "justification," like salvation, is used differently in different contexts, depending on what the writer is trying to prove. With Paul, in the first part of Romans, he is proving that the doers of the law, those circumcised in the heart (cf., Romans 2:13-29) will ultimately be justified before God. This is in contrast to the Jew who thought he had it made simply because he sat in the synagogue and heard the Word! In the rest of the doctrinal section of Romans, beginning with chapter 3 and going through chapter 11, Paul explains why neither Jew nor Gentile could ever expect to be justified by law-keeping. In James, the burden is to prove the man by an approval of his faith. From the first chapter of James to the end of James the issue is the soundness of a person's faith. Only a man who has a faith which produces good works can expect to be justified before God. Who are those who will have this approval? Are they the ones who endeavor to be "justified by works of the law?" No!

> "For as many as are of the works of the law are under the curse: for it is written, *Cursed [is] every one that continueth not in all things which are written in the book of the law to do them.* But that no man is justified by the law in the sight of God, [it is] evident: for, *The just shall live by faith.*" (Galatians 3:10,11)

We say "No" to those who are willing to drop the yoke of the Mosaic Law and substitute their own law-keeping for justification, whether they be the Roman Catholic or the evangelical Legalist:

"Are ye so foolish? having begun in the Spirit, are ye now made perfect by the flesh?" (Galatians 3:3)

"Now to him that worketh is the reward not reckoned of grace, but of debt. But to him that worketh not, but believeth on him that justifieth the ungodly, his faith is counted for righteousness." (Romans 4:4,5)

Neither of the above will be justified. Only those circumcised in the heart by the Spirit of God to see the need for a justification based solely on the merits of Jesus Christ will be justified both now and forever. Scripture presents a picture of the sinner being justified by *faith* in the work of Christ alone apart from any works of law or obediences. This *faith* is pregnant with good works which are brought forth during the life of the sinner to show forth the veracity of his *faith*. These good works are said to then justify the sinner having been produced from that original position of faith justification. These are not separate "works of merit" that warrant the ground of justification. They are rather intricately associated with justification as the fruit of it.

Jonathan Edwards seems to have captured the essence of this elusive construct. In answering the question, "In what way might evangelical obedience be concerned in the affair of forensic justification (Christ's righteousness imputed as the total ground)?", he concludes the following:

"God, in the act of justification, which is passed on a sinner's first believing, has respect to perseverance, as virtually being contained in that first act of faith; and it is looked upon, and taken by Him that justifies, as being as it were a property in that faith. God has respect to the believer's continuance in faith, and he is justified by that, as though it already were, because by divine establishment it will follow..."[1]

For Edwards, all future acts of faith and repentance are beheld by God in the first act of faith. The resulting acts of faith and repentance will of necessity follow in time that which occurred at the first act. Edwards seems to be saying that faith, wherein one believes, is indispensable for our justification, yet bears no merit in itself as being a righteous or meritorious ground. Likewise, all future acts of faith (good works) are nothing more than an extension of our first act and they bear no merit as well. However, they too are indispensable for justification in that they are necessary and conceived as having been performed already in the mind of God.[2]

---

[1] *The Works of Jonathan Edwards,* (Carlisle, PA: Banner of Truth Trust, ©1979) pg. 641
[2] Jonathan Edwards points out to us that either the word "faith" or the term "justify" has
continued on following page

Thus, Abraham can be said to be justified by faith apart from any works of law. God justifies the ungodly through faith. But also, in that faith, Abraham had works of faith yet future. The example James cites for us is the offering up of Isaac. James says that this justified Abraham. It is true! The justified man was justified as his first faith bore fruit to faithful acts. The original ground has not changed. The faith so indispensable to the fruition of that ground is still spilling out fruit that justifies.

The doers of the law will be justified. All those who are justified will do the law. How? They are in unity with Christ and by faith they fulfill the requirements of the law. This faith is productive of the fruit that was anticipated in the original ground of justification. It is very much analogous to forgiveness. The fact of original forgiveness gives us impetus to pursue ongoing forgiveness. We are forgiven completely by virtue of being in Christ via our first act of faith. Yet we seek forgiveness as we sin, i.e., sin-repentance-forgiveness. Likewise, we are justified in our first act of faith and yet we are justified by its evidence as we bear the fruit of being in Christ.

In summary, we have examined different ways of understanding how James and Paul must be brought together without contradiction.

We may understand justify in a demonstrative sense as meaning that Abraham was *shown to have been justified* by his works. Works are evidences of a declared state.

We may understand justify in a demonstrative sense as meaning that Abraham was *shown to be just* by his works. Works are evidences of a changed man.

We may understand justify in a non-technical sense of the term as meaning Abraham was *justified by his works* (a justification of his *Justification*). Works are viewed by all demanding the verdict of justification.

---

to be changed in the context of James. He notes that most want to understand James as using faith quite differently than Paul. Could we not say the same for the word "justify"? Edwards opts for altering the sense of justify as used by James:

> "We, on the other hand, suppose that the word *justify* is to be
> understood in a different sense than the apostle Paul."

Edwards then builds a case for justification by works, here in James, as meaning the evidences of justification. This would be in harmony with the demonstrative sense of justification as showing Abraham to be righteous:

> "It is by works that our cause appears to be good..." "And that we
> should understand the apostle, of works justifying as an evidence..."

We may understand justify in the sense that works are indispensable as is faith when viewed together as the *fruit of justification*. Neither are the ground, but it may be said that both are contemplated in the equation as faith is to union with Christ as the ground, and works is the fruit of the ground.

Regardless of the way in which the construct develops, there can be no relationship between faith, repentance and works which detracts from the absolutely unambiguous testimony of God that the righteousness of Christ ever remains the ground and righteousness of our justification.

We wish to end this discourse in total agreement with Dr. Edward's insight into the seriousness of the matter. To be wrong on justification is to embrace another gospel which Dr. Edwards calls "the opposite scheme."

> "The opposite scheme does most directly tend to lead men to trust in their own righteousness for justification, which is a thing fatal to the soul. This is what men are of themselves exceeding prone to do, (and that they are never so much taught the contrary), through the partial and high thoughts they have of themselves, and their exceeding dulness of apprehending any such mystery as our being accepted for the righteousness of another."[1]

---

[1] *The Works of Jonathan Edwards*, pg. 653

Chapter 17

Professional Anti-Catholics?

W E HAVE devoted this chapter to a dialogue with a modern Roman Catholic apologist who has a bone to pick with what he terms "professional anti-Catholics." We feel it is important to have some exchange, point for point, with a professional Romanist in order to show the flavor and intensity of our struggle with Roman Catholicism.

We have chosen Karl Keating of *Catholic Answers* as our representative. His books are popular and he represents conservative Catholicism. Although, we have been told by some Catholics that Keating is entirely too moderate for them. We cannot hope to pick a Catholic writer with whom all will be pleased. We have no doubt that even the pope has his detractors!

It is, evidently, difficult for those involved in defending the Catholic religion to steer away from the idea of "man-made" authority. Virtually all of the apologetic work found in Keating is centered on the false assumption that men who disagree with Rome must be following Dr. Boettner or some other "fundamentalist" guru. Thus, in six chapters of his book, Keating devotes himself to an assessment of various ministries which are contra-Rome. In so doing, he labors under the wrong assumption that these men and their ministries "have drawn their inspiration from Boettner."[1] We have already mentioned Dr. Boettner and his work entitled *Roman Catholicism*. It has not yet occurred to Keating that these men may have read the same Bible which Boettner cherished and thus have drawn their inspiration, not from human authority, but from the pages of the Scriptures.

We are convinced that Boettner is accurate in his assessment of Romanism, but we do not want the reader to be distracted from our stance that the Bible informed Boettner. Roman Catholic apologists cannot debunk Boettner because Boettner spoke the heart of Scripture.

In this next section we shall comment briefly on Keating's treatment of the various people and organizations whom he loves to call "anti-Catholic."

---

[1] Keating, *Catholicism and Fundamentalism*, pg. 50

This term is used to describe anyone who wishes to throw down the Catholic religion with the Word of God. It is our hope that all who read this book would understand that Christians are not Catholic-haters. Christians are keen to protect the gospel of Christ against the Roman Catholic religious system which sets itself against the gospel of Christ. In this sense and this sense *only* is Keating justified in using the terminology "anti-Catholic."

There are a number of organizations devoted to supplying Christian churches with literature and information on the history and theology of the Roman Catholic religion. For the most part Keating is accurate as he outlines the general organization and leadership among the more visible missions to the Catholic community. One soon finds out that Keating has varying degrees of disdain depending on which particular organization he is assailing. It is our intention to respond only in the arena of biblical truth and historical accuracy. We find no real value in bantering about things not really important. Suffice it to say that Karl Keating does not appreciate either the "method" or the "material" presented publicly by such men and women as former Catholic priests or nuns. He is equally rueful to those who have never been inside the Catholic religion and are attempting to witness to the Catholics. Much of what Keating writes is called *ad hominem*, or "against the man" argumentation. The idea is to make a man look foolish which has the effect of eroding any basis of confidence in what that man might be saying.

For the reader's convenience, we have simply itemized the chief complaints of Keating and endeavored to deal with them fairly.

Answering Common Catholic Complaints

COMPLAINT #1 *Catholic Rejoinders*

There is a great deal of concern among Catholic apologists that their position is not given equal time among those who wish to enlighten the Christian community to the Catholic religion. The complaint is that those who speak publicly skew both the history and the doctrine of the Catholic religion. While it is true that a number of well-meaning Christians have not done enough research of the history of the Catholics, it is going too far to say that history and doctrine are presented in a cursory fashion. This is certainly not the case of Dr. Boettner's book nor of any other of the more detailed analyses of the Romanist positions. Certainly no one can come away from one or two Bible studies and expect to have exhausted 1500 years of Romanistic thinking. Yet, we cannot minimize the obvious and drastic differences between the Bible and the Catholic religion which surface immediately in just a short discussion. Christians tend to play the game on the level field of biblical data. As such, they are accused of being "simple minded" or "unlearned." To the Romanist, giving equal time is tantamount to bringing an avalanche of extra-biblical opinions from myriads of historical sources.

This brings us to a point of consideration which has been more fully developed in a previous chapter. The Catholic apologist does not arm himself with Scripture alone because he is convinced that the revelation of God cannot be confined to the Bible alone. This would be quite foreign to his thinking. Rather, the Catholic likes to appeal to the traditions of the Catholic religion and the authority of the councils and popes to prove his point of view. In light of this, the scholarly Roman Catholic would be quite disappointed to hear *only* a presentation of what the Bible has to say on any given subject without taking into consideration any of the popes, councils, or traditions of men.

COMPLAINT #2 *Anti-Catholic or Pro-Gospel?*

There appears to be a general complaint that Christians have made the grave error of relying too much on what Keating calls "professional anti-Catholics" for their source materials. If there is any validity to such a complaint, we hope to have at least a portion of the antidote with the writing of this book. However, it is unclear to us what difference it makes *where* one finds the truth. What matters is the truth itself!

For that matter, on more than one occasion, Paul the preëminent evangelist to the Gentiles quoted from secular poets to prove his point. The source of the truth is not anywhere near as important as the truth. This is not to say that one should not fully investigate the veracity of the material. But to say that so and so cannot be given any credence because he or she is a "non-Catholic" or even a "non-Christian" does not make any sense. The truth is the truth and should not be disparaged by any character assassinations.

We have endeavored to avoid this particular charge by going directly to the highest sources available to the researcher to substantiate our points. We agree that the Catholic religion has written enough that we do not need to rely on what anyone else says the Catholic religion believes.

We would like to add one more observation to this discussion before moving on to the next complaint. Many times Christians will use poorly written or poorly reasoned Catholic materials to prove a point against Romanism. This is not the fault of the Christian any more than it is of the Catholic who uses poorly written or reasoned material from those professing Christianity against them. We are in agreement with the principle that when something is misrepresented it needs to be exposed as such. This principle applies both ways. We are unhappy with much of what has been done to build straw men of Catholic positions and then blow them away. Likewise, the Christian community has been overly caricatured by Catholic apologists. We applaud all efforts to end such nonsense. The grave issues of truth must not disappear in the fog of biased rhetoric which becomes a feeble smoke screen for an unwillingness to do proper homework.

COMPLAINT #3 *A Little Greek*

Christians will appeal to the original languages in their hopes of dissuading Catholics from thinking that Peter is the rock upon which Christ will build the Church. The passage of controversy has always been Matthew 16:18; "And I say unto you, you are Peter, and upon this rock I will build my church..." A common argument used by many fine Christian scholars, sees a difference between Christ's use of the words *petros* and *petra*. Matthew recorded, using the Greek language under inspiration, the following:

"That thou art *petros*, and upon this *petra* I will build my church."

The idea is that *petros* refers to Peter since it is in the masculine. However, the *petra* is in the feminine and therefore cannot refer to Peter who was a man. Thus, it is argued, that the feminine *petra* must refer to a rocky ledge or a rock which is not Peter. It is argued that the feminine *petra* can refer to Christ in context as it is the common Greek word for ledge or stone and does not have to agree with the gender of Christ to be used metaphorically of Christ.

Although having some merit and plausibility this understanding of the Greek use of *petra* and *petros* is by no means conclusive. It may well be that these two words mean essentially the same thing and are referring to the same person in context, i.e., *Peter*.

Saying this does not grant to Rome her insistence that Peter was the first pope nor does it grant apostolic succession. We covered this in more detail earlier on. What we want to clear up here is the validity of the method used by some Catholic scholars to avoid the previously mentioned use of the Greek text by some Christian scholars. Keating thinks he has answered the question of Matthew 16 by saying glibly:

"Brewer (a Christian writer) rests his argument on an examination of the Greek, a tactic that usually works when his Catholic reader knows no Greek and is not aware *the first Gospel was composed in Aramaic, the language Christ spoke*. In fact, the argument Brewer makes, *if applied to the Aramaic and not just the Greek*, actually backfires against him, but he does not let the reader in on that secret."[1]

We would point out to the reader that the manuscripts of the Gospel of Matthew are all in Greek and every English translation of the Gospel of Matthew is taken from the Greek manuscripts. There is some speculation that Matthew might have used some Aramaic sources to write his Gospel but this is not proven. What we know is that the Lord inspired the construction and writing of this Gospel in Greek from which we arrive at all of our translations.

We need to undo the damage that may have been caused by the Catholic assertion that the first gospel was composed in Aramaic. This cannot be substantiated and even if it were in any way true, it most certainly does not answer the questions of Matthew 16 as we have seen.

COMPLAINT #4 *Touto Esti*—*"this is"*

The complaint here is that Christians "blunder" when they insist that the Greek words *touto esti* mean "this represents" or "this stands for," rather than "this actually is," as the Catholics take it to mean. Of course the center of controversy is the statement of Jesus Christ at the Last Supper when He broke the bread and gave it to His disciples saying, "*labete phagete; touto estin to soma mou*" or, "take ye and eat; this is my body." The Catholic wants the *touto estin* (this is) to mean that the bread literally *is* the body of Christ. The Christian thinks that Christ used the words *touto estin* (this is) to represent his body.

Catholic scholars want us to believe that the primary meaning of *touto estin* carries with it a replacement meaning when used to qualify an inanimate object. Thus, if I take a snapshot of my son out of my wallet and say "this is" my son, then the picture would become in some miraculous way my actual son. Or if I were to turn in a term paper on which I spent a great deal of time and effort and then say to my instructor that "this is my heart," he would have to recognize the term paper to be my literal heart.

To begin with, *estin* is the third person singular of the word *eimi* in Greek which is the word for "is" or "existence." It is found in sentences beginning with "I am." If referring to something in the third person, we would say "this is." If referring to ourselves in the first person we would say "I am." On many occasions our Lord referred to himself in the first person by saying "I am" this, or "I am" that. The burden of proof is whether it can be proven that every time Jesus uses this word of "being" or "existence" he

---

[1] Keating, *Catholicism and Fundamentalism*, pg. 63. Emphasis added

becomes that which he says he is. For instance, Jesus says in John 15 "I am the vine." His words are "*Ego eimi*" or "I am." Does this mean that Jesus is literally the vine? Suppose Jesus were standing near some grape vines and He picked one up in His hands and said to His disciples, "Do you see this vine? I am this vine." Or, "This vine is Me (*touto estin*)." Then He said, "You are the branches." Are we to believe that Christ somehow wanted to make those with Him believe that the vine became Jesus Christ and the branches became His disciples?

The Christian does believe that "*touto estin*" means "is." But what does "is" mean? Certainly there is plenty of room for a symbolical meaning to these words spoken by Christ since He was standing there in His own body saying that He was giving out His own body. It is not a blunder to seek after the metaphor in the story itself.

COMPLAINT #5 *The Early Church Fathers*

Catholic writers, with good reason, like to appeal to the text of James 2 to defend their understanding of justification. It is not surprising. Along with this comes the complaint that those who speak out against Rome always ignore the clear teaching of James 2. Integrated with this complaint is the accusation that the Church Fathers are not consulted as they should be in matters pertaining to doctrine. Such is the complaint arising out of the interpretation of John 20:22-23. What the Fathers have to say about this should be determinative in the eyes of the Catholic.

While it may be true that popular tracts designed to appeal to the more glaring practices of the Catholic religion have not taken the time or the length to present all the arguments, it is not true that these positions have not been defended. We do however agree that the pamphlets and tracts should reflect a more intensive presentation of the issues as Boettner has done in his book and hopefully is accomplished in this book as well. We have already stated our differences with Rome on James 2 and justification in our previous chapters.

COMPLAINT #6 *Catholic Practices*

The Roman Catholic religion complains about Christians who attack them in areas of practice. The idea is that the Romanist has reserved for himself, in his religion, certain practices which are not to be confused with his doctrine. He wishes that the practices would be left alone and the doctrine would be the focus of our contention. This is fair enough! However, it is hard to distinguish where practice starts and doctrine leaves off—and vice versa. Christians are quite used to a separation between doctrine and practice as evidenced by the liberty we have in various forms and types of worship and ecclesiology. The Catholic religion appears to want it both ways. When something is discontinued from popular observance (e.g., not eating meat on Friday), it is said to have been a tradition or a practice not doctrine. Yet, they want to admit to a sort of elastic attitude toward doctrine also. In castigating the Christian for not understanding the Catholic approach to doctrine, Keating has this to say:

> "On the one hand they (anti-Catholics) seem to think there could be no proper development of doctrines as Catholics understand the term, no deeper understanding of them as centuries pass."[1]

The inference from this is that "doctrine" too is always subject to the interpretation of the Catholic religion. This is in line with the Catholic assertion that the Catholic religion stands above the Scriptures. We would have the reader understand that most everything the Romanist does by way of practice stems from a doctrinal base. However, the heart of the matter is *doctrine* and there is enough of a difference between Romanism and Christianity to focus on it alone. This is perhaps as it should be. We reiterate that this, in fact, has been done in Christian writings throughout the centuries, and we have endeavored to do the same.

COMPLAINT #7 *"Snickerings"*

As we stated at the outset, this portion of responding is almost impossible. Keating singles out Bart Brewer of *Mission to Catholics International*, Bill Jackson of *Christians Evangelizing Catholics*, Donald Maconaghie of *The Conversion Center*, Jimmy Swaggart, Keith Green and finally Jack Chick and Alberto Rivera.

The approach to these men and their writings is best described as "scatter-shooting." After giving a brief introduction to each particular ministry, Keating gives us pot shots mixed with anecdotal sayings about the veracity of this one or that one. Keating does not like the way Maconaghie writes, or the way Bill Jackson really does not understand the Catholic position because he does not list the Catholic response in his tracts. Keating wants everyone to know that Maconaghie used Cardinal Newman in an inappropriate way in one of Maconaghie's newsletters. Keating thinks that Maconaghie is a good example of "...the way fundamentalist opponents of the Church bend facts to the snapping point."[2] Keating thinks that the *Conversion Center* newsletters are bizarre, and thinks anti-Catholics "wear out Catholicism's defenders by inundating them with short remarks that

---

[1] Keating, *Catholicism and Fundamentalism*, pg. 66
[2] Keating, *Catholicism and Fundamentalism*, pg. 73

demand long explanations."[1] Keating is upset because the *Conversion Center* takes the position that all drinking of alcohol is wrong and has written a tract to compare the "wrongness" of alcohol with the "wrongness" of Rome. Keating thinks wrongly that all Christians therefore must think all drinking is wrong. Keating thinks also that most Christians are overly fond of the King James Version of the Bible because he has dealt with some who are zealous for the KJV.

When writing of Dr. Bill Jackson, who founded *Christians Evangelizing Catholics*, Keating is unhappy with Jackson's definition of a cult. He thinks it is a narrow "fundamentalist" mentality. However, Keating wants us to be happy and informed that the Roman religion has always recognized other religions as containing some truth more or less to the degree that they mirror Catholicism!

Keating thinks that Swaggart is "ignorant" when he speaks to the Roman Catholic religion because Swaggart does not understand the difference between "discipline" and "doctrine" when it comes to celibacy. Citing Swaggart's weakness in not researching some historical data, Keating is upset because Swaggart insists on paying attention more to the Bible than to the word of the Fathers. As far as Peter being the first pope, Keating is certain the Bible is incompetent to decide the issue. Perhaps we can capture the frustration of Keating by quoting him directly in the middle of his diatribe against Swaggart:

> "Fundamentalists' reverence for the word of God is often so extreme that it becomes distorted, and they think the Bible should be the last word on any matter occurring between the start of Christ's public ministry and the close of the first century."[2]

In correcting Swaggart's understanding of the Mass, Keating assures his readers that "no Catholic thinks Christ dies anew at each Mass."[3] We discussed this at length in a previous chapter.

We may sum up what this particular Catholic apologist thinks of James Swaggart's attempt to challenge the Romanist position with the following quotation. We get the impression this may stand for all who would dare to question Rome:

> "His (Swaggart) book is a fine example of the danger of mixing a little knowledge with considerable prejudice. If he were less

---

[1] Keating, *Catholicism and Fundamentalism*, pg. 75

[2] Keating, *Catholicism and Fundamentalism*, pg. 93

[3] Keating, *Catholicism and Fundamentalism*, pg. 93

prejudiced—that is, less inclined to accept blindly every unflattering thing said about the Catholic Church—and more knowledgeable, Jimmy Swaggart would be embarrassed that his name is on such a travesty, because he is not really a bad man, just a man badly informed."[1]

In his evaluation of Keith Green, Keating is not as punishing. He is disappointed with Green and all others who fail to take the *touto estin* of the Lord's Last Supper as literally the body of Christ in the sense the Romanists do. He is also bothered that the anti-Catholic Green did not understand that "the sacrifice can be perpetuated (presented again) even though the death occurred once."[2] But perhaps the Catholic's chief complaint is issued against Christians in general. Keating tells us that:

"Anti-Catholics (fundamentalists to Keating) memorize their lessons well, but they memorize selectively because they are taught only certain things. Although they read the entire Bible, with, naturally enough, special emphasis on the New Testament, verses that do not mesh with what their pastors have told them are either skipped or just not perceived as being trouble spots."[3]

Keating likens the "fundamentalist" to a communist who wakes up in a scream when his subconscious is constantly telling him that the parts of the puzzle of his ideology do not fit! He fights it as long as he can and then he finally gives in to what he has secretly known all along. We are left with the understanding that "fundamentalism" is left to its own doom as more and more people realize that the pieces of the puzzle do not fit.

It is worthy to note that in this section, Keating makes a large concession to what we have already observed. In responding to Green's assessment of the post Vatican II period, Keating gives us this information.

"There have been changes since the Council, but *there has been no alteration at all in basic doctrines or in principles of operation.*"[4]

This admission helps to prove why Christians have a point of departure with any movement of well-meaning but naïve Christians who wish to put Christians under the "unity of love" spell as promoted by the post-Vatican II Catholic religion.

---

[1] Keating, *Catholicism and Fundamentalism*, pg. 97

[2] Keating, *Catholicism and Fundamentalism*, pg. 101

[3] Keating, *Catholicism and Fundamentalism*, pp. 101, 102

[4] Keating, *Catholicism and Fundamentalism*, pg. 103. Emphasis added

Keating devotes his last bit of "scatter-shooting" to the work of Jack Chick and *Chick Publications*. Among those who are mixed in with Chick are Tony Alamo and Alberto Rivera. The Chick organization has relentlessly attacked the Romish traditions and doctrines through *Chick Tracts* and a comic book format. We will admit that the Chick organization has become a center for controversy due to their emphasis on the political arm of Rome and the implication of Romanists in such things as national conspiracies. It is, however, outside the universe of this discourse to devote any space to the validity of the Chick claims or those of Alberto Rivera. We would have the reader to know that one does not have to subscribe to the intrigue of these publications to see and to know the dangers of Romanism. We prefer to stand against Rome on the basis of solid biblical interpretation only. The great Protestant Reformation was fought to the death against the Roman Catholic religion without the need for an evaluation of the Romanistic influence on governments. The battle was rather pitched on the field of theological truth. "Who speaks for God?" was and remains the issue. In this light, we need to remind the reader that Karl Keating ends this section of his defense of Romanism very much like he begins. He is convinced that the rascals who are against the Catholics are nothing other than a band of "fundamentalists" who somehow have turned the nation's ear against Rome by use of misinformation and a gross misuse of the Bible.

Keating is right in his understanding of the way in which Christians perceive the Catholic religion. We do believe it to be the most nefarious institution on the face of the earth. The reasons have been expressed in a straightforward manner throughout the pages of this book. We have examined the heart of Rome and the doctrines which Rome is so eager to promote, defend, and carry to the ends of the earth and found them wanting!

Chapter 18

The Changing Face of Rome

THE Roman Catholic religion is an enigma in many ways and utterly maddening in its remarkable ability to speak out of both sides of its mouth. On the one side, there is an almost radical insistence on the *unchanging* dogmas of the "Mother Church." But on the other side, there is an outright contradiction and rapid departure from days gone by. For the Christian, this makes dealing with Rome doubly difficult. We are never sure whether we are dealing with the *unchanging* doctrines of Rome or the Roman propensity to expand and mature doctrine (deny the old in favor of the new). Now that Vatican II has come and gone there have been many opinions as to whether Rome has changed. If it has, has it been for the good or the bad?

After reviewing Vatican II, we conclude Rome has departed from some things, seemingly set in concrete, in early councils and canons. However, we cannot applaud the changes that are taking place. Our concern is only intensified as we regard the direction Rome has taken in light of these changes. It used to be standard fare to do pitched battle with an old time Catholic over the issues of justification and sacramental salvation along with other dogmas of the religion. But now we must deal with a hybrid Rome that is modernistic as well as ancient. These two streams have come together in Romanism to form a waterfall of free flowing theological constructs. For instance, what is one to do with modern Rome? What shall we say to existentialism in Rome, or to liberalism? How does a Christian respond to Rome's ideas of ecumenism? We personally have had the opportunity to speak in depth to a Roman Catholic priest who denied virtually all of Rome's historical moorings and their significance. We were not certain with whom or with what we were debating. But it certainly was not historical Rome!

All this leads to the changing face of Rome. Rome is changing but where is it going? Change is not enough unless that change is designed to bring one closer to the authority of God's Word and the gospel of Jesus Christ. We see Rome headed the other way! We need to be aware that many Evangelicals are in concert with this new direction of Rome. But we have found that this new direction offers nothing but bubbles and vapors mixed in with the old liberalism of 100 years ago. The nature of Rome's changing face looks very much like the modernism and neo-orthodoxy which swept through the Evangelical community 100 years ago. The infallibility of the Bible is questioned. The role of women is being questioned. The entire arena of homosexuality and gay rights has been a thorn in the side of Rome. Also, Catholics for choice have been vocal in Roman Catholicism. This is mixed in with a syncretism and ecumenical spirit which is bewildering. All the while, there is a conservative beat which repeats the emphasis on old line dogma. To this extent, there is a movement back to the Latin Mass! Could the Catholic religion be ready to splinter into a hundred different little Romanist religions? In the midst of this, there are some Evangelicals who are impressed with the positive buzz words and ecumenical elements in Rome. They may want to join in. There are always those who will desperately seek alliance and common ground with Rome regardless of the cost. Thus, one group Rome that is attracting is the dyed-in-the-wool liberal who shares Rome's ungodly view of the non-Christian world. Also, Rome is attracting many theologically illiterate who seek nothing more than to camp out under dangerous emotion-packed terms such as "love," "unity" and "brotherhood."

But though change is afoot and liberalism is knocking at the door, it has not radically changed Rome's understanding of the gospel and salvation. In this chapter we should like to point out that not one doctrine of the core of Rome has changed in terms of sacramental salvation. We have endeavored to show clearly that the Roman Catholic religion of the 1990's is the same doctrinally as that of the 16th and 17th century. They have added some things, but the heart of the matter remains the same. So on the one hand, we need to continually address the issue of the gospel with the Romanist. Until Rome forsakes the sacramental system complete with papal infallibility etc., we shall not consider Rome to be of Christ. Hopefully, this book has borne out the reasons why we do not hesitate to take, what for some, may seem to be a harsh stand. On the other hand, we see conflicts between modern Rome and historical Rome. We also see liberalizing tendencies and a desire to be a leader in a worldwide ecumenical movement.

We have often read and heard that Vatican II is the new Rome. Sweeping changes in Rome have been hailed by Protestant and Catholics alike as the dawning of a new Rome. We have been told of a softer Rome or a more conciliatory Rome. Perhaps Rome is now open to vital change and willing to see the error of previous policies and dogmas. Or so we are told. But is this the case? We answer, "Emphatically no!"

We find disturbing and incriminating language in our analysis of the documents of Vatican II. The disturbing aspect is that Rome has condescended to call Protestant Christians "separated brethren." This new terminology is a change, but for the Christian, it is also dreadful and dangerous. It appears that Rome wants to label Christians as brothers in hopes of lending credibility to Romanism. It also appears that Rome wishes to hide or minimize the eternal chasm which separates Rome from the gospel of Christ! Christians need to reject such manipulative language and stick to their faith that Christianity and Romanism are absolutely contradictory. Christians are indeed separated from Rome but in no way is a Christian a brother of the Romanist religion. They (Roman Catholics) are not fellow heirs of the grace of God nor are they members of the Body of Christ. For Rome to call Christians separated brethren is similar to Mormons or Hindus calling Christians separated brethren. We say, "No thank you!"

It is equally disturbing to read that Romanists think separated brethren have been given some light and have a hope of salvation. Listen to the sweet and enticing "honey" of Vatican II:

> "It follows that the separated Churches and communities as such, though we believe they suffer from the defects already mentioned, have been by no means deprived of significance and importance in the mystery of salvation. For the Spirit of Christ has not refrained from using them as means of salvation which derive their efficacy from the very fullness of grace and truth entrusted to the Catholic Church."[1]

We use the term "honey" here to describe the sweetness of Rome because such language becomes the bait either to ensnare people into Romanism or, perhaps worse yet, to lure them to Rome for approval when it comes to embracing the gospel of Christ! In a not-so-subtle manner, Rome has set itself up as the spiritual guru of the western world. Rome has unilaterally declared itself to be the judge of whether one's religion does or does not have the necessary elements to qualify as a Christian religion. This absorption by decree does two things. First, it attempts to legitimize Rome since Rome is making the proclamation as though it were the official judge in the matter! Secondly, it minimizes the opposition to insignificance should anyone disagree. The net effect of all this is the horror of a non-Christian religion setting criteria for Christianity even to the point of calling Christians separated brethren! This so-called "breaking down of walls and barriers" between Rome and the rest of the world is detailed in *Unitatis Redintegratio* or the *Decree on Ecumenism* of Vatican II. We say with tongue in cheek that one day the pope may declare *ex cathedra* the entire world to be Roman Catholic whether they like it or even know it. At least the attempt to do so would not surprise us.

---

[1] *Vatican Council II*, Volume II, Austin Flannery, general editor, (Northport, NY: Costello Publishing Company, ©1992) pg. 456

This then is the first danger. Christians should not allow themselves to be aligned with the false religion of Rome. They may cry "separated brethren" all they want. The facts are that Christians have nothing in common with the sacraments and antichrist doctrines of Rome. They never have and never will. The second danger is that in becoming so enamored with the syrup and honey language of Rome, one misses the real agenda and the not-so-hidden-face of Rome. Aside from the obvious doctrines that set Rome off from Christianity, we must come to grips with how Rome defines "ecumenical." All those who dance with Rome long enough will soon realize that it is a one-way street if you want Rome as a partner. Christians should shudder at these words from Rome's decree on ecumenism:

> "Such actions, when they are carried out by the Catholic faithful with prudent patience and under the attentive guidance of their bishops, promote justice and truth, concord and collaborations, as well as the spirit of brotherly love and unity. *The results will be that, little by little, as the obstacles to perfect ecclesiastical communion are overcome, all Christians will be gathered, in a common celebration of the Eucharist, into the unity of the one and only Church, which Christ bestowed on his Church from the beginning.* This unity, we believe, subsists in the Catholic Church as something she can never lose, and we hope that it will continue to increase until the end of time."[1]

Lest the reader remain unconvinced of Vatican II and the real agenda behind the ecumenical movement, we offer this citation from the same document.

> "The manner and order in which Catholic belief is expressed should in no way become an obstacle to dialogue with our brethren. It is, of course, essential that the doctrine be clearly presented in its entirety. *Nothing is so foreign to the spirit of ecumenism as a false irenicism which harms the purity of Catholic doctrine and obscures its genuine and certain meaning.* At the same time, Catholic belief must be explained more profoundly and precisely, in such a way and in such terms that our separated brethren can also really understand it."[2]

Such disturbing language of Vatican II typifies the audacity of Rome's attempt to absorb Christians by *defining* them into the fold! The child of God will resist this and realize it as a sham. But those involved in nominal denominations and the liberal element of the religious world seem to be beating a path to the doorstep of Rome. It is not surprising to this writer, in

---

[1] *Vatican Council II*, Volume II, pg. 457. Emphasis added
[2] *Vatican Council II*, Volume II, pg. 462. Emphasis added

view of our previous exegesis, that Vatican II has found the soft underbelly of state churches and starkly liberal Protestant denominations. This soft belly is the age old heresy of baptismal regeneration or membership by birthright in the Body of Christ. It is not entirely surprising that Romanists are appealing to what they call the common bond of baptism in order to proclaim salvation in non-Romanist, liberal, Protestant denominations. If you are a liberal Protestant involved in religion as a good work, then alliance with Rome on the basis of a common baptism may seem like another good idea to bring people together. However, we ask those of you who are strong Presbyterian, or confessing Episcopalian, or solid Lutheran, or historical Congregationalists if you would like to join the fold of Rome based on their assessment of your baptism?

> "For men who believe in Christ and have been properly baptized are put in some, though imperfect, communion with the Catholic Church. Without doubt, the differences that exist in varying degrees between them and the Catholic Church—whether in doctrine and sometimes in discipline, or concerning the structure of the Church— do indeed create many obstacles, sometimes serious ones, to full ecclesiastical communion. The ecumenical movement is striving to overcome these obstacles. But even in spite of them it remains true that all who have been justified by faith in baptism are incorporated into Christ; they therefore have a right to be called Christians, and with good reason are accepted as brothers by the children of the Catholic Church."[1]

We now turn our attention to the incriminating aspect of Vatican II. We have shown how Roman pride extends to the doctrine of infallibility for the pope as well as the councils when all are in agreement. Yet, we have found stark contradictions in comparing the statements of Vatican II with the earlier statements of Roman councils on the same subject. We preface this section by mentioning that we have restricted our research to Rome's view of religions outside of Roman Catholicism.

If Rome is absorbing anyone and everyone remotely naming the name of Christ, then what is Rome doing with those who do not recognize Jesus Christ as God incarnate? What is Rome's strategy for the millions of what Rome formerly called "pagans" who do not in the least hold to any Christian or Roman doctrines? It should be eyebrow-raising to the conservative Romanist and absolutely eye-popping to the Christian to see what Rome has declared concerning pagan religions. For the Christian, it is a matter of watching the blind leading the blind. Not only are we absolutely to avoid Rome because of antichrist doctrines and dogma, but also now much more

---

[1] *Vatican Council II*, Volume II, pg. 455

due to the startling open display of Vatican II's absorption of other pagan religions! This modern insistence of Rome to absorb those formerly labeled as pagan religions is incriminating evidence against Rome as it radically departs from its historical councils. With this inconsistency displayed openly, the doctrine of Magisterium infallibility falls in a heap. A further eye-opener for the Christian is to see first hand the possibilities of a one world religious system with Rome at the head.

Any doubt that Rome is a massive tangle of religious contradictions and antichrist elements evaporate in light of the evidence when comparing early Rome and *Nostra Aetate* (Declaration on the Relation of the Church to Non-Christian Religions). *Nostra Aetate* seems to absolutely defy the earlier Catholic councils with respect to the status of non-Christian religions. The initial Catholic councils did not tolerate the kind of brazen universalism as expressed in this Vatican II document.

From the annals of early Romanist councils we may glean some very unambiguous dogma concerning the status of anyone outside of Rome as regards the value and worth of their religious affections. Let us start with the Athanasian Creed:

> "Whoever wishes to be saved, needs above all to hold the Catholic faith; unless each one preserves this whole and inviolate, he will without a doubt perish in eternity."[1]

We move next to Pelagius II about 585 A.D.

> "If anyone, however, either suggests or believes or presumes to teach contrary to this faith, let him know that he is condemned and also anathematized according to the opinion of the same Fathers …Consider (therefore) the fact that whoever has not been in the peace and unity of the Church, cannot have the Lord (Galatians 3:7)…"[2]

The words of Innocent III cannot be mistaken. They were written December 18, 1208.

> "By the heart we believe and by the mouth we confess the one Church, not of heretics but the Holy Roman, Catholic, and Apostolic (Church) outside which we believe that no one is saved."[3]

---

[1] Denzinger, pg. 15
[2] Denzinger, pg. 95
[3] Denzinger, pg. 166, 167

The Fourth Lateran Council of 1215 spells out for us Romish dogma in no uncertain terms:

> "One indeed is the universal Church of the faithful, outside which no one at all is saved, in which the priest himself is the sacrifice, Jesus Christ, whose body and blood are truly contained in the sacrament of the altar under the species of bread and wine; the bread (changed) into His body by the divine power of transubstantiation, and the wine into the blood, so that to accomplish the mystery of unity we ourselves receive from His (nature) what He Himself received from ours."[1]

Boniface VIII wrote these words as part of the Bull *Unam Sanctam* in November of 1302:

> "With Faith urging us we are forced to believe and to hold the one, holy, Catholic Church and that, apostolic, and we firmly believe and simply confess this (Church) outside which there is no salvation nor remission of sin."[2]

We ask the reader what could be more direct than the teaching of the Council of Florence in 1438?

> "It (the Council) firmly believes, professes, and proclaims that those not living within the Catholic Church, not only pagans, but also Jews and heretics and schismatics cannot become participants in eternal life, but will depart 'into everlasting fire which was prepared for the devil and his angels' (Matthew 25:41)..."[3]

Pope Gregory XVI writing on the dangers of indifferentism has these strong and caustic remarks:

> "Now we examine another prolific cause of evils by which, we lament, the Church is at present afflicted, namely indifferentism, or that base opinion which has become prevalent everywhere through the deceit of wicked men, that eternal salvation of the soul can be acquired by any profession of faith whatsoever, if morals are conformed to the standard of the just and the honest... And so from this most rotten source of indifferentism flows that absurd and

---

[1] Denzinger, pg. 169
[2] Denzinger, pg. 186
[3] Denzinger, pg. 230

erroneous opinion, or rather insanity, that liberty of conscience must be claimed and defended for anyone."[1]

As recent as 1878 we read the opinion of Pius IX:

"But, as is Our Apostolic duty, we wish your episcopal solicitude and vigilance to be aroused, so that you will strive as much as you can to drive from the mind of men that impious and equally fatal opinion, namely, that the way of eternal salvation can be found in any religion whatsoever."[2]

From these, and other citations too numerous to recount, it can be clearly seen that the Romanism of the past had little use for other religions. These councils and declarations of popes appear to wear the garment of infallible dogma since there was universal agreement and teaching on the matter. Keating, quoting from *Lumen Gentium,* reminds us of the nature of Romish infallibility:

"This authority (of the Bishops) is even more clearly verified when, gathered together in an ecumenical council, they are teachers and judges of faith and morals for the universal Church. Their definitions must then be adhered to with the submission of faith."[3]

With this in mind, how does the ancient religion of Rome measure up with today's moderns? Well, it depends on if you are talking with pre- or post-Vatican II Rome. Pope Pius the IX, writing in the mid-1800's, wrote a syllabus of condemned errors:

"Errors of indifferentism condemned:

"1. Everyone is free to embrace and profess the religion which by the light of reason he judges to be true.

"2. Men can find the way of eternal salvation and attain eternal salvation by the practice of any religion whatever.

"3. We should at least have good hopes for the eternal Salvation of all those who are in no way in the true Church of Christ."[4]

---

[1] Denzinger, pg. 403

[2] Denzinger, pg. 415, 416

[3] Keating, *Catholicism and Fundamentalism*, pg. 216

[4] Neuner, J., and Dupuis, J., *The Christian Faith in the Doctrinal Documents of the Catholic Church*, (New York: Alba House, ©1981) pg. 283

As late as 1950 Pope Pius XII condemned indifferentism and syncretism. Notice this citation from the plenary council of India:

"We therefore reject the view so widely spread in our regions which holds that all religions are equal among themselves, and that, provided they are adhered to with sincerity, all are various ways to one and the same end, namely God and eternal salvation. We equally reject the syncretism according to which the ideal religion or the religion of the future is conceived as a sort of synthesis to be worked out by men from various religions that exist."[1]

We ask the reader to compare the above documented data with the writings of Vatican II. We compare over 1500 years of Roman councils with *Lumen Gentium* (1964), (The non-Christians and the People of God).

"There are finally those who have not yet received the Gospel; they too are ordained in various ways to the People of God... The plan of salvation includes those also who acknowledge the Creator; foremost among these are the Muslims: they profess fidelity to the faith of Abraham and, with us, adore the one and merciful God who will judge mankind on the last day. Nor is God far from those who in shadows and images seek the unknown God; ...Nor does divine Providence deny the help necessary for salvation to those who, without fault on their part, have not yet reached an explicit knowledge of God, and yet endeavor, not without divine grace, to live a good life, for whatever goodness or truth is found among them is considered by the Church as a preparation for the Gospel."[2]

We offer this lengthy yet absolutely critical citation from *Nostra Aetate* (October, 1965):

"The religions which are found in more advanced civilizations endeavor by way of well-defined concepts and exact language to answer these questions. Thus, in Hinduism men explore the divine mystery and express it both in the limitless riches of myth and the accurately defined insights of philosophy. They seek release from the trials of the present life by ascetical practices, profound meditation and recourse to God in confidence and love. Buddhism in its various forms testifies to the essential inadequacy of this changing world. It proposes a way of life by which men can, with confidence and trust, attain a state of perfect liberation and reach

---

[1] Neuner and Dupuis, pg. 285
[2] Neuner and Dupuis, pg. 287

supreme illumination either through their own efforts or by the aid of divine help. So, too, other religions which are found throughout the world attempt in their own ways to calm the hearts of men by outlining a program of life covering doctrine, moral precepts and sacred rites.

"The Catholic Church rejects nothing of what is true and holy in these religions. She has a high regard for the manner of life and conduct, the precepts and doctrines which, although differing in many ways from her own teaching, nevertheless often reflect a ray of that truth which enlightens all men. Yet she proclaims and is in duty bound to proclaim without fail, Christ who is the way, the truth and the life (John 1:6). In him, in whom God reconciled all things to himself (2 Corinthians 5:18-19), men find the fullness of their religious life.

"The Church, therefore, urges her sons to enter with prudence and charity into discussion and collaboration with members of other religions. Let Christians, while witnessing to their own faith and way of life, acknowledge, preserve and encourage the spiritual and moral truths found among non-Christians, also their social life and culture.

"The Church has also a high regard for the Muslims. They worship God, who is one, living and subsistent, merciful and almighty, the Creator of heaven and earth, who has also spoken to men. They strive to submit themselves without reserve to the hidden decrees of God, just as Abraham submitted himself to God's plan, to whose faith Muslims eagerly link their own. Although not acknowledging him as god, they venerate Jesus as a prophet, his virgin Mother they also honor, and even at times devoutly invoke. Further, they await the day of judgment and the reward of God following the resurrection of the dead. For this reason they highly esteem an upright life and worship God, especially by way of prayer, alms-deeds and fasting.

"Over the centuries many quarrels and dissensions have arisen between Christians and Muslims. The sacred Council now pleads with all to forget the past, and urges that a sincere effort be made to achieve mutual understanding; for the benefit of all men, let them together preserve and promote peace, liberty, social justice and moral values."[1]

---

[1] *Vatican Council II*, Volume II, pp. 739-740

Pope Paul VI showed no reluctance to approve pagan cultures and their searchings after God. Modern popes (post Vatican II popes) seem to reserve their contempt for thumping what they call "fundamentalists." We have already suggested that this Roman derogatory name (fundamentalist) is synonymous with what we call Christian![1]

We offer a further sampling of the wisdom of Rome's vicar of Christ on earth!

Encyclical letter *Ecclesiam Suam* (1964), by Pope Paul VI:

> "Then we see another circle around us. This too is vast in extent; yet it is not so far away from us. It is made first and foremost of those men who adore the one, supreme God, whom we also worship. We refer here to the children of the Hebrew race, worthy of our respect and love. They are faithful to the tradition proper to what we call the Old Testament. We refer also to those who adore God according to the conception of monotheism, especially that of the Muslims, whom we rightly admire for the truth and goodness found in their religion.

> "The Catholic Church holds in great regard the moral and religious values proper to the African traditions, not only because of their own significance but also because she sees them as a providential and most fruitful foundation on which the preaching of the Gospel can be based and a new society centered on Christ can be built... In fact the doctrine and redemption of Christ fulfills, renews and perfects whatever good is found in all human traditions. Therefore, the African who is consecrated as a Christian is not forced to renounce his own self, but assumes the ancient values of his people 'in spirit and in truth' (John 6:24)(sic)."[2]

We offer two citations from the current pope, John Paul II:

> "Does it not sometimes happen that the firm belief of the followers of the non-Christian religions—a belief that is also an effect of the spirit of truth operating outside the visible confines of the Mystical Body—can make Christians ashamed at often being themselves so disposed to doubt concerning the truths revealed by God and

---

[1] In a scorching article found in the *Boston Globe,* the modern pope has blasted the work of Evangelicals in South America. "In a scorching blast at evangelical Protestant sects, Pope John Paul II accused them yesterday of seducing with false mirages and misleading with distorted simplifications." (*Boston Globe*, October 14, ©1991)

[2] Neuner and Dupuis, pp. 293, 295-296

proclaimed by the Church and so prone to relax moral principles and open the way to ethical permissiveness?

"What seems to bring together and unite, in a particular way, Christians and believers of other religions is an acknowledgment of the need for prayer as an expression of man's spirituality directed towards the Absolute. Even when, for some, He is the Great Unknown..."[1]

What then of the changing face of Rome? We can see that Rome has not changed its doctrine one iota. Rather, Rome has changed its own rules with regard to the pagan world and anyone willing to listen in the "christianized" world. Rome seeks to expand by assimilation! Duped liberals lead their religions in a drum-beat to the waiting arms of Rome. We look for this shift to increase dramatically.[2]

Insofar as paganism is concerned, in hopes of global absorption, Rome has visited the planet with a grotesque form of ecumenism which stretches the imagination of even Rome's faithful. As Christians, we must steadily hold the line and resist all of this in simple obedience to the gospel once delivered to the saints. In the final analysis, if truth is relegated to the realm of the relative whimperings of the philosophers of any age then there is no truth! Rome's courting of the pagan religions of this age will ultimately bring about either the destruction of Romanism or a powerful one-world religious force. Either way, the current status of Rome keeps it strictly out of bounds for the Christian.

Rome has not been infected with the gospel of our Lord and Savior Jesus Christ. She remains doubly inoculated to placing herself under biblical authority.

---

[1] Neuner and Dupuis, pp. 298, 300

[2] We suggest that any interested reader should consult the *1990 Catholic Almanac* (pg. 280 and following) for a succinct background on Ecumenism and the United States as well as the world. Of particular significance is the *Anglican-Catholic Final Report*, pg. 289

Post Script

IF YOU have read this book and wish to witness back to those you love who are still caught in the bondage of Rome, we suggest that you keep the main thing the main thing. It is perfectly normal for a Christian to want to witness to a Catholic. Begin with the meaning and significance of the sacramental system and slowly lead your Catholic friends to the finished work of Christ and the complete acceptance and forgiveness to be found in Him alone. I hope that God will use the truth of His Word and this humble attempt to preserve it for His glory and the salvation of His own. May this treatise be used as a portion of His providential means to accomplish His will for their salvation. May His saints be strengthened and thus return praise to Him for what He has done in our Lord and Savior Jesus Christ. *Soli Deo Gloria.*

Dear Roman Catholic friends,

I have written this book out of a motive to proclaim the truth of the gospel of Christ. For many years I was a dutiful participant in the religion of Rome. I was born and confirmed into the Catholic religion. But I had never read the Bible nor was I encouraged to do so. I grew up on the Catechism, but I was never challenged with a comprehensive understanding of the Word of God. I was also ignorant of history. It was not so much that I denied Jesus Christ. As a Catholic, I affirmed Jesus Christ. But I did not know the Jesus of the Bible. I knew only a "jesus" of my own imagination. I was like most of you. I lived in a gray world of being Roman Catholic without knowing the gospel of Jesus Christ. I urge you to read the Word and ask questions. I also urge you to go to God through Jesus and submit to His Word.

Many of you have relatives and friends who have become born again. They have witnessed to you about their newly formed faith in Jesus Christ. Perhaps this book will help you understand why they feel an urgency to present to you the gospel of Christ. Please do not hide away or run from the gospel. It will do no good to say, "I am a Catholic!" What really matters eternally is that you believe the Christ of Scripture and do not embrace the religion of men.

> "But as we were allowed of God to be put in trust with the gospel, even so we speak; not as pleasing men, but God, which trieth our hearts." (1 Thessalonians 2:4)

Disturbing Alliances—Evangelicals and Catholics Together

FOR the past two years a task-force of Evangelicals and Roman Catholics has been working together to forge a document which is written to express some common convictions about the Christian faith and mission. This document, entitled *Evangelicals and Catholics Together: The Christian Mission In The Third Millennium*, has been hammered out and signed by a number of prominent people.[1]

The beginning of the document contains a disclaimer. "This statement cannot speak responsibly for our communities."[2] This means that this document has no official sanction within the Roman Catholic religion. There exists no official Evangelical worldwide authority. Evangelicals are not unified under one hierarchy as is the Roman Catholic community.

This manuscript is disturbing. It is disturbing because it is an attempt to mollify the absolutely incompatible differences of belief between the Roman Catholic religion and the Evangelical community. The clear goal of the document is to place the pressing social ills of the upcoming Third Millennium

---

[1] Among the signers are Mr. Charles Colson of Prison Fellowship; Father Juan Diaz-Vilar of St. Peter's College; Bishop Francis George of the Diocese of Yakima; Dr. Kent Hill, President of Eastern Nazarene College; Dr. Richard Land, Christian Life Commission of the Southern Baptist Church; Dr. Larry Lewis, Home Mission Board of the Southern Baptist Convention; Dr. Jesse Miranda of the Assemblies of God; Msgr. William Murphy of the Archdiocese of Boston; Father John Neuhaus of The Institute on Religion and Public Life; Mr. Brian O'Connell of World Evangelism Fellowship; Mr. Herbert Schlossberg of The Fieldstead Foundation; Archbishop Francis Stafford of the Archdiocese of Denver; Mr. George Weigel of Ethics and Public Policy Center and Dr. John White, President of Geneva College.

[2] *Evangelicals and Catholics Together: The Christian Mission in the Third Millennium*, March 29, 1994, pg. 1

ahead of any clear presentation of the gospel of Christ. In so doing, the gospel of Jesus Christ has been sacrificed on the altar of social concern.

The framers of this writ speak out of both sides of their mouths. With one side of their mouth, they purport to advance the one mission of Christ (though the mission of Christ is not clearly defined in the document). With the other side, they expunge the gospel of any meaningful content by "ecumenizing" it into something which might be called Evangelical Catholicism. Using very carefully chosen language (so as not to offend either community), a new gospel emerges void of content and embraceable by all! The Catholic religion is said to have the gospel as well as the Evangelical community. This is maintained even though the two gospels are antithetical and contrary to each other.

Armed with a self-prescribed mandate for unity, this document begins by assuming Roman Catholicism is Christian. Herein lies the heart of the matter. Is Roman Catholicism a Christian religion? The authors of this accord say, "Yes!" What is their logic?

> "As Christ is one, so the Christian mission is one. That one mission can be and should be advanced in diverse ways. Legitimate diversity, however, should not be confused with existing divisions between Christians that obscure the one Christ and hinder the one mission."[1]

As can be seen, Catholicism is defined as nothing worse than a "legitimate diversity." This preëmptive theological strike declares that the war is over before the battle has begun! By sheer fiat the writers affirm that Roman Catholicism, with all its attendants (Sacramentalism, Papal authority, Catholic traditions, Marian worship, Penance, Purgatory, Substantive grace, unbloody Sacrifice of the Mass, Priestly class and Baptismal regeneration, to name a few), is nothing more than legitimate diversity within the Christian community!

Furthermore, under the theme song of unity, we are asked to repent of our sins against "the unity that Christ intends for all His disciples"[2] We are told that to withstand Rome is to sin in the eyes of Christ. Essentially, Evangelicals are asked to repent of the Protestant Reformation. By what principle? The principle of unity!

This attempt to reverse history makes sense to those who grant the premise that Roman Catholicism is, in fact, a Christian religion. Evidently, many

---

[1] *Evangelicals and Catholics Together,* pg. 2
[2] *Evangelicals and Catholics Together,* pg. 2

Evangelicals
"Emphaticall
compromisir
dare to decl;
Rome, to b/
Evangelic;
attempt. L'

  "As
  love'
  ene/

We be
Cathc
twist
Cath

We
W/
re
te...
Evangelica...
correction from the ...
ridiculed. Systematic theology ...
seminaries are judged on their winsom...
abilities to teach and preach God's Word. Growth ...
the church has become the barometer of success. Is it any w...
this climate there would arise such an assault on the gospel of Jesus Chr...
We have opened ourselves up to the Roman Horse. Today, more than ever
before, language is stripped of its meaning. Evangelical preachers are taught
to sound like politicians. Distinctions of theology, once so clear, have
become a muddled mess. With so much mist in the pulpit is there any
wonder why there is so much fog in the pews?

Entering into this milieu is the Catholic sympathizer playing on the obvious.
The nation is in trouble morally. Homosexuality has taken the center stage
of the social debate. The Catholic religion has always stood against this
abomination. The right to life in the womb has taken center stage in the
moral argument of the nation. The Catholic religion has always fought for
the life of the unborn infant. Euthanasia has swept the headlines. The
Catholic religion has always stood against aided and unaided suicide. The
Catholic religion rails against such things in the name of God and Christ!

---

[1] *Evangelicals and Catholics Together,* pg. 4

214

The deduction is that the Catholic religion is asked to embrace Rome, we are asked to repe...

In the midst of this challenge sits an Eva...
theologically that it can barely whimper...
The net effect is the soft and slow d...
America!

One need only read the "Affirm...
to see how far we have drift...
prophets. The collaborators...
the following words.

"We affirm toget...
because of Chri...
than the love...

"All who...
Christ.
Christ...

To the...
of...
d...

Christian. We are not only
nt of our resisting Rome.

ngelical community so weakened
a reply. The net result is acceptance.
eath of the gospel of Jesus Christ in

ation" section of this treatise on ecumenism
ed from discerning the gospel from the false
of this affirmation would have us rally around

her that we are justified by grace through faith
st. Living faith is active in love that is nothing less
f Christ..."[1]

ccept Christ as Lord and Savior are brothers and sisters in
Evangelicals and Catholics are brothers and sisters in
."[2]

naïve this sounds legitimate. But it is as stone cold dead as the heart
he unregenerate. First, the term "justified" is never defined by the
cument. The Romish religion understands "justification" as an ongoing
process of God rewarding merit in and through the sacramental system.
This *process* justification has its origins in the waters of Romish baptism.
Catholic theology views good works of men, done in faith, as the ground of
their ongoing justification. Grace is not defined in this document either. The
Romish understanding of grace is substantive. Grace is said to be poured
into the soul at baptism and given through the sacraments for obedience.
The Romish religion defines grace as that which God infuses based on
obedience. It can increase or decrease. "Through faith" is not defined. The
Romish religion understands "through faith" as an ongoing trust in the Mass
for forgiveness of sins. Faith, to Catholics, is trusting that Christ has given
them a share to suffer for the expiation of their sins through Penance and
Purgatory.

The Evangelical world knows nothing of this kind of gospel! Justified by
faith through grace means that the righteousness of Jesus Christ is imputed
to us through the agency of faith for our righteousness. It is a transaction
freely given by God. The merits of Christ become ours by faith. Our

---

[1] *Evangelicals and Catholics Together,* pg. 5
[2] *Evangelicals and Catholics Together,* pg. 5

salvation is not suspended on our own merits or a sacramental system. Grace is the disposition of God wherein He grants His unmerited favor to unworthy sinners for the sake of Christ. The gospel is faith alone in the finished work of Jesus Christ.

The unity of the Body of Christ is dependent upon all those who embrace this gospel. Rome does not. It is one thing to *say* Christ is Lord and Savior. It is another to believe *the gospel* He gave to us! There can be no doubt that the Jew of the first century had a healthy belief in one God sovereign over all. The first century Jews believed with all of their heart and soul and mind that there was but one God, the creator of Heaven and earth. What they did not believe was the gospel of God. Seeking to establish a righteousness of their own, they did not obey the righteousness of God. Likewise, the Roman Catholic community has a zeal for God. But it is a prideful zeal which rejects the gospel of God. Like their predecessors of the first century, they stumble over the stumbling block. They pursue God, not in accordance with knowledge, but with their vain religion. We cannot declare them brothers and sisters in Christ on the basis of their mere assent that Jesus is Lord and Savior. The demons can say as much and the Mormons do say as much!

We encourage Evangelicals everywhere to repent of their own involvement with Rome. We reject the proposal, which has been put forth in the following citation, that Rome represents nothing other than a distinctive pattern of discipleship:

> "That we are all to be one does not mean that we are all to be identical in our way of following the one Christ. Such distinctive patterns of discipleship, it should be noted, are amply evident within the communion of the Catholic Church as well as within the many worlds of Evangelical Protestantism."[1]

This contention confuses the substance of the gospel with the diversity of expression, in worship and ecclesiology, of the gospel. Evangelicals may vary in their expression of worship but not in the substance of the gospel! We affirm the gospel of Rome to be a false hope and not merely a distinctive pattern of discipleship within the Christian community.

Also, we refuse any call which asks us to stop the practice of witnessing to the Roman Catholic community. The following excerpt should warn us how easily these men recommend an end to evangelism. Using carefully selected language to camouflage an agenda of ecumenism, Rome is being declared exempt from Christian witness:

---

[1] *Evangelicals and Catholics Together,* pg. 22

"We condemn the practice of recruiting people from another community for purposes of denominational or institutional aggrandizement."[1]

This declaration violates the command of our Lord to preach the gospel to those lost in religions of their own making. We affirm that Rome is in need of the gospel of Jesus Christ.

We further reject the assumption that aberrant gospels can be brought together under the guise of differing worshipping communities. The citation given below illustrates how far some have gone to close their eyes, cover their ears and stop up their mouths for the sake of unity with Rome.

"Three observations are in order in connection with proselytizing. First, as much as we might believe one community is more fully in accord with the Gospel than another, we as Evangelicals and Catholics affirm that opportunity and means for growth in Christian discipleship are available in our several communities. Second, the decision of the committed Christian with respect to his communal allegiance and participation must be assiduously respected. Third, in view of the large number of non-Christians in the world and the enormous challenge of our common evangelistic task, it is neither theologically legitimate nor a prudent use of resources for one Christian community to proselytize among active adherents of another Christian community."[2]

The above citation spells the death knell of the gospel witness to the Roman Catholic religion. It is reprehensible to assault the gospel of Jesus Christ with such brazen idolatry. We affirm there is one Body confined and defined by virtue of a common belief in the gospel of Christ which is antithetical to the gospel of Rome.

In addition, the notion that individual decisions (such as where to worship) have no bearing on the honor of Christ (therefore must be protected from evangelism) is patently non-biblical and must be rebuffed. We consider the sentence below, extracted from the text of the document, to be of utmost danger to the health and vitality of the gospel in America.

"Similarly, bearing false witness against other persons and communities, or casting unjust and uncharitable suspicions upon them, is incompatible with the Gospel. Also to be rejected is the practice of

---

[1] *Evangelicals and Catholics Together*, pg. 22
[2] *Evangelicals and Catholics Together*, pp. 22, 23

comparing the strengths and ideals of one community with the weaknesses and failure of another."[1]

This injunction destroys the God-given mandate to qualify all religious communities by the gospel of Jesus Christ. We reserve the right to examine all and any religious systems using the measure of the faith once delivered. It is grotesque to shut out the gospel in deference to a promotion of peace and unity among those who seek common ground with foreign religions!

We affirm that there are false gods in this age and temples of worship that are abhorrent to Jesus Christ. We reject the assertion that matters of regeneration, baptism and new birth are tangential to the gospel. We affirm that these precious truths must not be diluted and compromised by admitting all manner of description and definition. We reject the supposition that Catholicism and Christianity can be Christian together. We affirm that Catholicism must give way to Christianity either through evangelism or the return of our Lord.

In the final analysis, such declarations as *Evangelicals and Catholics Together* do not serve the cause of God and truth. The premise of such declarations is the avoidance of what are perceived to be minor differences between the Christian and Catholic community. But these differences, in reality, are as sharp and clear as any throughout the history of Christ's Church. We cannot emphasize enough that Roman Catholicism has a completely distinctive set of beliefs about the gospel of Jesus Christ. Honest Roman Catholics will not shy away from this statement. Honest Evangelicals will not seek out ways to emulsify the gospel by blending in contradictory ideas from other religious sources.

We accept the observation that the nation is becoming increasingly morally bankrupt. We accept the fact that we are in troubled times. But the remedy is not to redefine the gospel in hopes of gathering massive numbers to speak out politically against unrighteousness. The remedy is rather to reaffirm the gospel and take it in to all religions. The remedy is to encourage Christians to take their stand in a non-Christian pluralistic society and grapple for a share of voice in the market place.

We would be fools to think the bottoming out of America can be fixed through a redefinition of basic Christianity. This is the worst kind of myopic thinking. We warn American Evangelicals that Rome is a worldwide religion. We are free only in America to evangelize this imposing contradiction to the heart of God's gospel. We pray that God's people will discipline those who have undermined the gospel with such documents.

---

[1] *Evangelicals and Catholics Together*, pg. 23

Make your voice heard here first. We recommend that support for evangelical organizations which maintain such a stance prescribed in the document *Evangelicals and Catholics Together,* be withdrawn.

[The Strange Fire of Dr. J. I. Packer

Perhaps the two most sobering articles ever to appear in the pages of a reputed Evangelical magazine have been printed in *Christianity Today,* December 12th, 1994. I refer to articles written by the venerable and highly esteemed J. I. Packer and Alister E. McGrath. Dr. Packer and Alister McGrath are both of Regent College, Vancouver, British Colombia, and are highly respected Evangelicals whose writings and teaching have blessed millions of God's people. This is what makes a review, especially of J. I. Packer's article, so difficult to write. He, in particular, is a giant of our age.

However, truth is at stake. A redefining of the gospel and a new way of looking at Christianity has been rammed right into our living rooms and we are left with no choice but to respond. In endorsing the recently publicized statement entitled *Evangelical and Catholics Together* (ECT), Dr. Packer shocked many in the Christian community. The response has been harsh from many sources. Now, in an article from *Christianity Today,* Dr. Packer defends his decision.[1]

In defending his signing of *Evangelicals and Catholics Together*, Dr. Packer has, in effect, asked us to re-evaluate the gospel. For this we are grateful. For in the final analysis, it is the gospel which must be clarified. If this be so and Dr. Packer is found to have violated the basic principles of the gospel, then he stands under its correction as any man must.

The Review

Dr. Packer begins his defense by getting some weight off his chest. He has been chastised by the Evangelical community for selling out the gospel. He has been vilified by his peers for having made a mistake of gigantic proportions. To off-load some of the criticism, Dr. Packer refers to his critics as "isolationists," and "fear" mongers.

> "Many isolationists are unwilling either to rethink or, under any cir-
> cumstances, to change. I was surprised at the violence of initial

---

[1] *Christianity Today*, December 12, 1994, J. I. Packer, "Why I Signed It," pp. 34-37

Protestant reaction, but I should not have been. Years ago, I came to realize that fear plays a larger part in North American motivation than is ever acknowledged. The sitting-on-a-volcano feeling is very American and is easily exploited. But fear clouds the mind and generates defensive responses that drive wisdom out of the window."[1]

Having cast those who would oppose his signing of *Evangelicals and Catholics Together* as isolationists and driven by fear, Dr. Packer goes on to say that he,

"...ought to have anticipated that some Protestants would say bleak, skewed, fearful and fear-driven things about this document."[2]

His aim is to set the record straight. The *Evangelicals and Catholics Together* statement is not what all those fear-driven isolationists think that it is. Dr. Packer would have us enter into wisdom with him and see just how valuable a document this really is!

All the "defensive" rhetoric aside, it is necessary that we look at the issues. We have already reviewed the *Evangelicals and Catholics Together* document and found it to be extremely dangerous. We do not consider our review motivated by fear or isolationism. Hopefully, we are driven by the truth of the gospel. We are motivated by honor to defend the gospel and contend for the faith once delivered to the saints. There are good and proper motivations for denying the accuracy or benefits of a particular thing. We regret that Dr. Packer feels it necessary to impute motives to those who have for the right reasons warned Evangelicals about *Evangelicals and Catholics Together*. If there are no right reasons to defend the gospel, then Paul was wrong to encourage the Galatians to do so. He was equally wrong to encourage Timothy and Titus:

"O Timothy, keep that which is committed to thy trust, avoiding profane [and] vain babblings, and oppositions of science falsely so called: Which some professing have erred concerning the faith." (1 Timothy 6:20,21)

"This witness is true. Wherefore rebuke them sharply, that they may be sound in the faith; Not giving heed to Jewish fables, and commandments of men, that turn from the truth." (Titus 1:13,14)

Most people who vigorously oppose *Evangelicals and Catholics Together* do so on the basis of their understanding that the gospel is being compro-

---

[1] *Christianity Today*, pg. 34
[2] *Christianity Today*, pg. 34

mised. There is nothing wrong with this. We have no doubt that when he feels the gospel to be threatened, Dr. Packer rises to the occasion. He need not chastise Evangelicals for rising on this occasion where he is unable. We believe Dr. Packer is wrong both in his assessment of motives in those who oppose him and in his assessment of *Evangelicals and Catholics Together*.

Nuts and Bolts

We are struck by the discordant language so uncharacteristic of Dr. Packer in the presentation of his defense. It is as though he is struggling to use language to make opposite things seem to be the same. For instance, he openly admits that he maintains Reformed theology as taught by Calvin but thinks collaboration with Roman Catholics is the most fruitful sort of ecumenism. Listen to his words:

> "But in fact, while maintaining what Reformed theology has always said about official *tradition of the Church of Rome*, I have long thought informal grassroots collaboration with Roman Catholics in ministry is the most fruitful sort of ecumenism that one can practice nowadays."[1] (italics ours)

We pick up a glimmer of hope early in his defense. Perhaps, we hope, Dr. Packer is only talking about joint cooperative efforts such as picketing abortion clinics or conservative politics. Such co-belligerency is a well-established fact among politically oriented Evangelicals and Roman Catholics. Perhaps he only wants more of that! But we become concerned when, in reading the above quotation, Dr. Packer chooses the word "tradition" when referring to Roman Catholic practices rather than "theology" or "gospel." We take objection early on in our efforts at clarification. The Reformers did not quibble with Rome on matters of inconsequence. They fought a bloody war over the meaning and content of the gospel itself. Dr. Packer errs in trivializing the vast expanse of difference between Rome and Christianity in the eyes of the Reformers. His use of "tradition" here bodes ill for the gospel later!

Is the Gospel at Stake?

The heart of Dr. Packer's defense begins with his reasons why he could not become a Roman Catholic. This is the crux of the entire issue. Dr. Packer

---

[1] *Christianity Today*, pg. 35

treats his differences with Rome as significant enough to prevent him from entering Rome, but not significant enough to disqualify Rome as a Christian community. Though Dr. Packer points out accurately Rome's foibles, he does so with less than exclusionary language. To Dr. Packer, Rome is "theologically flawed," but not dead wrong! Rome is "historically flawed," not dead wrong! Rome's belief in merits, the Mary cult, purgatory and indulgences serve merely to "damp down" full assurance, but do not kill the liberating gospel of Jesus Christ! The belief of Rome that the pope is infallible (in matters of faith and morals), and that the Church at Rome is impossible to correct is "very cramping," but not deadly to *Sola Scriptura* and *Sola Fide*! Rome's doctrine of justification "cuts across" Paul's teaching but does not ruin the gospel! Thus, Dr. Packer cannot enter Rome because Rome is "flawed," "cramping," "damps down security," and "cuts across Pauline justification." Evidently, that is it! Four hundred fifty years of Protestantism is reduced to a matter of personal tastes as to which worshipping community one desires!

He describes Rome as if Rome were not troubling to the gospel. These things would prevent Dr. Packer from joining Rome but not necessarily anyone else! The clear implication here, and later in Dr. Packer's direct testimony, is that these are not *critical* differences. Incredibly, according to Dr. Packer, these Romish beliefs do not constitute another gospel! Apparently, Rome's position on the Mass, purgatory, papal infallibility, traditions, penance, justification, baptismal regeneration and Maryolatry do not diminish the gospel of Jesus Christ. Is it a wonder why some have been so boisterous in their incredulity with Dr. Packer? Is this what the Reformers gave up their lives for? Did they only die for the right to have worship according to their individual tastes? Did they believe the Romish system was only a bit "cramping" or "theologically flawed?" We fear Dr. Packer has fallen off the track here to say the least! He cannot, with any reasonable integrity, hold to the Reformation gospel, as championed by Calvin and others, while essentially dismissing their claims that Rome had abandoned the gospel!

The Rationale

Having taken what appears to us an absolutely untenable stand, Dr. Packer gives us his reasoning. We are given three reasons why we should join in with Rome and become one within the limits of our conscience.

"First: Do we recognize that good evangelical Protestants and good Roman Catholics—good, I mean, in terms of their own church's

– No -one good

stated ideal of spiritual life — are Christians together? We ought to recognize this, for this is true."[1]

"But I am not the only one who is thus made aware that evangelicals and Catholics *who actively believe* are Christians together."[2]

Dr. Packer enunciates for us why he believes good Catholics are Christians. He quotes from *Evangelicals and Catholics Together* which accepts Jesus Christ as Lord and Savior, affirms the Apostles' Creed, and that we "are justified by grace through faith because of Christ," and understands the Christian life as conversion to Jesus Christ.

We are surprised and perturbed. Since when are we to judge the gospel on the basis of a particular religion's "stated ideal of spiritual life?" Dr. Packer has missed the point! All religions on the face of the earth have a stated ideal of spiritual life. Does this make them Christian? What is at stake here is a definition of Christianity. By Dr. Packer's loose standards of "stated ideal of spiritual life" and "actively believing community" all must be included. Do not the Mormons have an "active belief?" Are not the Moonies involved in participation with their "stated ideal of spiritual life?" Dr. Packer mentions the Apostles' Creed. Are we to believe those who affirm the Apostles' Creed are *ipso facto* Christian? We are convinced that one can embrace the Apostles' Creed and not be a Christian. The reason for this is the institution of the Apostles' Creed as a formula in many Roman and Eastern Churches. Furthermore, the Apostles' Creed says nothing about *how one is saved*! It is a scant reminder of the essential facts of Christ's mission but lacks in any necessary detail. One could actually believe the Apostles' Creed while filling in the *"how one must be saved?"* question with absolute heresy.

We notice further that Dr. Packer makes no mention of the object or content of faith. That a religious community is "actively believing" means little unless they are "actively believing" the right thing! Rome does not actively believe the right thing about the gospel of Jesus Christ. Rome's active faith is in baptismal regeneration, penance, purgatory, priests who dole out temporal punishments for sins committed, bloodless propitiation of Christ in the Mass, infallibility of the pope and Romish tradition placed on a par with Scripture. Rome "actively believes" that no one can have assurance of his salvation. Rome "actively believes" the way of salvation is through the sacraments. Rome has set a "stated ideal of the spiritual" that denies *Sola Fide* (faith only) as the entrance into the Kingdom of God! Rome denies the imputation of Christ's righteousness as our ground of justification.

---

[1] *Christianity Today*, pg. 35
[2] *Christianity Today*, pg. 35

We are shocked and bewildered. Dr. Packer may want to chastise us for being too picayune when it comes to the gospel, but we are not alone. The apostle Paul threw a fit over the simple inclusion of the time honored practice of circumcision into the gospel equation. Was he a bit picayune? Why not say, "let the Jews have their 'worshipping community,' no harm done. We all believe in Jesus after all." Was Paul boorish in his zeal to protect the gospel against circumcision? Why did he not say, "leave them alone, at least they have 'lively faith.'" Obviously, Paul saw something that Dr. Packer is quite unwilling to see. Judaizers were not simply adding on a few optional accessories to the gospel. They were tinkering with the heart of the message. Circumcision and any part of the law would ruin the gospel. That is why Paul says he did not tolerate it for a minute. What words would Paul have for those accusing him of being an "isolationist" and "fear-driven"? What words would he have for the new Pharisees of Rome with their doctrines and dogmas which crush the gospel? We are convinced if circumcision ruins the gospel then Rome obliterates it! Dr. Packer has given away the farm without a fight. We shall not grant him his first assumption. Rome is not Christian. It is not Christian because it does not know or preach the gospel of the grace of Jesus Christ.

We are put on notice, by Dr. Packer, that justification based on the imputed righteousness of Christ alone is relegated to a footnote of fine print which the framers of *Evangelicals and Catholics Together* could not be expected to agree. We caution the reader at this junction to red flag all talk of justification. The *Evangelicals and Catholics Together* statement uses careful language, "justified by grace through faith because of Christ." Any theologian will immediately recognize that the door is deliberately left open for the Romish doctrine of justification. Rome believes "by grace" is grace infused through their sacramental system. Rome believes "through faith" is faith that Christ gave us a sacramental system administered by priests to bring the grace of God to its people. Rome believes "because of Christ" means that Jesus Christ is the *meritorious* cause but baptism is the *instrumental cause* without which no man is justified. This is not the Christian faith. Christians believe "by grace" to be the absolute unmerited loving disposition of God. Christians believe "by faith" to mean faith only in the accomplished work of Christ whose righteousness becomes our own upon believing. Christians believe "because of Christ" to mean that Christ's death was sufficient to pay for all of our guilt and debt to God without our having to suffer or pay penance. His righteousness is the absolute ground of our justification. For the Christian, justification is a declaration of acquittal based upon the righteousness of Christ. For the Roman Catholic, it is a renewal which starts in baptism and can be lost through sin and failure to attend the Catholic sacraments. We are at a loss as to how these two radically opposed concepts of salvation can ever be confused as being the same.

We should add that we know many good Mormons and many good Jehovah Witnesses as well as Christian Scientists. Shall they also be considered Christians? Evidently error as to the Person of Christ (deity, two natures, God/man) disqualifies some worshipping communities from being considered Christian. But error as to the *way of salvation* and the *gospel message* apparently constitutes little ground for criticism. Roman Catholics may affirm the deity of Christ and His resurrection and His return, but they do not affirm His gospel! Is this not important anymore?

The second reason Dr. Packer wishes to embrace Rome could have been anything really. Once you have conceded that Rome is a gospel-carrier then any second reason will make sense. We take the time to review Dr. Packer's second reason because it is disturbing in and of itself.

"Vital for the church's welfare today and tomorrow in the United States and Canada is the building of the strongest possible transdenominational coalition of Bible-believing, Christ-honoring, Spirit-empowered Christians who will together resist the many forms of disintegrative theology—relativist, monist, pluralist, liberationist, feminist, or whatever—that plague both Protestantism and Catholicism at the present time."[1] ~ Not by ~~regulus~~ by ~~power~~ -

What are we to say to this? Our first thought is that the social ills of the day have been put squarely in front of the integrity of the gospel. It is not to the Church's welfare to sacrifice the gospel on the altar of social concern! This would be a grave error.

Once again we are surprised at how easy it is for someone as brilliant as Dr. Packer to fall for such rationale. Dr. Packer does not see that his cure is worse than the disease. Any deals with the devil to fend off social decay will soon come back in total annihilation of the Body of Christ by Her enemies. It is vital for the Church's welfare that She not sell her collective soul to the pragmatists and utilitarians who seek aid from the enemy! The gospel does just fine under duress and persecution. It needs to be clarified and preached in our Bible colleges, seminaries and in our churches across North America. We cannot fight the liberal with the unbeliever can we? Yet, this is Dr. Packer's proposal. We need, says he, to round up good Catholics to unite them into a coalition of Bible-believing Christians. The problem is that Catholics are taught to not trust the Bible only! The problem is Catholics are taught a different gospel of salvation. What are they going to tell the world? It is one thing to tell people that killing babies in the womb is morally reprehensible. The Mormons and Buddhists do that. But now, what is their gospel?

---

[1] *Christianity Today*, pg. 35

Dr. Packer forgets his history. There has never been a time when the gospel has not been hated. We need to stop pleading for unity at the expense of the truth and be about our business of teaching and preaching the gospel to all those outside of it, be they a religious community or not!

Dr. Packer makes a dreadful impassioned plea that Christians link up. Who are Christians? According to Dr. Packer they are those who believe the following:

> "...that adherents to the key truths of classical Christianity, a self-defining triune God who is both creator and Redeemer, this God's regenerating and sanctifying grace; the sanctity of life here, the certainty of judgment hereafter, and the return of Jesus Christ to end history—should link up for the vast and pressing task of re-educating our secularized communities on these matters. Again, it is the theological conservationists, and they alone—mainly, Roman Catholics and the more established evangelicals—who have resources for the rebuilding of these ruins, *and their domestic differences about salvation and the Church should not hinder them from a joint action in seeking to re-Christianize the North American milieu.*"[1] (emphasis ours)

There you have it. Not a word about what the gospel might be. Not a sentence about repentance and faith in Jesus Christ. Not a morsel about sin and its remedy through simple faith in the finished work of Jesus on the cross. The entire course of the Protestant Reformation and subsequent history of the establishment of North America is reduced to "domestic differences about salvation." We are almost speechless! Have we gone mad? Have we actually read from one as highly esteemed as Dr. Packer that we need to join with the Roman Catholic religion to re-Christianize North America? Evidently those who left England and Europe in the 1600's had it all wrong. They should have brought the Society of Jesus with them!!

Dr. Packer goes on to say that "propagating the basic faith remains the crucial task." What faith? Are we now confined to preach monotheism coupled with "name-your-own" ideas about regenerating grace and judg-ment? Dr. Packer seems to reduce the Christian message to God, Christ, Grace, Sanctity of Life, Personal Judgment and the Return of Christ with various religious communities filling in the blanks as to how one is saved or how one enters the Kingdom!

Contrary to Dr. Packer's sentiments, we are not ready to give up the gospel for any social cause. When what is at stake is truly understood, Christians

---

[1] *Christianity Today*, pg. 36

will come together. But it will not be to emulsify the gospel through dilution. It will be to clarify and rebuild what has been eroded through compromise with false systems. Our goal should be the uplifting of the gospel and then penetration into society. Furthermore, history knows nothing of the "Christianized" North America that Dr. Packer wants to get back to. At best, we find the new colonies founded on the two principles of the Protestant Reformation: *Sola Fide* and *Sola Scriptura*. How ironic that Dr. Packer wishes to enlist the endorsement of Rome to return North America to her Christian roots. Early North America had no toleration for the false hope of Rome!

Dr. Packer offers as his third rationale for pressing us into the Catholic fold the fact that it is already happening! Naturally, he attributes the "already happening" to the work of the Holy Spirit. He cites three illustrations. Offered are Francis Schaeffer's principle of co-belligerence, evangelistic methods of Billy Graham and charismatic get-togethers where distinction between Protestants and Catholics vanish "in Christ centered unity of experience."

It is a quantum leap from walking a sidewalk in protest to claiming that all those walking are Christians. If I picket with a Muslim and a Jew over the protection of private schools from government interference am I saying that they are Christian? No, and co-belligerency on social issues should not be used as a bridge for the dilution of the gospel.

Also, we are not at all impressed with the willingness of Dr. Graham to be excitedly indiscriminate as to the nature of the gospel and the laxity he has exhibited in involving disparate religions in his campaigns.

Thirdly, we are remorse that Dr. Packer could possibly be so influenced by the "experience" movement. Does not solid biblical data protect us from the outrageous claims of those with an experience? Shall we now say it is "of the Spirit" simply because it is the experience of the masses? Should we not test the spirits to see if they are of God?

The final word from Dr. Packer on this entire matter is summed up in his ending remarks which we produce verbatim:

> "May ECT realistically claim, as in effect it does, that its evangelical and Catholic drafters agree on the gospel of salvation? *Yes and no. If you mean, could they all be relied on to attach the same small print to their statement, "we are justified by grace through faith because of Christ" no.* (The Tridentine assertion of merit and the Reformational assertion of imputed righteousness can hardly be harmonized.) If you mean, do all present-day Catholics focus on the living Christ,

Lord, Savior, and coming King as the direct object of the sinner's faith and hope in the way ECT does, no again. (I imagine some traditional Catholics have problems with ECT at this point, though today's Catholic theologians observably do not.) But if you mean, does ECT's insistence that the Christ of Scripture, creeds, and confessions is faith's proper focus, and that "Christian witness of the necessity aimed at conversion," not only as an initial step but as a personal life-process and that this constitutes a sufficient account of the gospel of salvation for shared evangelistic ministry, then surely yes. *What brings salvation, after all, is not any theory about faith in Christ, justification, and the church, but faith itself in Christ Himself.*[1] (emphasis ours).

We would ask an open and honest question. When God deems fit to save a person and gives that person the light of the revelation of Christ in his heart, what is the belief that ensues? Is it a belief that embraces the Romish religion? If so, then Rome must be counted in as fully Christian. If not, then we must be prepared to stand opposed to those who wish to credit the Romish system with focusing on the living Christ.

We further ask if it be possible for the Spirit of God to produce a faith within the Body of Christ that is irreconcilable? In other words, has God produced the faith of the Roman Catholic as well as the absolute antithesis of that faith all in one Body of Christ? We read with all too much vividness the fact that our forefathers in the faith were hunted like animals and butchered for their insistence on a gospel contrary to historic Rome. Rome has not rescinded Trent. Trent curses the very heart of our faith. Shall we now give in to Trent to allegedly "save" the world?

Furthermore, there is a new Roman presence on the block. A short excursion into Vatican II presents the Christian with all the more reason to avoid Rome. Vatican II in essence has subverted even Rome's historical attempts to draw the line with Romish notions. Old Rome used to curse to Hell those who did not follow her into idolatry. Recent Rome now embraces one and all and invents yet another gospel for the world's religions. We find this from Vatican II:

"Let Christians, while witnessing to their own faith and way of life, acknowledge, preserve and encourage the spiritual and moral truths found among non-Christians, also their social life and culture. The Church also has a high regard for the Muslims. They worship God, who is one, living and subsistent, merciful and almighty, the Creator of heaven and earth, who has also spoken to men. They

---

[1] *Christianity Today*, pp. 36, 37

strive to submit themselves without reserve to the hidden decrees of God, just as Abraham submitted himself to God's plan, to whose faith Muslims eagerly link their own. Although not acknowledging *him as God*, they venerate Jesus as a prophet, his virgin Mother they also honor, and even at times devoutly invoke. Further, they await the judgment and the reward of God following the resurrection of the dead. For this reason they highly esteem an upright life and worship God, especially by way of prayer, alms-deeds and fasting."[1]

If this does not sound enough like the *Evangelicals and Catholics Together* statement then we ask you to evaluate the next paragraph.

"Over the centuries many quarrels and dissensions have arisen between Christians and Muslims. The sacred Council now *pleads with all to forget the past, and urges that a sincere effort be made to achieve mutual understanding;* for the benefit of all men, let them together preserve and promote peace, liberty, social justice and moral values."[2]

We issue you a warning cry. The name of the game today is unity at any price. We ask you to consider the far-reaching tentacles of Rome. Today, it is acceptance of its false gospel. Tomorrow it is the acceptance of the world's false gospels. It will not end until we are under dominion of a one world religious system. This is not fear-mongering. This is a "gut check" and a "reality check" for those who profess the gospel of our Lord Jesus Christ.

We regret having to write such a strong review against one who has been used by God to such a great extent. And yet, the glaring inconsistencies between the J. I. Packer we have come to know and love and the one we read of now, cannot go unnoticed or unchallenged.

When is Another Gospel Another Gospel?

We would like now to interact with Alister E. McGrath, Professor of Systematic Theology at Regent College, Vancouver, British Columbia. Dr. McGrath has given us another eye-opening article found in the same issue of *Christianity Today*, (December 12, 1994, pages 28-33). Paged in front

---

[1] *Vatican Council II*, Volume II, pp. 739-40
[2] *Vatican Council II*, Volume II, pg. 740

of Dr. Packer's apology, this article is more analytical and theological than Dr. Packer's. We shall have to pay careful attention.

We applaud Dr. McGrath's article because he has handled the Reformation issues with a succinct clarity found in few writings. Dr. McGrath has gotten to the point on Justification and other critical doctrines of the Reformation which have separated Evangelicals from the Roman Catholic religion for almost 450 years.

However, we applaud only moderately. Despite Dr. McGrath's accuracy on the theological differences which separated the Reformers from Rome, we find Dr. McGrath to have failed to grasp the essence of Romanism on salvation. Also, Dr. McGrath fails to give the doctrinal differences their proper weight.

Dr. McGrath has made two grave errors. The first is not grasping Rome's use of terminology in such phrases as *salvation by the grace of God*. The second is not concluding from the evidence on justification that Rome preaches (*heteron euaggelion*) another gospel! In effect, Dr. McGrath has loaded the proverbial theological gun, pointed it at Rome's gospel, taken careful aim and failed to pull the trigger! The trigger, for the sake of the gospel, needs to be pulled.

The problem begins with Dr. McGrath's misunderstanding of Catholic terminology. While accurately observing that Rome rejects Pelagianism (that we are justified on the basis of our works) he misleads in saying that the Catholic Church, "does, indeed, uphold the principle of salvation on the basis of God's grace."[1] He also misleads when speaking of Catholic justification as being *from the grace of God*.

Here is the point. Rome can say, "we are justified by the grace of God" and reject justification based upon *our own works* simply because Rome attaches preceding grace to all of man's works. Hence, to Rome, *good works* are not strictly *our own works* but those works wrought by God. God's grace is behind good works. These good works are then added as a part of the ground of justification. Any Catholic theologian will tell you that he is not justified on the basis of *his good works*. No, he is justified on the basis of good works, wrought by God, through graces given freely by God in the Romanist sacramental system. It is misleading to frame Catholic terms of justification *by the grace of God* as though they mean the same thing as the evangelical gospel of justification *by the grace of God*. It is the evangelical gospel that the grace of God is the imputation of the righteousness of Christ for our declared justification. Good works have their role as the necessary

---

[1] *Christianity Today,* pg. 30

result, but only after having been declared justified by God's grace based upon the imputation of Christ's righteousness alone.

The same thing holds true of salvation. Catholic theologians uphold the principle of salvation on the basis of God's grace, but what do they mean? The phrase *by God's grace* is critical. The Roman Catholic sees *God's grace* everywhere, and so inflates the concept of grace as to make it meaningless! It is well-documented that *God's grace* can be construed by Rome to mean God allowing us to suffer for our own sins! (See pages 102-103, above.) Incredibly, Rome says we must, *by the grace of God*, discharge the debt of sin by suffering! Trent is straightforward:

> "If anyone says that after the reception of the grace of justification the guilt is so remitted and the debt of eternal punishment so blotted out to every repentant sinner, that no debt of temporal punishment remains to be discharged either in this world or in purgatory before the gates of heaven can be opened, let him be *anathema*."[1]

By *God's grace* we can have a shorter stay in purgatory! By *God's grace* we can be regenerated in the Catholic sacrament of baptism! By *God's grace* we can acquire more grace through the eating of Christ's actual body and drinking of His actual blood in the Catholic Eucharist! By *God's grace* we can earn indulgences, buy Masses for the dearly departed and go directly to Mary to ask a favor of the Son!

It is the height of naïveté to suggest that Roman Catholics believe in salvation *by the grace of God* as though these words had any correspondence to Paul's gospel of justification by faith apart from works of law or deeds of righteousness. They do not!

Evangelicals who try to explain the Roman gospel may get a bit zealous and say that Rome believes in a "works salvation." This is more a matter of compressing the essence into a short dictum than a serious misrepresentation of the Catholic religion. For in the final analysis, Rome teaches the ground of our justification includes good works wrought by God. It utterly rejects alien righteousness in the verdict of justification. Also, the big work (after a passive baptism) in the Roman system is to avail oneself of the means of grace. Grace, in Rome, is a supernatural enabling which is procured! Thus, justification is dependent upon dedication to the sacramental system to get more grace, to do more works in order to suffer less penance or spend less time in purgatory. The minute the Romanist stops doing his part he is lost. Dr. McGrath apparently has missed this point.

---

[1] Schroeder, pg. 46. From the 6th Session of Trent, chapter 16, canon 30

It is also entirely misleading for Dr. McGrath to say that Catholics are somehow orthodox with the gospel by saying they hold, "Salvation is only possible through the cross of Christ."[1] A Mormon or a Jehovah Witness could say this, not to mention an entire parade of quasi-christian cults. It is equally misleading to say that,

> "Roman Catholicism, from the Council of Trent in 1547 onwards, has unequivocally rejected this [justified on the basis of our works] doctrine."[2]

In the first place, no one accuses Rome of saying that being justified on the basis of his own raw, inherent, non-baptized works! What we do accuse Rome of is proclaiming a gospel of salvation based upon faith plus *grace-produced works* stemming from participation in Rome's sacramental system. This faith plus a *grace-induced works* gospel is foreign to the gospel of Jesus Christ.

To say that Rome does not believe works *uninitiated* by God can save us is of little comfort! Especially when Rome attaches merit to the initiated works of God! Listen to Trent.

> "Hence, to those who work well unto the end and trust in God, eternal life is offered, *both as a grace mercifully promised to the sons of God through Christ Jesus, and as a reward promised by God Himself,* to be faithfully given *to their good works and merits.*"[3]

> "...we must believe that nothing further is wanting to those justified to prevent them from being considered to have, *by those very good works which have been done in God,* fully satisfied the divine law according to the state of this life and *to have truly merited eternal life,* to be obtained in its due time, *provided they depart this life in grace.*"[4]

> "If anyone says that justifying faith is nothing else than confidence in divine mercy, *which remits sin for Christ's sake, or that it is this confidence alone that justifies us, let him be anathema.*"[5]

---

[1] *Christianity Today,* pg. 29
[2] *Christianity Today,* pg. 29
[3] Schroeder, pg. 41. From the 6th Session of Trent, chapter 16
[4] Schroeder, pg. 41. From the 6th Session of Trent, chapter 16
[5] Schroeder, pg. 43. From the 6th Session of Trent, chapter 16

"If anyone says that the justice received is not preserved and also not increased before God through good works, but that those works are merely the fruits and signs of justification obtained, but not the cause of its increase, let him be *anathema*."[1]

We believe Dr. McGrath has chosen his words very carefully so as to oblige the Romanist gospel. It is totally inaccurate to let stand Dr. McGrath's summary that,

"We have already observed that today's Catholic church does, indeed, uphold *the principle of salvation on the basis of God's grace*."[2] (italics ours)

This statement is dangerous and not worthy of a careful biblical theologian.

Why Not Pull The Trigger?

We are at a loss as to how Dr. McGrath can so carefully and expertly clarify our differences with Rome and not call Romanism another gospel! Look, he finds Rome to be totally outside of the evangelical understanding of justification. He finds Rome's teaching on the Church, assurance, indulgences, purgatory and Mary (just to name a few) to be absolutely contrary to the evangelical understanding of the gospel. Yet, he will not say that Rome is outside of Christianity.

Ostensibly, we feel his reluctance stems from a greater fear of living in a post-Christian world than a fear of unfaithfulness to the gospel of Jesus Christ! Dr. McGrath, like his colleague Dr. Packer, has a healthy fear of non-Christian religions *but little fear of Rome.* We are absolutely baffled! Rome does not preach nor teach the gospel of our salvation. Rome has not changed theologically since Trent. On top of this, Rome is leading the cavalcade in accommodations to the Muslims and Hindus of the world. Vatican II and post Vatican II speeches should make Evangelicals extremely uncomfortable. Rome is engrossed in ecumenism while claiming to be Christ's Bride here on earth. Rome also comes close to declaring all religions to be, in some way, related to Rome, albeit only in Rome will there be the fullness of spirituality. If Rome's gospel is not enough to keep us out of Rome (and it most assuredly is) then what of Rome's ecumenism? Has not Dr. McGrath read Vatican II? Rome embraces what Dr. McGrath dreads the most. We offer an illustration taken from *Lumen Gentium,* and a

---

[1] Schroeder, pg. 45. From the 6th Session of Trent, chapter 16

[2] *Christianity Today*, pg. 30

speech given by John Paul II. In referencing the Muslim and Hindu religion, Vatican II states:

"The plan of salvation includes those also who acknowledge the Creator; foremost among these are the Muslims: they profess fidelity to the faith of Abraham and, with us, adore the one and merciful God who will judge mankind on the last day. Nor is God far from those who in shadows and images seek the unknown God; for He gives to all men life and breath and all things..."[1]

We find these sobering words given by Pope John Paul II at Manila in February of 1981, while addressing several Asian churches.

"All Christians must therefore be committed to dialogue with the believers of all religions, so that mutual understanding and collaboration may grow; so that moral values may be strengthened; so that God may be praised in all creation. Ways must be developed to make this dialogue become a reality everywhere, but especially in Asia, the continent that is the cradle of ancient cultures and religions... Christians will, moreover, join hands with all men and women of good will who share a belief in the inestimable dignity of each human person. They will work together in order to bring about a more *just and peaceful society in which the poor will be the first to be served*. Asia is the continent where the spiritual is held in high esteem and where the religious sense is deep and innate: the preservation of this precious heritage must be the common task of all."[2]

It appears to us that Rome is treating the other religions of the world precisely as Dr. McGrath and other Evangelicals are asking us to treat Rome. The language is imprecise. The words are carefully chosen so as not to offend. The meat of the matter is lost in reconciliation language. The focus of the gospel and the gospel message is buried under an avalanche of poetic semantics.

In every theological disputation and argument there is a turning point where the entire article can be summed up as to its essence. We find that turning point on the last page of Dr. McGrath's article.

He calls our differences with Rome "continuing doctrinal disagreements." He identifies the real enemies of the gospel as mainline liberal

---

[1] *Vatican Council II*, Volume II, pg. 367
[2] Neuner and Dupuis, pg. 300

Protestantism, secularism and, ironically, Islam! He then asks the question, "Can feuds between Christians be allowed when non-Christians seem to be winning the cultural battles?"[1] At this point the entire issue of the gospel has been compromised! Dr. McGrath considers the gospel of Rome to be nothing more than a "doctrinal difference" which can be ironed out later when the world is safe for the gospel.

Essentially, we are being asked by a reputable theologian to set aside the gospel until the world is safer for the gospel! We are absolutely dumbfounded. We are asked to erase 450 years of history, throw out the gospel and join ranks with Rome to make this world a better place to live!

Although, Dr. McGrath expresses his uneasiness with the direction the train is headed, he does not withhold his fuel! He thinks that we can set aside our differences and get on with the task of quieting the world. But how shall we do this? Shall we preach the Roman Catholic gospel to Muslims? Hardly, they are to be esteemed and their doctrines held in high regard, according to Vatican II. Even so, are we willing to say a Muslim converted to Catholicism is now Christian? Shall we turn the tide of secularism using the mighty gospel of Rome? Shall we elect Roman governors and presidents so that we can be safe and free to worship as our fathers did? We speak as if insane!

Another Gospel

There are no doubt some who have lost their identity, their mooring and have gone apostate. Things are pretty bizarre when people are leaving liberal Protestant churches to join conservative Roman Catholic churches. True enough! But it is even more bizarre for high profile professing Christians to get rattled over this. Since when is the barometer of healthy Christianity measured by people jumping from liberal ships on fire into the frying pan of Roman slave ships? There are plenty of conservative Bible-believing churches to accommodate those who want to flee liberalism!

Christians have long given up on liberals who are looking for that elusive combination of meaningful ritualistic religion without any accountability to the God of Scripture. In Rome they may find the ritual, but with it comes eternal death through a false hope.

Furthermore, we are extremely concerned at how easy it is for some to quickly desert the One who called them by the *grace* (Evangelical definition) of Christ to a different gospel.

---

[1] *Christianity Today*, pg. 33

Suddenly truth is in the way of some who are in a hurry to usher in the third century united around moral, social and political causes. Hold on here! Perhaps we should take a lesson from the apostle Paul. He lived in dangerous times (cf., 2 Corinthians 11:23f). The gospel was underground! The prospects for a long life upon becoming a Christian were slim. The Body of Christ was tiny and frightened by the great Roman empire. What to do? According to today's alleged consensus, the Church should have pursued needed allies to bring in a safer social, moral and political environment. Why not join in with the Jewish nation? After all the early Christians had more in common with Judaism then they did with the Temple of Zeus! Now what should they have given up to form a political and social alliance against the dreaded Roman pagans and gods of the Canaanites? How about something insignificant like circumcision? Why not just include it as part of being a Christian? After all, it is a minor doctrinal difference between Christian and Jew. For that matter, how about the Law of Moses? We can think of nothing more moral than the Law of Moses.

Hopefully the reader gets the point! The apostle Paul thundered against the inclusion of anything that took away from the righteousness of Christ for our justification. He would not allow for even a minute the innocuous doctrine of circumcision! According to today's evangelical standards, Paul must have been narrow-minded indeed. Perhaps he was ignorant that belief in monotheism, Christ as the Son of God, and the judgment in the end were enough to make one a Christian. If we can form a political, moral and social consensus with those who preach circumcision, or the law, or the sacraments, or 5 steps to Heaven, or baptismal regeneration, or "oneness" pentecostalism, then all the better! After all, are not we all simply Jehovah's witnesses? We speak as if mad!

We are not aware of any passage of Scripture which informs us that having begun by faith we are to continue by ritual or sacrifice, or sacrament or evangelical obedience! However, we do see a tiny band of faithful refusing to blend Christianity in with another gospel. We do see the early Fathers willing to suffer death rather than compromise the gospel to an amalgamation of political strength! We do see Christians unwilling to set aside the gospel for even a second to accomplish some wide-eyed idea of world peace!

We ask a basic question. If the apostle Paul considered the simple rite of circumcision an intrusion on the gospel of Jesus Christ, to the point where he called it another gospel, what are we to think of Roman Catholicism? The Judaizers were moral, monotheistic, willing to believe that Christ was the Son of God and sold out to Moses. Why not adjust the gospel? We believe the answer lies in the uniqueness of the gospel and the power of God when it is preached. To the Jews it was a stumbling block, to the Greeks it was foolishness. The Roman Catholic gospel, having its origin with men, is neither foolishness nor a stumbling block to a world that relishes in fatal attempts to please God with its own righteousness.

Perhaps if the Christians of the world would not be afraid to call a false hope, *a false hope* we could begin to recapture the lost ground with the only message of mankind's salvation.

We have been sufficiently warned by Dr. McGrath that there is a great deal of confusion and fear among Evangelicals. He is at the forefront. These anxieties stem from a wavering commitment to the gospel of Jesus Christ which could lead to alliances with pagan gospels for political safety. As the nation of Israel forged alliances, which would later turn on them and take them captive, so now our leaders are asking us to open up our gates and welcome the Roman Horse! We say, "No." We say, "Let our fear be in forsaking the gospel of the living God."

Veritas Formidabilis (Formidable Truth)

A Vindication of Loraine Boettner contra Karl Keating

THIS appendix is a defense of the gospel of Jesus Christ through a refutation of one popular Roman Catholic writer[1] who has endeavored to "debunk" the research and conclusions of the late Dr. Loraine Boettner. Though Dr. Boettner has gone home to be with the Lord, his book entitled *Roman Catholicism* still speaks clearly to the issues of distinction between the Romanist religion and the gospel of Jesus Christ. Dr. Boettner understood the issues and was not afraid to speak up. We join in the debate since it is a timeless struggle between light and darkness. We highly recommend the work of Boettner. Though somewhat dated, it is still accurate in its assessment of the never changing doctrines of the Romish religion. The following pages will unfold Catholic apologetics interacting with Boettner, followed by our commentary. We have spent much time in this appendix carefully checking Dr. Boettner and the Catholic allegations in order to give the reader a good look at how a modern Romanist writer defends his religion against Boettner. In so doing, we feel we have brought out into the open the real animosity between the religion of Rome and the doctrines of Christianity. We encourage the reader to stay with us through this appendix in its entirety. Many are wondering whether Boettner's work can be trusted. It can. Others are somewhat overwhelmed by the blasting diatribe against Boettner by Catholicism. This appendix will give you a bird's-eye view of just how the debate rages and how truth is uplifted. Hopefully, it is written in such a way that one does not have to read the

---

[1] Karl Keating is the director of *Catholic Answers*, a lay organization which explains and defends the beliefs of the Catholic religion. Although he has no technical authority within his religion, Keating's book has been given the *Nihil Obstat* and *Imprimatur* of the Catholic religion by an Archbishop and a Monsignor. This is a stamp of approval that the book carries no doctrinal or moral error. Keating's book is available through Ignatius Press, San Francisco, CA, ©1988, 343p

entirety of Boettner or Keating. We do, however, highly recommend that both books be read by Christians.

We have written in direct response to Karl Keating, of *Catholic Answers,* who has written a scathing review of Dr. Boettner in his own book entitled *Catholicism and Fundamentalism.* We find it suitable that Karl Keating devotes one entire chapter to Loraine Boettner and his book. *We conclude that Boettner remains a well-reasoned and powerful rejoinder to the error of Roman Catholicism.*

> "Dr. Boettner was born on a farm in northwest Missouri. He is a graduate of Princeton Theological Seminary (Th.B., 1928; Th.M., 1929), where he studied Systematic Theology under the late Dr. C.W. Hodge. Previously he had graduated from Tarkio College, Missouri, and had taken a short course in Agriculture at the University of Missouri. In 1933 he received the honorary Doctor of Divinity, and in 1957 the degree of Doctor of Literature. He taught Bible for eight years in Pikesville College, Kentucky."[1]

In the preface of his book, Boettner sets forth his purpose in writing:

> "The primary purpose of this work is to set forth in strong contrast the differences between the evangelical Protestant and the Roman Catholic churches, both in regard to doctrine and in regard to the practical effects where these two systems have been effective in the lives of the people."[2]

Thus, we shall take Boettner at his word and inquire to see if he has done what he intended to do. Boettner recently died and we believe him to be at home with the Lord. One wonders what the Catholic Church would say regarding the whereabouts of Boettner at this time. Boettner denied the efficacy of infant baptism. He denied the Mass as a real partaking of the body of the Lord. He was adamantly opposed to the Romish teaching on the authority of the pope, penance, purgatory, justification, confirmation, confession to priests, veneration of Mary, assumption of Mary, the sacramental system and the efficacy of the Mass. He did not believe that any of these beliefs or practices had anything whatsoever to do with the gospel of Jesus Christ. He openly challenged Rome and proclaimed to the world that Rome carries the disease of heresy within her very heart. One cannot read Boettner and confuse his efforts with trying to promote an ecumenical alliance with Rome.

---

[1] Taken from the jacket cover of Boettner's book, *Roman Catholicism*

[2] Boettner, Loraine, *Roman Catholicism*, (Phillipsburg: Presbyterian Reformed, ©1962) preface to the 5th edition, pg. x

If the Roman Catholic apologists can debunk the work of Boettner, they will have gone a long way toward convincing the world that Catholicism is truly the religion of Christ. We wish to examine very carefully Keating's handling of Boettner and what he likes to call "the Anti-Catholic's Sourcebook."[1]

To say that Keating does not think much of Boettner's work is an understatement! His assessment begins with some serious accusations and proceeds to get worse. Keating believes Boettner violated the rules of fair play:

> "Nowhere, perhaps, are these rules of fair play violated with greater regularity than in the writings of fundamentalists who attack the Catholic religion."[2]

He then spends the next 23 pages trying to prove his observation is accurate. We shall follow his reasoning and let the reader decide if Boettner and others who write against Catholicism display a "real lack of intellectual rigor,"[3] or "push unadorned bigotry,"[4] or "market the lurid,"[5] or publish that which, in the case of Boettner, is "nil in scholarly attainment."[6]

To begin with, Keating builds a straw man in his opening salvo against Christianity by asking the reader to "understand" that the credibility of the anti-Catholic movement depends largely on the credibility of Boettner's book. We find this statement to be false. The credibility of the movement which denies Roman Catholicism the legitimacy of the Christian label does not rest upon the work of one man let alone his book! The source of credibility is the Bible, from which Dr. Boettner would be the first to attribute the conclusions of his work. We wish to clarify that Dr. Boettner was not infallible. His writings are credible when they represent the truths found readily in the Bible. Part of Roman Catholicism's problem is its natural tendency to attribute authority to a mere man.

The Romanist system is accustomed to looking to man for authority rather than the Scriptures. Keating wrongly concludes that people who expose the error of Romanism "plagiarize" Boettner. It is a matter of fact that without Boettner men have been exposing the Romanist religion for over 1600 years!!

---

[1] Keating, *Catholicism and Fundamentalism*, pg. 27
[2] Keating, *Catholicism and Fundamentalism*, pg. 27
[3] Keating, *Catholicism and Fundamentalism*, pg. 29
[4] Keating, *Catholicism and Fundamentalism*, pg. 32
[5] Keating, *Catholicism and Fundamentalism*, pg. 32
[6] Keating, *Catholicism and Fundamentalism*, pg. 31

Keating complains that Dr. Boettner "skips from the Bible to nineteenth-and twentieth-century anti-Catholic works."[1] In Keating's estimation, one does not display intellectual rigor unless one interacts with the Patristic Fathers or the Traditions of Catholicism. This is an untenable position. Dr. Boettner does not have in mind a perusal of 1900 hundred years of ecclesiastical history. He saves his rigor for the careful articulation of the Romanist position and how it squares with the Bible. It remains to be seen whether Dr. Boettner has misused sources that were not accurate or used the Bible in such a way as to disqualify his work.

What about Scholarship?

The first serious charge against Boettner is given by Keating who concludes that Boettner's book is "nil" insofar as scholarly attainment is concerned. He determines this in part on the accusation that Dr. Boettner improperly relies upon William Cave, chaplain to King Charles II, who wrote *The Lives of the Apostles*. Boettner uses Cave to prove a point about Peter being in Rome.

Boettner quotes Cave as follows:

> "It cannot be denied that in St. Jerome's translation it is expressly said that he (Peter) continued twenty-five years as bishop in that city (Rome); but then it is evident that this was his own addition; who probably set things down as the report went in his time, *no such thing being found in the Greek copy of Eusebius*."[2]

It is absolutely clear, from this quote and the context of Boettner, that his point from Cave is that Eusebius, historian and Bishop of Caesarea (265-339, A.D.), makes no mention of Peter having been in Rome for 25 years as the *Bishop of Rome*. Jerome added "bishop in that city" to his work from Eusebius, but it is not found in the Greek of Eusebius. Keating makes an absolutely false conclusion from Boettner's use of Cave. After reading page 118 of Boettner, Keating fantastically concludes:

> "Take as an example his (Boettner's) reliance on William Cave, chaplain to King Charles II, who wrote *The Lives of the Apostles* that in the Greek original of Eusebius Pamphilius' Ecclesiastical History, completed about 325, there is no reference to Peter being Bishop of Rome. Boettner accepts this as sufficient proof that the

---

[1] Keating, *Catholicism and Fundamentalism*, pg. 30
[2] Boettner, *Roman Catholicism*, pg. 118. Emphasis in original

apostle was *never in the capital of the Empire,* a fact he wishes to use in debunking the papacy."[1]

First, we must read what Cave has said in the above citation as given by Boettner. As we read the citation we find out that Cave says, "that there is no such thing being found in the Greek of Eusebius." What is the "no such thing"? It is Jerome's assertion that Peter was bishop of Rome for 25 years! Keating betrays scholarship when he ignores the clear meaning of Boettner's use of William Cave. Neither Boettner nor Cave say there is no reference to Peter ever having visited Rome. Boettner cites Cave to show that there is no evidence in Eusebius that Peter was the Bishop of Rome for 25 years! Boettner does not withhold his opinion that Peter may have visited Rome. He does so by recognizing Eusebius:

> "The first reference that might be given any credence at all [to Peter being in Rome] is found in the writings of Eusebius, and that writing is doubted even by some Roman Catholic writers."[2]

Boettner agrees that Eusebius may have put Peter in Rome. But Eusebius does not have Peter the Bishop of Rome for 25 years. But this is not the real point. The point is that Keating accuses Boettner of relying upon William Cave to prove that Peter was never in Rome.

> "Boettner accepts this as sufficient proof that the apostle was never in the capital of the Empire..."[3]

We ask, "Where does Boettner conclude this?" If Keating wanted to be honest with Boettner, he would have quoted Boettner accurately.

> "Exhaustive research by archaeologists has been made down through the centuries to find some inscription in the catacombs and other ruins of ancient places in Rome that would indicate that Peter at least visited Rome. But the only things found which gave any promise at all were some bones of unknown origin."[4]

Keating wishes to set the reader straight with his brand of rigorous scholarship. He challenges the reader to read Volume I and Volume II of *Ecclesiastical History*. In so doing he promises us that we will find, "what Cave said

---

[1] Keating, *Catholicism and Fundamentalism*, pg. 30. Emphasis added
[2] Boettner, *Roman Catholicism*, pg. 30
[3] Keating, *Catholicism and Fundamentalism*, pg. 30
[4] Boettner, *Roman Catholicism*, pg. 118

was not there."[1] Remember, Cave said that there was no such thing (referring to the 25 year episcopacy of Peter at Rome) being found in the Greek of Eusebius. Well, what do pages 144 and 190 of Volume I and page 48 of Volume II in *Ecclesiastical History* say?

> "Tradition says that he (Mark) came to Rome in the time of Claudius to speak to Peter, who was at that time preaching to those there."[2]

> "...but Peter seems to have preached to the Jews of the Dispersion in Pontus and Galatia and Bithynia, Cappadocia, and Asia, and at the end he came to Rome and was crucified head downward, for so he had demanded to suffer."[3]

> "...when Peter had publicly preached the word at Rome..."[4]

We cannot find here what Keating said would be here. Boettner used Cave correctly. It appears clear also that Cave used Eusebius correctly. In the above citations, Eusebius does not tell us that Peter was *Bishop at Rome for 25 years*!

We suspect Keating may have relied upon Jerome's translation (*Chronicles of Jerome*)[5] to enlist Eusebius' voice for Peter being the Bishop of Rome for 25 years. When Boettner quotes Cave, the point of Cave is that Jerome probably inserted into the *Chronicles of Eusebius* the alleged 25-year Bishopric of Peter at Rome.

In the first place, it is grievous to this writer that Keating lashes out at Boettner for not proving a point which Boettner did not ever claim! Secondly, The *Chronicle of Eusebius* is not totally reliable as a source of ancient history. Listen to what at least one expert says:

> "The Chronicle of Eusebius does not survive in its original language and format. Eusebius completed the work shortly after its terminus

---

[1] Keating, *Catholicism and Fundamentalism*, pg. 30

[2] Eusebius, *The Ecclesiastical History*, Volume I (Cambridge, MA: Harvard University Press, ©1953) pg. 144

[3] Eusebius, *The Ecclesiastical History*, Volume I, pg. 190

[4] Eusebius, *The Ecclesiastical History*, Volume I, pg. 48

[5] We have found what appears to be the source of Keating's citation in *The Chronicle of Jerome*. The reader is encouraged to consult *Eusebius Werke* (Siebenter Band) *Die Chronik Des Hieronymus* (Hieronymi Chronicon) by Rudolf Helm (Leipzig: J. C. Hinrichs' sche Buchhandlung, ©1913) pp. 179 and 185. Even though the title of the book is the *Work of Eusebius*, it is in reality the *"Chronicle of Jerome."* The citation belongs to Jerome and not Eusebius!

at the Vicennalia of Constantine in 325. Within fifty years of his death in the late 330s, translations, epitomes, redactions and extensions began to circulate."[1]

We also notice that Keating is disturbed with those whom he perceives as "not being of an intellectual bent"[2] who do not verify a claim when "verification of a charge is easy."[3]

Nit-Picking

It is evident that Keating does not like the way in which Boettner has organized his material. He is also highly critical of the sources to which Boettner refers in some of his findings. Boettner is accused of quoting only those interested "in pushing unadorned bigotry—from which Boettner gets his juiciest information."[4] By smashing the sources without refuting them, Keating is comfortable to smear Boettner's work as merely tales from angry ex-Catholics or disgruntled former Catholics. He accuses Boettner of having no appreciation of the Catholic religion from the inside. The result, says Keating, is that Boettner only gives a parody of the Catholic view or a caricature of the Catholic position. Of course, in all these accusations there is not one shred of evidence from Keating to illustrate where Boettner has misrepresented the Catholic religion on matters of doctrine and practice. In the main body of Keating's work there are ample opportunities to show where Boettner is refuting a caricature of the Catholic position. We are not surprised to find that Keating begins defending the Catholic positions rather than proving that they are a figment of Boettner's imagination!

We have shown in this section how easy it is to smear an opponent by attributing to him some conclusion or deduction and then blowing it away. We turn our attention now to a continuation of answering the criticism of Keating as it gets more specific. To set the tone, let us set out clearly in Keating's own words his unabridged assessment of Boettner's work.

"But that is not all. There are literally hundreds of errors of fact in this book. In any ten consecutive pages one can find ten palpable blunders. These are real mistakes, not innocent things like typographical errors. There are major errors, and there are minor

---

[1] Mosshammer, Alden A., *The Chronicle of Eusebius and Greek Chronographic Tradition,* (London: Associated University Press, ©1979) pg. 29

[2] Keating, *Catholicism and Fundamentalism*, pg. 20

[3] Keating, *Catholicism and Fundamentalism*, pg. 30

[4] Keating, *Catholicism and Fundamentalism*, pg. 32

ones, and they lead one to ask at what point does sloppiness become more than mere negligence? When does it show actual bad faith, a deliberate unwillingness to do one's homework?"[1]

How ironic that the author who complains the most about a lack of footnoting and bibliographic referencing should make such a claim without the gumption to show forth these hundreds of dreadful blunders. As we have shown, Boettner has withstood the test of accuracy in the case of Eusebius. The remainder of this section will be devoted to an evaluation of the few instances Keating has given to us which, in his mind, substantiates such audacious criticism.

Contextual Criticism

Boettner is accused of being unscholarly by quoting only a few lines from the Roman Catholic historian, Philip Hughes. This kind of criticism is undeserved. Citations from others are to serve the point of the author. They are useful tools when trying to buttress a point or drive home a particular thought. Real error occurs if an author is quoted out of context or represented as positing something which he is clearly against. Keating accuses Boettner of misquoting Hughes:

> "As it turns out, Boettner refers to only a few lines from Hughes' book, and those *are taken out of context.*"[2]

This is a serious charge and we need to investigate. In his footnote on page 32, Keating blames Boettner for misusing Hughes:

> "...Boettner says Hughes is admitting that Gregory was the first Pope."[3]

But, does Boettner say that Hughes is admitting that Gregory was the first pope? If he did then this would be misquoting Hughes and Keating would have a legitimate complaint. But Boettner does not claim what Keating says he claims. In the context of Boettner it is clear that he wishes to start the idea of papal *supremacy* with Gregory I. There is no indication at all that Boettner wishes to deny that Hughes did in fact recognize previous bishops of Rome as taking for themselves the title of pope. Indeed, the citation from Hughes used by Boettner referring to Gregory begins with "...is generally

---

[1] Keating, *Catholicism and Fundamentalism*, pp. 33, 34
[2] Keating, *Catholicism and Fundamentalism*, pg. 32. Emphasis added
[3] Keating, *Catholicism and Fundamentalism*, pg. 32. Emphasis added

regarded as the greatest of his *line*."[1] It is the burden of Boettner to show that the Catholic historian does understand that, "in a real sense he (Gregory I) is the founder of *papal monarchy*."[2]

We do not find Boettner misquoting Hughes or putting words in the mouth of Hughes to the effect that Gregory was the first pope. On the other hand, Keating does not reference his footnote to any direct quote of Boettner. He simply attributes this statement to Boettner. Who is taking whom out of context? Boettner does say:

> "The papacy really began in the year 590, with Gregory I, as Gregory the Great, who consolidated the power of the bishopric in Rome and started that church on a new course."[3]

However, Boettner does not attribute his conclusion to Hughes. Boettner understands the supremacy of Rome really began its ascendancy with Gregory the Great. He cites Hughes who agrees with Boettner that Gregory I was the first to exert such *supremacy*. Keating's allegation that Boettner takes Hughes out of context is unfounded. It appears to us that the opposite is true. Keating has violated his own standard by attributing to Boettner what, in fact, was not said by Boettner!

The Enigmatic Strossmayer!

Joseph Georg Strossmayer was a Bishop of Diakovar in Croatia-Slavia at the time of Vatican I (1870). He was distinguished as one of the leading opponents of papal infallibility. The *Old Catholic Encyclopedia* lists him as one of the most "notable" adversaries of papal infallibility (for further reference see *The Old Catholic Encyclopedia*, Vol. 14, pg. 316). Karl Keating refers to Boettner's understanding of Joseph Georg Strossmayer's resistance to papal infallibility at Vatican I as a "gaffe." According to Keating, Boettner misrepresented Strossmayer. But did he? There can be no question of Strossmayer's resolve to stand against the infallibility of the Bishop at Rome. We know that he delivered a dramatic speech of some two hours before his peers. We also know that he voted *non placet* (i.e., no place), when the final vote was taken. In fact, Strossmayer did not stay for the official ratification of the doctrine of papal infallibility. Precisely what he said at the council cannot be accurately retrieved. The Roman Catholic religion has asserted as forgery a pamphlet distributed throughout Europe

---

Boettner, *Roman Catholicism*, pg. 127. Emphasis added
Boettner, *Roman Catholicism*, pg. 127. Emphasis added
Boettner, *Roman Catholicism*, pg. 126

claiming to contain Strossmayer's address. However, Boettner's use of a portion of this pamphlet is not a "gaffe." Had Boettner been able to consult the *New Catholic Encyclopedia* of 1967 under the heading of Strossmayer, he would have found nothing of the alleged forgery. Boettner would have had to consult the 1913 edition of the *Catholic Encyclopedia*, which is now outdated, to "easily" find the Catholic Church's position on the Strossmayer speech. Here are the contents of the Strossmayer article in the outdated *Catholic Encyclopedia*:

> "At the Vatican Council he was one of the most notable opponents of papal infallibility, and distinguished himself as a speaker. The pope praised Strossmayer's 'remarkably good Latin.' A speech in which he defended Protestantism made a great sensation. Afterwards another speech, delivered apparently on 2 June, 1870, was imputed to him. It is full of heresies and denies not only infallibility but also the primacy of the pope. The forger is said to have been a former Augustinian, a Mexican named Dr. Jose Augustin de Escudero."[1]

Notice the wording of this article. A speech in which Strossmayer defended Protestantism, "made a great sensation."[2] Also, the article seems unclear as to the identity of the forger: "...the forger is *said* to have been."[3] Evidently, the verdict is still out on whether Strossmayer actually spoke what the infamous pamphlet attributed to him! We grant that the Catholic historians are convinced enough to claim it a forgery. But is it? We find it interesting that the entire article on Strossmayer in the *New Catholic Encyclopedia*, which is farther removed from the time of Vatican I, contains not a single reference to either his speech or the alleged forgery. Could it be that the farther removed we are from the actual events the more unclear history becomes for the Romanist?

The September 1905 issue of *Catholic World*, contains an article devoted to Strossmayer. This article mentions the alleged forgery calling it "the bitterest trial of his career."[4] The author defends the "impossibility" of authenticity of what he calls "this infamous document."[5] However, he gives us a curious note as to the resolution of the controversy:

> "Silenced in Germany, the calumny still subsisted in England and America, and as late as 1889 we find the Bishop writing to the

---

[1] *Catholic Encyclopedia*, Vol. 14, (Encyclopedia Press, ©1913) pg. 316

[2] *Catholic Encyclopedia*, Vol. 14, pg. 316

[3] *Catholic Encyclopedia*, Vol. 14, pg. 316

[4] *The Catholic World*, April-September, (New York: Paulist Fathers, ©1905) pg. 785

[5] *The Catholic World*, pg. 785

Bishop of Covington on the matter. Meanwhile Strossmayer had received a letter from a priest in America who had received the confession of the forger. The man, who had been an apostate, entreated Bishop Strossmayer's forgiveness, and died full of remorse."[1]

No further information than this is given in this article. The name of the mysterious forger is not given to us. Who possibly could determine the real facts given such propensity for the notorious in the Roman Catholic religion? If Boettner is to be criticized, it can only be on the grounds of not having given the Roman Catholic view of history. One last note, the Old Catholic Church movement which sprang up within the ranks of Romanism, denied the infallibility of the Bishop of Rome.

> "The term Old Catholic implies that Vatican Council I introduced into the Roman Catholic Church innovations that left Old Catholicism as the repository of traditional Catholic traditions."[2]

It is noteworthy that in the previously mentioned article of *Catholic World*, the author makes mention of the Old Catholic use of Strossmayer's speech.

> "...and the Old Catholics of Germany employed it (Strossmayer's speech) as their chief weapon at the council of Constance in 1873."[3]

It appears that Protestants are not the only ones guilty of using Strossmayer against papal infallibility. It should not be lost on the reader that this was in fact his position. Strossmayer did not stand alone. The *New Catholic Encyclopedia* lists as "considerable" the number of those who opposed the definitions of Vatican I on infallibility.[4]

Of Popes and Chairs

Keating hopes to discredit Boettner further by crediting to Boettner yet more of what Boettner did not affirm. This flap is over the chair of St. Peter. Keating accuses Boettner of actually restricting the authority of the Catholic dogma of *ex cathedra* (speaking out of the chair of Peter) to the actual physical chair of Peter! According to Keating, Boettner thinks that the pope has to be sitting on the actual chair of Peter to speak *ex cathedra*. Keating arrives at this ludicrous conclusion because Boettner has a footnote on the

[1] *The Catholic World*, pg. 786
[2] *New Catholic Encyclopedia*, Volume 10, pg. 672
[3] *The Catholic World*, pg. 786
[4] *New Catholic Encyclopedia*, Volume 10, page 672

same page of his commentary on papal authority which mentions the current physical "chair of St. Peter" cannot be dated back to the first century. Keating puts the two together and attributes to Boettner a silly conclusion nowhere even intimated by Boettner. Upon reading Boettner's historical footnote, Keating first attributes convoluted logic to Boettner and then mocks him:

> "The point [of Boettner] is that Peter's real chair does not exist, so a Pope cannot sit in it. Since, by official decree of Vatican I, he is infallible only when sitting in Peter's chair, he cannot issue infallible definitions at all. The Catholic Church is refuted by its own archaeology!"[1]

The reader is to be reminded that this use of Boettner is written by the same author who boldly laments,

> "Nowhere perhaps, are these rules of fair play violated with greater regularity than in the writings of fundamentalists who attack the Catholic religion."[2]

Boettner does not conclude from his historical footnote what Keating says he does. It was not Boettner's intention to refute *ex cathedra* by noting that Peter's original and literal chair is not in Rome. Keating is guilty of blatant misrepresentation which seriously damages his credibility in giving an honest appraisal of Boettner's work. This is nothing more than a fabricated deduction attributed to Boettner with the idea to discredit the entire book.

Faith, Morals, and "Elastic Authority"

At the Council of Trent, in April of 1546, the Catholic religion formally adopted the old *Latin Vulgate Edition* as the standard of the Church upon the pain of *anathema* for those who reject this decision. The Vatican Council of 1870 reaffirmed the *Latin Vulgate* as the authoritative text of the Catholic religion. This same council set forth the doctrine of the infallibility of the popes when speaking in matters of faith and morals. Boettner makes mention of an apparent discrepancy between the "infallibility" of Pope Sixtus V and the Council of Trent. Sixtus had arranged for another translation of the *Vulgate* which he declared to be the final authority of the text. Was he speaking infallibly when he made his pronouncement? If so, then how could his decision have been overturned by Clement VIII a mere two years

---

[1] Keating, *Catholicism and Fundamentalism*, pg. 37
[2] Keating, *Catholicism and Fundamentalism*, pg. 27

later? This is a fair question. The answer given by Keating is that Sixtus V was not speaking on matters of faith and morals when he declared which Bible the entire Catholic religion should be using! Keating puts this decision of Sixtus V on the same plane as predicting tomorrow's weather or solving today's arithmetic problem when compared with what might be said of speaking on faith and morals. We notice also that Keating glosses the glaring contradiction by dodging the bullet of the Sixtus decree. Keating says,

> "But a Pope's order that no one should publish a version of the Vulgate differing from the official version has nothing to do with faith and morals."[1]

This statement may or may not be true. But this is not what Sixtus V did. Sixtus V reversed the decision of the Council of Trent and was himself reversed by Clement VIII. It does not take a scholar to ask the question, "If changing the translation of the Bible which a religion is supposed to trust does not fall under the category of faith and morals, then what does?" We must assume that when a pope is proven to have made an error the decision is said to be outside the category of faith and morals. Who will decide how elastic this category shall be? When does the decision of a pope become merely disciplinary and not define a point of faith and morals? Boettner understood only too well the outrageous doctrine of papal infallibility. His 18-page treatment of it is not even mentioned by Keating in the complaint section of Keating's work.

Heresies and Inventions

On pages 7 through 9 of his book, Boettner gives his readers a list of what he calls Roman Catholic heresies and inventions. This list mentions some Roman Catholic practices and the date of their adoption into the Catholic religion. There is no comment on any of the items listed in this section of *Roman Catholicism*. This list falls in the general introduction of the book. Dr. Boettner does not purpose to deal with every single item on the list. The list is meant to give the reader a quick glance look at the history of Catholic traditions. Nevertheless, Keating wants to work from this itemized list to refute Boettner. But upon analysis, Keating can only refute what he thinks Boettner is trying to conclude from this itemized list. For instance, Keating is certain that Boettner lists "making the sign of the cross ...300,"[2] because Boettner wants to disparage anything not found directly in the pages of the Bible. Yet, Boettner nowhere makes this point. Keating attributes this to

---

[1] Keating, *Catholicism and Fundamentalism*, pg. 37. Emphasis added
[2] Keating, *Catholicism and Fundamentalism*, pg. 38

Boettner. Dr. Boettner puts a disclaimer on this itemized list which is
ignored by Keating:

> "Not all dates can be given with exactness since some doctrines and
> rituals were debated or practiced over a period of time before their
> formal acceptance."[1]

All Boettner wants the reader to understand is that the rituals of Catholicism
have come over a long period of time. This gives evidence of the Romanist
accepting some things which are not only missing from the Bible, but are
actually contrary to the Bible. For instance, making the sign of the cross is
not found in the Bible. We readily consent to the practice of this tradition by
Tertullian. Yet, how is it incorrect to mention that it may have become a
common practice of the emerging Catholic religion around 300? Keating is
accurate and to the point when he says what really matters is whether "what
purports to be his Church has kept all the same beliefs."[2] The question of
signing the forehead or the dress of the Catholic religious leaders will not
settle the issue of whether the Catholic religion has kept the faith of the Lord
once delivered in the Scriptures. Other items on the list will serve much
better to show forth the vast chasm which exists between Romanism and
Christianity. Boettner lists some of them while others are, in Luther's
terminology, *adiaphora* (of no consequence). Thus, in tracing Keating's
challenge we will respond as briefly as possible to these inconsequential
rabbit trails and visit the important items with greater intensity. Of the
thirteen items presented by Keating from the list of Boettner, we consider
five of them to be interesting but of no great theological value to our
discussion. Hence, an attempt at brevity will be necessary where these are
concerned. To satisfy the desire to group Keating's thirteen items, the order
has been changed from both Boettner and Keating. Let the reader first
consider working from the inconsequential to the more marked contrasts
between Catholicism and Christianity.

ITEM: "Making the sign of the cross ...[A.D.] 300."[3]

As we have stated above, Keating presses the reader to conclude with him
that Boettner is trying to make a point nowhere mentioned by Boettner.
Keating informs us that, "The reader is to conclude that it must be contrary
to Christianity, yet that makes little sense."[4] It is more to the point that any
case for a binding practice of anything must undergo strict scrutiny from the
Scripture before becoming a required part of any liturgy. Making the sign of

---

[1] Boettner, *Roman Catholicism*, pg. 7

[2] Boettner, *Roman Catholicism*, pg. 38

[3] Keating, *Catholicism and Fundamentalism*, pg. 38

[4] Keating, *Catholicism and Fundamentalism*, pg. 38

the cross is not right or wrong; however, what could be wrong is a false deduction from the practice such as ascribing to it any kind of efficacious power or authority before God. We hasten to add that the Romanist, to our knowledge, does not ascribe such to this practice. However, we would caution the reader to be suspect when an appeal is made by Rome for support of their practices to historical figures such as Tertullian. Tertullian had this to say about the sign of the cross:

> "...we make the sign of the cross on our foreheads at every turn, at our going in or coming out of the house, while dressing, while putting on our shoes, when we are taking a bath, before and after meals, when we light our lamps, when we go to bed or sit down, and in all the ordinary actions of life."[1]

The use of Tertullian by Keating should be tempered by the fact that Tertullian wrote *De Corona* after he defected from third century Christianity and embraced Montanism. In the same work, Tertullian declares unlawful both military service and the acceptance of public office! If Tertullian was fond of the practice of the sign of the cross, was it due to alleged apostolic tradition or Tertullian's personal rituals?

An objection must be made also to some rather glib assertions by Keating under this subsection. Contrary to Keating, the Catholic religion did not decide Sunday to be a day of worship for Christians. Christians meet on the first day of the week by way of apostolic example. "And upon the first [day] of the week, when the disciples came together to break bread" (Acts 20:7). There is no Church authority which restricts worship to Sunday. The Bible sets the example and Christians, in the absence of a clear-cut command as to when to meet, follow the example. Keating also slips in the notion that no mention is made of the New Testament form of worship "other than that set out at the Last supper, which gives the outline of the Mass."[2]

It has been shown that the Catholic religion's ideas of the Last Supper have nothing in common with biblical Christianity. In fact, for those who wish for a "coming together" of the two religions, we would invite your particular attention to the chapter devoted to the Mass.

ITEM: "Priests began to dress differently than laymen ...500."[3]

Does the clothing of the priest have anything to do with the religion of the Catholic? Keating insists, "They did not adopt special dress for Mass, but,

---

[1] Tertullian, *The Chaplet*, paragraph 4, chapter 1, pg. 237

[2] Keating, *Catholicism and Fundamentalism*, pg. 38

[3] Keating, *Catholicism and Fundamentalism*, pg. 39

as everyday fashions changed over time, their dress began to stand out."[1]
This is somewhat misleading when one considers an article on the Chasuble
found in the *New Catholic Encyclopedia*:

> "Its use was not at first restricted to priests or to the celebration of
> the Mass. The restriction came about with the gradual introduction
> of an investiture ceremony as part of the rite of ordination."[2]

It is apparent that priests dress differently than other men in the Catholic
religion with a purpose to set them aside in their dress. This is carefully
orchestrated to give the constant awareness of the Romish opinion that
priests are somehow set apart from the rest of the Body of Christ and have
high priestly functions to go with their garb.

ITEM: "Extreme unction ...526."[3]

Keating's complaint is that Boettner only has a single line about Extreme
Unction which is intended (Keating supposes) to "make the reader believe
the Catholic Church invented this sacrament."[4] In the first place, Boettner
reserves his comments on Extreme Unction for the section of his book on
the seven sacraments of Rome. Nothing which Boettner writes is inaccurate. The fact that he does not go into detail over Extreme Unction speaks of
his choice of limiting his work more than any misrepresentation of the so-
called sacrament. Boettner was not oblivious to James 5:14,15. His whole
point is that James 5 does not support the Romish claims deducted from the
text. What is the Romish claim? Listen to the Council of Trent:

> "If anyone says that the anointing of the sick neither confers any
> grace nor remits sins nor comforts the sick, but that it has already
> ceased, as if it had been a healing grace only in the olden days, let
> him be *anathema*."[5]

> "If anyone says that the priests of the Church, whom blessed James
> exhorts to be brought to anoint the sick, are not priests who have
> been ordained by a bishop, but elders in each community, and that
> for this reason a priest only is not the proper minister of Extreme
> Unction, let him be *anathema*."[6]

---

[1] Keating, *Catholicism and Fundamentalism*, pg. 39
[2] *New Catholic Encyclopedia*, Volume 3, pg. 517
[3] Keating, *Catholicism and Fundamentalism*, pg. 39
[4] Keating, *Catholicism and Fundamentalism*, pg. 39
[5] Schroeder, pg. 105
[6] Schroeder, pg. 105

To this could be added an update from the *1990 Catholic Almanac*:

> "This sacrament, promulgated by St. James the Apostle (James 5:13-15), can be administered to the faithful after reaching the age of reason who begin to be in danger because of illness or old age. By the anointing with blessed oil and the prayer of a priest, the sacrament confers on the person comforting grace; the remission of venial sins and inculpably unconfessed mortal sins, together with at least some of the temporal punishment due for sins; and, sometimes, results in an improved state of health."[1]

Boettner's point is well-taken that James 5 teaches an expected recovery of the sick person, whereas the Roman Catholic sacrament treats James 5 as a preparation for death. This is something quite foreign to the text. Also, Keating is guilty of confusing the event with the actual meaning of the event. No one would argue that James did not call for the elders of the church to anoint the physically sick and pray over them. Also, no one would argue that the benefits were not forthcoming from these prayers and anointings. The sick man was to recover and if there was sin related to the cause of his sickness, it would be forgiven.

But this practice of the first century bears little resemblance to the importation of the so-called sacrament of Extreme Unction as fashioned by Roman Catholic theologians. In other words, James 5 does not teach the Catholic Extreme Unction and therefore Extreme Unction was not practiced in the first century. We agree with Dibelius and Greeven:

> "Only in the Middle Ages did there develop from the practice of anointing the sick the sacrament of Extreme Unction for the person who is dying. This is a transition in which the curative intention at the very least recedes into the background. Quite by contrast to the sacrament of Extreme Unction, the healing aspects stands in the foreground in James 5:15."[2]

ITEM: "Worship of the cross, images, and relics authorized in ...786."[3]

Keating accuses Boettner of not understanding the story when it comes to the Catholic practice of worshipping images and relics. Keating tries to cleverly reduce the iconoclastic controversy in Romanism down to mere

---

[1] *1990 Catholic Almanac*, pg. 228

[2] Dibelius, Martin and Greeven, Heinrich, *A Commentary on James*, (U.S.A. Fortress Press, ©1976) pg. 254

[3] Keating, *Catholicism and Fundamentalism*, pg. 40

differences surrounding the "allowance" of first century customs which "permitted artistic representations."[1]

We marvel at the ease with which history can be reduced to trifles depending on whose hand is holding the pen. What Keating fails to inform us of is that the eastern wing of the Roman Catholic religion was convicted that so many people were worshipping idols and images that something should be done about it. Thus, the Councils of Constantinople were convened in 730 and 754 where 338 oriental bishops condemned the worship and undue veneration of images. We shall allow the Roman Catholic historians to give us the story:

> "Held in 754, upon the same subject, by Emperor Constantine Copronymus. It consisted of three hundred and thirty-eight oriental bishops, and assumed the title ecumenical; no patriarch was present, nor any deputies from the great sees of Rome, Alexandria, Antioch, and Jerusalem. A decree was published, condemning not only the worship and undue veneration of images, &c., but enjoining the absolute rejection, from every church, of every image or picture of what kind soever, and forbidding all persons to make such in future, or to set them up in any church or private house, under pain, if a bishop, priest, or deacon, of deposition, if a laymen or monk, of *anathema*, over and above the punishment enjoined by the imperial edicts."[2]

These decrees of Constantinople were overturned by the Council of Nicea in 787. In the second session of Nicea a letter from Pope Hadrian was read which denounced Constantinople and endorsed the adoration and relative worship of images. Hadrian called the council of Constantinople "violent and ill advised" proceedings and defended the use of images. In the defense of images, Hadrian made the distinction between what the Romanists call *latria* (worship reserved for God) and relative worship which they say can be exercised toward the images and the idols. Landon gives us the upshot of the essence of Hadrian's letter at the council of Nicea:

> "Salutation and the adoration of honour ought to be paid to images, but not the worship of Latria, which belongs to God alone: nevertheless, it is lawful to burn lights before them, and to offer incense to them, as is usually done with the cross, the books of the gospels, and other sacred things, according to the pious use of the ancients.

---

[1] Keating, *Catholicism and Fundamentalism*, pg. 41

[2] Landon, Edward H., *A Manual of Councils of the Holy Catholic Church*, (Edinburgh: John Grant, ©1909) Vol. 2, pg. 412

For honour so paid to the image is transmitted to the original, which it represents."[1]

We think Boettner understood the story all too well. At Nicea in 787 the western wing of Romanism overruled the eastern wing and declared adoration and honor was to be given to images. It is interesting to note that the Council of Constantinople was considered to be bogus by the western bishops, especially Rome. The rationale for not accepting the council as authentic was that there were not in attendance enough of the western bishops. And yet, the Council of Nicea itself was not recognized by the French bishops who opposed it on the grounds that no western bishops except the pope were present. Again, Landon captures the historical moment for us.

"This council was not for a long period recognized in France. The grounds upon which the French bishops opposed it are contained in the celebrated Caroline Books, written by order of Charlemagne. Their chief objections were these. 1. That no Western bishops, except the pope, by his legates, were present. 2. That the decision was contrary to their custom, which was to use images, but not in anyway to worship them. 3. That the council was not assembled from all parts of the church, nor was its decision in accordance with that of the Catholic Church."[2]

Can there be any doubt that even in Catholic history a double standard exists? Rome appears to wield the power among the lesser bishops and the criteria of decision making does not apply to the Bishop at Rome. Also, we are left with one portion of the Catholic religion saying one thing and the other portion saying something different. The idea of Roman Catholic unity is a myth perpetrated onto its unsuspecting followers in hopes of keeping them in line on the basis of some type of ongoing perpetual ecclesiastic authority. History gives us the real story.

In all this, Boettner is certainly correct. We object to the pedantic quips of Keating such as found on page 40 of his work. Here, Keating decides that Boettner "seems to say" that Catholics give slivers of wood, carvings of marble and pieces of bone the same adoration they give to God. This is not true of Boettner. If Keating wanted to know the points Boettner was making in the item list of pages 7 and 8, he could have turned to Boettner's treatment of this subject on pages 279-297. Anyone can see clearly exactly what Boettner is saying about the Catholic adoration of images and idols. Two facts emerge which should be considered by the reader. The Bishop of

---

[1] Landon, pg. 412

[2] Landon, pg. 413

Rome was successful in overturning the Council of Constantinople which forbade the adoration of relics and images. Second, the Scriptures do not allow for the false distinction between *latria* for God and worship for the images. This is nonsense. We urge the reader to digest Boettner's section on the worship of images and compare it with the biblical teaching.

ITEM: "Bible forbidden to laymen, placed on the Index of Forbidden Books by the council of Valencia ...1229."[1]

We tend to agree with Keating that Boettner probably had in mind Toulouse rather than Valencia as the council which placed the Bible on a forbidden book list. It appears Boettner's citation of "Valencia 1229" should read "Toulouse 1229." However, the contention of Keating that Boettner errs as to the content of the council is unfounded. Keating would restrict the prohibition of the Scriptures to a group of people called the Albigensians.[2] The point of Keating is that the Catholic Church had to "restrict the use of the Bible until the heresy was ended."[3] The alleged heresy was that the Albigensians were misusing the Bible to substantiate their theories. The Roman solution was to take the Bible away from them until they came to their senses and agreed with Rome! If I were living in the 13th century I would not have a Bible to read or consult if I dared to differ from the mind of Rome. Keating assures us that this was a local problem as if this justifies the conduct of Rome. E. H. Landon chronicles for us the prohibitions of the council at Toulouse in which 45 canons were published. Canon 14 speaks to the issue of forbidden reading.

> "Forbids the laity to have in their possession any copy of the books of the Old and New Testament (except the Psalter, and such portions of them as are contained in the Breviary, or the Hours of the blessed Virgin), most strictly forbids these works in the vulgar tongue."[4]

One wonders how the Romish religion expects anyone to justify the confiscation of the Bible (even locally) from the laity, in hopes of squelching honest inquiry into the Word of God. Toulouse, along with the Index of Forbidden Books, gives one a historical perspective of how Rome has taken the Bible away from those who may disagree.

---

[1] Keating, *Catholicism and Fundamentalism*, pg. 44

[2] For further discussion on the origin and beliefs of the Albigenses one should consult a number of historians. There are wide and varied accounts of these people from Albi, France. Our point is to illustrate the failure of Rome to tolerate them and allow them to have the Scriptures regardless of their dissent!

[3] Keating, *Catholicism and Fundamentalism*, pg. 45

[4] Landon, pg. 172 (from the Council of Toulouse, 1229, Canon 14)

The *New Catholic Encyclopedia* recounts the somewhat sordid history of the Index. We are intrigued with the conclusion of this article:

> "The purpose and effectiveness of the Index of Forbidden Books was re-evaluated at the time of Vatican II, when the sentiment in favor of abolishing the Index was going around. Finally, in the early part of 1966 Cardinal Alfredo Ottaviani, the head of the Congregation for the Doctrine of the Faith, declared there will be no more additions to the Index; as such it remains only as a historical document. This does not mean, however, that whatever has continued on the Index is now automatically permitted reading for all Catholics."[1]

ITEM: "Transubstantiation proclaimed by pope Innocent III ...1215,"[2] "Adoration of the wafer (host), decreed by pope Honorius III ...1220."[3]

We have placed these two items together since they cannot be separated. If one rejects the notion of transubstantiation then it logically follows that one will reject the adoration of the wafer. It is true that the Catholic religion adores the wafer because they believe by some mystery the wafer turns into the actual body of Christ. Thus, to say that the wafer is adored is technically not true. The Catholic is adoring, what for them, used to be a wafer, but is now the actual body of Jesus Christ. But, let us rest assured that the Bible nowhere teaches the doctrine of transubstantiation. Neither do the biblical texts of John 6 or 1 Corinthians 11 render such an outlandish interpretation. Right here we turn our attention to Keating's lament that Boettner

> "...should direct his complaint not at some nonexistent worship of ordinary bread, but at Catholics' notion that the bread becomes something other than bread."[4]

We have been happy to oblige with this request, but not because Boettner has not! We again wonder if Keating has taken the time to read much past pages 7 and 8 of Boettner's 460-page book. Boettner devoted 25 pages to the Mass and in that section fully six pages to transubstantiation! We find it incredible that Keating should desire that Boettner direct his complaint against the Catholics' notion of transubstantiation when it is so obvious that he has done exactly that! Under the next ITEM of Boettner's book, auricular confession, Keating says,

---

[1] *New Catholic Encyclopedia*, Volume 7 pp. 434-5
[2] Keating, *Catholicism and Fundamentalism*, pg. 42
[3] Keating, *Catholicism and Fundamentalism*, pg. 44
[4] Keating, *Catholicism and Fundamentalism*, pg. 44

"...it is charges such as this that make one doubt the good faith of professional anti-Catholics."[1]

We find these words ironic. Let us now turn our attention to this next item.

ITEM: "Auricular confession of sins to a priest instead of to God, instituted by pope Innocent III, in Lateran Council ...1215."[2]

Under this item, Keating is disturbed that Boettner would make such a charge. Exactly what "charge" Boettner makes is unclear. Evidently, Keating is unhappy that Boettner did not "discover the antiquity of Auricular Confession."[3] Also, Keating is upset that Boettner does not understand that Catholics do not tell their sins to the priest instead of to God. Rather, Catholics tell their sins to God through the priest. Catholics allege that the priest is an *alter Christus*, or other Christ, standing in the place of Christ. Surely the reader will understand that whether a person is confessing his sins through the priest to God or to the priest, the Catholic emphasis is the same. The point is that people involved in the Roman Catholic religion understand that forgiveness of their sins comes from God by way of the priest. They believe that Christ has ordained a system of confession and penance which must go through the priest. The priest is the central figure in the Catholic method of obtaining forgiveness of sins. The priests hear the penitent's confession and then prescribe penance for the sins committed.

With respect to the Catholic allegation that auricular confession has its roots in the early Church it should be observed that conclusive proof is an impossibility according to the *New Catholic Encyclopedia*:

> "Though confession was a necessary presupposition to the reception of the Church's sacramental Penance, it is not always certain what sort of confession was required. At one time and place it could have been the acknowledgement by a person of his sin expressed by the mere fact that he took his place among the ranks of public penitents; it might also have been a verbal but generic admission of sinfulness similar to our Confiteor (a possible interpretation of the Didache 14.1; Quasten MonE 13). Some documents suppose or clearly call for a detailed confession of grievous sins. But to repeat, documents of the patristic period are difficult to interpret on this score, and unanimous agreement has not been reached among scholars."[4]

---

[1] Keating, *Catholicism and Fundamentalism*, pg. 43

[2] Keating, *Catholicism and Fundamentalism*, pg. 43

[3] Keating, *Catholicism and Fundamentalism*, pg. 43

[4] *New Catholic Encyclopedia*, pg. 131

Keating seeks to find proof for the antiquity of confession from the writings of Origen, Cyprian of Carthage and Aphraates. But do these ancients support the modern Catholic notion of confessing sins to a priest for forgiveness with the corresponding receiving of penance? We think not.

Let's take Origen first. In his Homily on the book of Leviticus, Origen is discussing the sacrificial system of the Old Testament Israelites. His commentary is on Leviticus 1-16. At the end of his discussions on the Old Testament sacrificial system and the role of the priest in that system he asks a question for the New Testament Church. He essentially asks whether the New Testament saint might lament that it might have been better with the ancient saints since they had such a diverse ritual in their scheme of sin forgiving through the sacramental system. Origen notes that the Old Testament saints had he-goats, cattle, birds and fine wheat flour for sacrificing. Yet, all the New Testament has is the Son of God killed. He then makes a comparison between the number and variety of ways in which sins are forgiven in the New Testament so that the reader will see that the New Testament saint is not short-changed by not having the diverse and varied rituals of the Old Testament.

Origen goes on to give (in his estimation) seven ways in which sins are forgiven in the New Testament. They are: baptism, martyrdom, giving, forgiving, converting a sinner, love and finally penance. It is after saying that penance is one of the ways in which God forgives sins that Origen says,

> "...when the sinner washes 'his couch in tears' and his tears become his 'bread day and night' when he is not ashamed to make known his sin to the priest of the Lord and to seek a cure according to the one who says, 'I said, 'I will proclaim to the Lord my injustice against myself,' and you forgave the impiety of my heart.'"[1]

We find it difficult to square the teaching of Rome on confession with this citation from Origen. In the first place, the emphasis on Origen's seventh way to receive forgiveness is on penance as exposed in the reference to Psalm 31 in his footnotes of this section. Furthermore, in repentance, one goes to the Lord directly as evidenced by the sinner having no fear of hiding his sins. In Origen's own commentary of his analogy, between the seven New Testament ways to have forgiveness and the Old Testament sacrificial system, he bypasses any reference to confession. If we were to take the time to read the next two pages of his commentary we would discover that, to Origen, if you have been consumed in mourning, you have offered fine

---

[1] Origen, *Homilies On Leviticus 1-16*, Homily 2, from: *The Fathers of the Church*, (Washington, DC: The Catholic University of America Press, ©1963) pg. 47

wheat flour. There is not a word about the necessity of confession nor a hint at the modern Catholic practice. We would further caution the reader to examine the context of any citation which endeavors to substantiate a point especially when the quote represents only one-third of a sentence.

If not Origen, then perhaps Cyprian of Carthage can substantiate the claims of Rome that auricular confession is ancient. Keating quotes from Cyprian who wrote a treatise entitled *De Lapsis* (*The Lapsed*). The context of the quote which Keating uses to prove the antiquity of confession is Carthage in A.D. 249-250. Cyprian had just been elected Bishop when Decius became emperor and published a cruel edict against Christians. Bishops were put to death and Cyprian fled for his life. During this period many professing believers apostatized from the faith. Evidently, many became heretics and never wanted anything to do with the Catholic (universal) Church after all had settled down. However, a number of these lapsed wanted restoration. A split within the community at Carthage soon developed between those who favored immediate restoration and those who did not. Cyprian wanted to wait. His detractors took matters into their own hands and defied the wishes of Cyprian to wait. Upon the return of Cyprian to Carthage, he had to undo what had been done and in so doing, he wrote *De Lapsis*.[1]

Keating quotes chapter 28 of this treatise to give proof that the early Church actually practiced Catholic confession. He does so in this manner:

> "Finally, of how much greater faith and more salutary fear are they who ...confess to the priests of God in a straightforward manner and in sorrow, making an open declaration of conscience."[2]

What Keating leaves out speaks volumes. Those to whom Cyprian was referring were those who had not obeyed the emperor, by sacrificing to idols, nor had they signed a certificate *saying* that they *had sacrificed* in order to save their skin. Cyprian is referring to those people who *thought* about doing such things. He is citing the example of those who are so grieved at even thinking about such things which would deny the Lord. This is not auricular confession in a confessional. This is public confession before a council. Those who wished to be restored had to undergo strict scrutiny before being readmitted. The citation which Keating uses references those who are willing to be contrite for *even thinking* of sacrificing to an idol. This, says Cyprian, is the much greater faith and more salutary fear. The entire context of *The Lapsed* is the restoration of those who publicly and privately denied the Lord. Open confession of wrongs done before the

---

[1] Cyprian, *Treatises, The Lapsed*, paragraphs 26-30, from: *The Fathers of the Church,* (NY: The Fathers of the Church, Inc., ©1958), pp. vi-vii

[2] Keating, *Catholicism and Fundamentalism*, pg. 43

Body of Christ is healthy and healing for the true Church. But this is a far cry from the Romish practice of confessional booths for the forgiveness of sins.

ITEM: "Celibacy of the priesthood, decreed by pope Gregory VII (Hildebrand) ...1079."[1]

We cannot find anything in the writings of Boettner to substantiate the deduction by Keating that Boettner thinks the "Catholic religion scorns marriage."[2] What we do find is the scorning of the indefensible discipline of the Catholic custom of celibacy. We wholeheartedly agree with Boettner that this Romanist policy is worthy of no small degree of scorn.

We find it peculiar that the Romanist defends celibacy by saying it is not required that any Catholic be celibate unless he decides to go into the priesthood. It is not, as Keating cleverly writes, that priests choose to be celibate in order to become better priests. No, if one is to be a priest at all then he must become celibate. And what gives the Catholic religion the right to impose such discipline? Keating takes a half-hearted pass at 1 Corinthians 7 as "proof" for the custom of Rome. But what is the real story?

In the first place, 1 Corinthians 7 was not written to a group of persons contemplating religious orders. It was written to every member of the Body of Christ. The advice Paul gives can in no way be construed to support a supposed priestly class. Secondly, Paul's advice is for men and women to get married unless gifted to remain unmarried. Notice 1 Corinthians 7:2, "Nevertheless, [to avoid] fornication, let every man have his own wife, and let every woman have her own husband." Paul did say that he wished that all men were "even as I," but subordinated this wish to the particular gift of the Lord. Notice 1 Corinthians 7:7, "But every man hath his proper gift of God, one after this manner, and another after that." Also, when Paul wishes that all men be as he was, what does he mean? Surely, the heart of the apostle was not in renouncing marriage for a supposed future priestly class. Rather, Paul wished for a single-minded devotion to the Lord for those who were so gifted. There is strong evidence in the context that Paul may have been widowed and chosen to stay unmarried even though he had a right to have a wife (cf., 1 Corinthians 9:5).

A further consideration of this is found in the advice of Paul to those not so gifted: "But if they cannot contain, let them marry: for it is better to marry than to burn" (i.e., with passion, cf., 1 Corinthians 7:9). Again, Paul asks

[1] Keating, *Catholicism and Fundamentalism*, pg. 41
[2] Keating, *Catholicism and Fundamentalism*, pg. 42

the questions, "Art thou bound unto a wife? seek not to be loosed. Art thou loosed from a wife? seek not a wife" (1 Corinthians 7:27). Remember, this advice is for all—not just to some supposed priestly class. And why would Paul tell these not to seek a wife? The answer is that Paul would have them devote time to the service of the Lord (if they could) since marriage will take time away from undivided attention. All this is governed by the fact that not all are gifted to remain single. This is why Paul says in verse 28, "But and if thou marry, thou hast not sinned." Furthermore, Paul gives this advice under the current conditions of his audience. He says in verse 26, "I suppose therefore that this is good for the present distress." Whether we take this as the stress of being a Christian in the first century or the stress associated with marriage in any century, the point is well-taken for those who have been gifted to comply with remaining single.

We should also note that Peter was married and when it came time for Paul to write down the qualifications for the eldership and bishops of the church, he was not afraid to say that the elder should be, "the husband of one wife." Also of the deacons, "Let the deacons be the husbands of one wife, ruling their children and their own houses well" (1 Timothy 3:1-12).

What then of the Roman policy of forbidding marriage to those who want to go into their priesthood? The real issue is the priesthood itself. The fact that we are willing to correct a faulty view of Romanist teaching on celibacy from the Scriptures is not to be taken as an endorsement for the Catholic concept of the priesthood. In parting from this ITEM, we would remind the reader that any elevation of celibacy will automatically devalue the gift of marriage that God has given to all mankind for his good and joy. The early Church, including the apostles, would never have so raised celibacy to the extent the Romanist religion has done. The sanctity of marriage is too precious to risk. It is the marriage union that best depicts the relationship between Christ and His Church. And we are yet reminded that in the later times some "shall depart from the faith, ...Forbidding to marry" (1 Timothy 4:1-4). Calvin was correct in his comments on a small group who tried to enforce celibacy at the council of Nicea. He said:

> "...there are never wanting little men of superstitious minds, who are always devising some novelty as a means of gaining admiration for themselves."[1]

We are convinced that there prevailed in Rome a too superstitious admiration of celibacy which has been continued down through the ages within Romanism. The sobering footnote to all this is that tradition without truth is nothing more than error grown old.

---

[1] Calvin, *Institutes*, Book 4, Chapter 12, paragraph 26

ITEM: "Apocryphal books added to the Bible by the Council of Trent ...1546."[1]

Under this ITEM, Keating is very brief but direct in his assessment of history. He states boldly:

> "The fact is that the council of Trent did not add to the Bible what Protestants call the apocryphal books. Instead, the Reformers dropped from the Bible books that had been in common use for centuries."[2]

Notice that Keating is very careful in selecting his words here. He only says that the Reformers dropped books from the Bible *that had been in common use* for centuries. There is a world of difference between books *in common use* and books which belong in the Bible as *canonical*! Keating could not say that the Apocryphal books of the Catholic religion were recognized before Trent as being canonical. In fact, every major figure of the first four centuries of the Church denied the canonicity of the Apocryphal writings. Yes, the Apocryphal books were around to read as they are today. But, they were not accepted by the Jews, by Christ, by the apostles or the early Church as being on a par with the Scriptures. The one exception to this group would be Augustine who left us with a list of books to be included with the canon. It is interesting to note that Augustine included into his list 1 Esdras, a book rejected by the Council of Trent. Also Augustine's view of canonicity may have been tiered as his notations in *The City of God* may indicate. In commenting about the books of Esdras and the books of Maccabees, Augustine gives us a somewhat perplexing statement:

> "From this time when the Temple was rebuilt, down to the time of Aristobulus, the Jews had not kings but princes; and the reckoning of their dates is found, not in the Holy Scriptures which are called Canonical, but in others, among which are also the books of the Maccabees. These are held as canonical, not by the Jews, but by the Church, on account of the extreme and wonderful sufferings of certain martyrs..."[3]

We would encourage the reader to examine the fine work written by R. Laird Harris entitled, *Inspiration and Canonicity of the Bible* for a

---

[1] Keating, *Catholicism and Fundamentalism*, pg. 46

[2] Keating, *Catholicism and Fundamentalism*, pg. 46

[3] Augustine, *The City of God*, book 18, paragraph 36. From: *Nicene and Post-Nicene Fathers*, Volume 2, (Grand Rapids, MI: Eerdmans, ©1979) Emphasis added. Compare also book 18, chapter 26 for more attestation that the Jewish community did not and does not accept the apocrypha as the Word of God.

comprehensive review of the way in which the early Church recognized the Bible. It is ironic that the Roman Catholic Church, by decree of Trent, has to inculcate into their Bible these particular books. Especially so since Trent adopted the *Latin Vulgate* from Jerome as the only translation suitable for the Roman Church. This is the same Jerome who, in fact, rejected the Apocryphal books from his understanding of the canon. Let the reader understand that it was neither the witness of antiquity nor the universal witness of the Catholic religion prior to Trent that these books were in fact canonical. Harris in quoting from W. H. Green maintains that both Gregory the Great and Cardinal Ximenes understood the apocryphal books to be read only for edification and not canonical. According to Harris:

"Gregory the Great, pope in approximately 600 A.D., in quoting I Maccabees, says, 'We address a testimony from books, though not canonical, yet published for the edification of the church.'"

He goes on,

"And the learned Cardinal Ximenes, in the preface to his Complutensian Polyglot, 'dedicated to Pope Leo X and approved by him,' states that the Apocryphal books printed therein were not in the canon but used for edification."[1]

Keating's glib assertion that the "Catholic Church, in the fourth century, officially decided which books composed the canon of the Bible and which did not,"[2] is palpably false. His comments to this effect betray a stark and fundamental difference between the Catholic understanding of authority and the Christian understanding of authority. Here, we would leave this ITEM with a clear distinction. The Christian believes that the Word of God established the Church and ever remains the basis upon which to judge the Church. The Roman Catholic believes that the Catholic religion established the Word of God and ever remains in judgment of it. These are utterly contradictory views, both of which cannot be right or reconciled.

ITEM: "Cup forbidden to the people at communion by Council of Constance ...1414."[3]

At the Last Supper of our Lord, He told His disciples to remember His death until He would come again. In so doing, He gave to them the bread

---

[1] Harris, R. Laird, *Inspiration And Canonicity Of The Bible*, (Grand Rapids, MI: Zondervan, ©1957, ©1969) pg. 192.

[2] Keating, *Catholicism and Fundamentalism*, pg. 47

[3] Keating, *Catholicism and Fundamentalism*, pg. 46

and the wine as symbols of His covenant with them. This memorial was instituted by the Lord and it is expected that His followers throughout the ages will participate in memory and anticipation of His return by sharing in the same manner as His disciples. We question the authority of the Catholic religion to forbid the congregation from doing what Christ asked His followers to do. The wine and the bread were shared in by all. It was not just the bread. We question further the audacity of the Romanist to get around this point by sheer promulgation that the wine is unnecessary to take since it is one and the same with the bread. It appears to us the Lord did not have in mind any future declarations that the bread and wine were actually His real body and blood and thus it would be too dangerous to take the wine to the common people lest they spill it! The entire reason for the refusal to obey the Lord's table properly in the Roman Catholic religion is wrapped up in their insistence that the wine is the actual body and blood of Christ and likewise the bread. If this be so, they reason, then it is not wrong to withhold either of the elements since they both contain all of Christ!! Here we see the *invention of transubstantiation* has led to the erroneous conclusion that the Body of Christ does not need to take the bread *and* the wine. Contrary to Christ's ordinance and Paul's command, Catholics omit the other element of the Lord's table. So convoluted is their reasoning, it is actually posited that eating *solely the bread* of their communion is emphasizing the true doctrine, since some people think that Christ may not be fully present in only one of the elements! In short, the Catholic invents transubstantiation and then worries that some people might think that Christ is not fully present in both elements, so they withhold the one to prove that both are fully Christ. Yet, if the original invention of transubstantiation is wrong (and it is) then the Catholics are guilty of withholding from their participants precisely what Christ ordered His followers to do!

Vindication!

We shall conclude this portion of our investigation into the accuracy of Loraine Boettner's book as reviewed in the first 50 pages of Karl Keating's work by responding to the broad-based assault by Keating on some nit-picking points. But lest we get lost in the nit-picking, the reader should realize that the Catholic religion has carefully woven together traditions and deductions from traditions to form a gospel tapestry which absolutely and irrevocably cannot be reconciled with the Christian gospel. We maintain that the Catholic religion has not maintained the deposit of Faith once delivered to the saints. It is not a question of whether the Church has the liberty to change and add this or that to the worship service or the time of meetings, etc.. No, the real question is whether the substance of the Catholic belief system passes the test of biblical scrutiny when it comes to the substance of the gospel. We say emphatically, "No!"

We would like to clarify that which may not have been precise enough in the writings of Boettner. We would agree that "orders" are given to priests and technically, nuns cannot receive "orders." However, nuns are consecrated by strict vows to work in the Catholic religion. Also, to our knowledge, "Purgatory Day" is merely the Protestant name given to the Romanist "All Souls Day." Regardless of what it is called, it is still a day set aside in the Catholic religion to commemorate the "Faithful Departed."[1] It is the day after "All Saints Day" in which the Catholic religion celebrates all the blessed in Heaven. It appears to us that calling it "Purgatory Day" may better describe the actual essence of "All Souls Day" since it is a remembering of the countless souls who are now suffering in the Roman chamber of terror called purgatory. Could the name "All Souls Day" be a softening of the reality of the Roman Catholic dogma of personal purgation of sins in a mythical place called purgatory?

We take exception to the quip against Boettner concerning monasticism. The Catholic religion, according to Keating, would have us believe Christ's withdrawal into the wilderness for forty days constitutes all the proof they need for the monastic life. Leaving aside the rather obvious observation that Christ went into the wilderness for a specific purpose and then went right back to work in the world, there is yet a greater flaw to the Catholic thinking. Underneath the "Monastic Mask" is the theology of appeasement. The idea is to suffer by self-denial in order to merit the grace of God. The Romanist cannot see the difference between "denial of self" and "self-denial." The Christian recognizes that one continues to deny the sin which remains after conversion to Christ. This is done out of love and obedience to the gospel of Christ. The Catholic, since he cannot see the absolute forgiveness of Christ at the cross, continues to mortify himself in order to gain acceptance which the Christian knows can only come by faith. When Christ prayed for His disciples, He prayed that they would be kept from the evil one, not that they would be taken out of the world. Listen to the words of Paul when he exhorted the Corinthians about living in the world:

> "I wrote unto you in an epistle not to company with fornicators: Yet not altogether with the fornicators of this world, or with the covetous, or extortioners, or with idolaters; for then must ye needs go out of the world." (1 Corinthians 5:9,10)

The idea is that the Christian is to be *in* the world but not *of* the world. Compare also John 17:16. We agree with Boettner that true Christian service is to be found in the world, ministering to those in desperate need to hear and participate in the gospel of Christ.

---

[1] *1990 Catholic Almanac*, pg. 246

We would like to point out that Keating evidently thinks it ludicrous that Christians think Catholics believe in Mary as some sort of fourth member of the Trinity. But, what is a Christian to think in light of such statements of the Catholic religion on Mary as found below?

> "Mary's co-redemptive activity, obviously, has no gap to cover up in her Son's work. All she has she has received from Christ. What she received was power to act with the Redeemer for mankind's salvation. She stands next to the Redeemer, as co-redemptress subordinate to Him, and she can act only in dependence on Him. But dependence does not exclude productivity. Mary's redemptive office is wholly derived from Christ, for it is the cooperation of a subordinate associate, which supposes His activity; *yet she truly acts with Him.*"[1]

In closing our analysis we agree that Boettner's comments on the Roman Catholic "gangsters" could be seen as "red baiting" in their force unless one takes the time to read them in context. Boettner saw a hypocrisy, not reserved for the Catholic religion alone, which gave a church-going member *good standing* despite the ethical demeanor of the church-member the remainder of the week.

Certainly, Roman Catholics do not have a monopoly on this type of hypocrisy! However, Boettner's point is that the Roman system lends itself to this on an ongoing basis because there is no true internal reform since the Catholic religion does not preach the gospel of Christ. Boettner, as a Presbyterian, held to a high respect for the Lord's Day and set aside the entire day unto the Lord. He does not misrepresent the Catholic practice that when Mass is over one soon forgets, what is for the Roman Catholic, an *empty* religious moment.

We also must point out that Boettner quotes extensively from men and women who have come out of Romanism. They should be listened to as those who have experienced, on an everyday level, the Roman Catholic system. These are understandably going to give very poor reviews of the Romanist religion. But this fact alone does not make null and void their testimony. It would be ludicrous to think that first-hand testimonies to actual events and beliefs should be discarded because they stand against the belief system. It might be quite shocking to some refugees to find out that their testimony is absurd simply because they are speaking out against that from which they were once involved.

---

[1] *Catholic Encyclopedia*, pg. 356. Emphasis added

We shall close this section by asking the reader to weigh the conclusions given to us by Keating. He insists that Boettner made "gross" and "frequent" mistakes.[1] He goes on to say Boettner "does not present the other side's point of view."[2] Keating is convinced that Boettner has found an enemy of "his own fashioning."[3] His biggest bomb is that Boettner does not present the true Catholic religion:

> "He castigates it, misrepresents it, ridicules it, but it is not the Catholic religion as Catholics know it, and the 'history' he presents is not the history of the Catholic Church."[4]

In this section we have ventured to see if these allegations are indeed accurate. We conclude that they are not. Instead, we have found a high degree of accuracy in Loraine Boettner. We have also found some disturbing elements to the writing style and veracity of Karl Keating. Aside from some very minor corrections, Boettner still stands.

---

[1] Keating, *Catholicism and Fundamentalism*, pg. 49

[2] Keating, *Catholicism and Fundamentalism*, pg. 49

[3] Keating, *Catholicism and Fundamentalism*, pg. 49

[4] Keating, *Catholicism and Fundamentalism*, pg. 49

Bibliography

1990 Catholic Almanac, the, (Huntington, IN: Our Sunday Visitor Publishing, ©1990)

Althaus, Paul, *The Theology of Martin Luther*, (Philadelphia: Fortress Press, ©1966)

Ambrose, *Theological and Dogmatic Works*, from: *The Fathers Of The Church*, (Washington, DC: The Catholic University of America Press, ©1963)

Augustine, *Homilies on the Gospel of John*, from *Nicene and Post-Nicene Fathers of the Christian Church*, (Grand Rapids: Eerdmans, ©1978)

Augustine, *The City of God*, book 18, paragraph 36. From: *Nicene and Post-Nicene Fathers*, Volume 2, (Grand Rapids, MI: Eerdmans, ©1979)

Boettner, Loraine, *Roman Catholicism*, (Phillipsburg: Presbyterian Reformed, ©1962), Fifth edition

Calvin, John, *Institutes of the Christian Religion*, (Grand Rapids, MI: Eerdmans, ©1957)

Catholic Encyclopedia, the, (Encyclopedia Press, ©1913)

Christianity Today, J. I. Packer, "Why I Signed It," pp. 34-37

Cyprian, *Treatises*, from: *The Fathers Of The Church*

Cyprian, *Treatises, The Lapsed*, from *The Fathers of the Church*

Denzinger, Henry, *The Sources of Catholic Dogma*, (St. Louis, MO: B. Herder Book Co., ©1954)

Dibelius, Martin and Greeven, Heinrich, *A Commentary on James*, (U.S.A. Fortress Press, ©1976)

Doeswyck, Peter, *Ecumenicalism and Romanism*, (Long Beach CA: Knights of Christ, Inc., ©1961)

Doeswyck, Peter, *The Roman Way of Salvation*, Volume 3, (Long Beach, CA: Knights of Christ, Inc., ©1963)

Dunn, James, *Baptism in the Holy Spirit*, (Philadelphia: Westminster Press, ©1970)

Eusebius, *The Ecclesiastical History*, Volume I (Cambridge, MA: Harvard University Press, ©1953)

Evangelicals and Catholics Together: The Christian Mission in the Third Millennium, March 29, 1994

Handbook for Today's Catholic, (Liguori, MO: Liguori Publications ©1978)

Harris, R. Laird, *Inspiration And Canonicity Of The Bible*, (Grand Rapids, MI: Zondervan, ©1957, ©1969)

Hodge, Charles, *A Commentary on 1 & 2 Corinthians*, (Edinburgh: Banner of Truth, ©1978)

Holy Bible, Douay-Rheims Version, (Rockford, IL: TAN Books and Publishers, Inc., ©1971)

Hughes, Philip E., *Second Epistle to Corinthians*, NIC, (Grand Rapids, Eerdmans, ©1962)

John Paul II, Apostolic Letter *Salvifici Doloris* (On the Christian Meaning of Human Suffering), February 11, 1984

Keating, Karl, *Catholicism and Fundamentalism*, (San Francisco, CA: Ignatius Press, ©1988)

Landon, Edward H., *A Manual of Councils of the Holy Catholic Church*, (Edinburgh: John Grant, ©1909) Vol. 2

Lewis and Demarest, *Challenges to Inerrancy*, (Chicago: Moody Press, ©1984)

Manning, Michael, *Questions and Answers for Today's Catholics*, (Nashville: Thomas Nelson Publishers, ©1990)

Mosshammer, Alden A., *The Chronicle of Eusebius and Greek Chronographic Tradition*, (London: Associated University Press, ©1979)

Neuner, J., and Dupuis, J., *The Christian Faith in the Doctrinal Documents of the Catholic Church*, (New York: Alba House, ©1981)

New Catholic Encyclopedia, the, (Washington, DC: Catholic University of America Press, ©1967)

Origen, *Homilies On Leviticus 1-16*, Homily 2. From: *The Fathers of the Church*,

Pinnock, Clark, *Biblical Revelation*, (Chicago: Moody Press, ©1971)

Schroeder, H. J., *The Canons and Decrees of the Council of Trent*, (Rockford, IL: TAN Books, ©1978)

Subilia, Vittorio, *The Problem of Catholicism* (*Il Problema del Cattolicesimo*), (Great Britain: SCM Press, Ltd., ©1964)

Tertullian, *The Chaplet*, paragraph 4, chapter 1

The Catholic World, April-September, (New York: Paulist Fathers, ©1905) pg. 785

Vatican Council II, Volume II, Austin Flannery, general editor, (Northport, NY: Costello Publishing Company, ©1992)

Watson, T. E., *Should Infants Be Baptized?*, (Grand Rapids: Baker House, ©1976)

Webster, William, *Salvation: The Bible And Roman Catholicism*, (Edinburgh: Banner of Truth, ©1990)

White, James R., *Answers to Catholic Claims*, (Southbridge MA: Crowne Publications, ©1990)

White, James R., *The Fatal Flaw*, (Southbridge, MA: Crowne Publications, ©1990)

Williamson, G. I., *Westminster Confession of Faith*, (Philadelphia: Presbyterian and Reformed, ©1978)

Works of Jonathan Edwards, the, (Carlisle, PA: Banner of Truth Trust, ©1979)

Zacchello, Joseph, *Secrets of Romanism*, (Neptune, NJ.: Loizeaux Brothers, ©1948)

Zins, Robert M., *Salvation By Grace Or Merit?* (booklet) (St. Croix Falls, WI, ©1988)

Recommended Reading

Butlin, C. C. J., A.L.C.D., *Traditional Doctrines of the Catholic Church Examined*, (Cheshire, England: Wright's (Sandbach) Limited, ©)

Calvin, John, *Tracts and Treatises in the Reformation of the Church*, 3 Vols., (Grand Rapids, MI: Eerdmans, ©1958)

Chemnitz, Martin, *Examination of the Council of Trent*, 4 Vols., (St. Louis, MO: Concordia, ©1971)

Fournier, Keith A., *Evangelical Catholics*, (Nashville: Thomas Nelson Publishers, ©1990)

Foxe, John, *Foxe's Book of Martyrs*

Hawthorne, Gerald F., *Philippians,* Word Biblical Commentary (Waco, TX: Word Books, ©1983) pp. 96-97

Hendricksen, William, *New Testament Commentary*, (Grand Rapids, MI: Baker Book House, ©1973)

Jewett, Paul K., *Infant Baptism & the Covenant of Grace*, (Grand Rapids, MI: Eerdmans Publishing Company, ©1978)

Kauffman, Timothy F., *Graven Bread: The Papacy, the Apparitions of Mary, and the Worship of the Bread of the Altar*, (Huntsville, AL: White Horse Publications, ©1995)

Kauffman, Timothy F., *Quite Contrary: A Biblical Reconsideration of the Apparitions of Mary*, (Huntsville, AL: White Horse Publications, ©1994)

Luther, Martin, *Luther's Works*, 56 Vols., (St. Louis, MO: Concordia, ©1958)

Pentecost, J. Dwight, *Romanism in the Light of Scriptures*, (Chicago, IL: Moody Press, ©1962)

Vanhuysse, T., *The Gift of Grace: Roman Catholic Teaching in Light of the Bible*, (Darlington, England: Evangelical Press, ©1992)

Warfield, B. B., *The Plan of Salvation*, (Grand Rapids: Eerdmans Publishing Co., ©1980)

Webster, William, *Salvation: The Bible And Roman Catholicism*, (Edinburgh: Banner of Truth, ©1990)

Westminster Theological Journal, Vol. XLII, Spring 1980, Number 2. See articles written by Robertson, O. Palmer, and Reid, Stanford

Zins, Robert M., Th.M., *Professor Norman Shepherd On Justification: A Critique* (Dallas Theological Seminary, 1981), thesis

Zins, Robert M., Th.M., *Salvation: By Grace or Merit?*, (Robert M. Zins, ©1988)

Subject Index

Scripture Index

About the author:

Robert M. Zins, a former Roman Catholic, is a graduate of Alma College
(B.A.), Springfield College (M.Ed.) and Dallas Theological Seminary
(Th.M.), and is currently the director of *A Christian Witness to Roman
Catholicism*, an apologetic ministry to the Roman Catholic community.
Aside from writing, Mr. Zins travels extensively, giving seminars in
evangelical churches and debating Romanist apologists. He is also Teaching
Elder at the Reformed Bible Church in Rutland, Vermont. Mr. Zins and his
wife, Nancy, live in Proctor, Vermont, along with their two sons,
Zechariah (13), and Luke (12).

Other Material Available From
PEACEWAY Productions
A Christian Apologetics Ministry Based In Austin, Texas

Call 512-346-6771

- For a free resource catalogue of our videos and books.
- For additional copies of *Romanism: The Relentless Roman Catholic Assault on the Gospel of Jesus Christ!*
- For materials on Christianity or the cults.
- To speak to someone about spiritual concerns.

Videos featuring Robert M. Zins, available from
PEACEWAY Productions:

ROMAN CATHOLICISM SERIES WITH ROBERT M. ZINS, TH.M.:

Justification by Faith $15.00
The Mass $15.00
Old Testament Religion Revisited $15.00
The Pope $15.00
Purgatory $15.00
Roman Catholic Apologists (Part 1) $15.00
Roman Catholic Apologists (Part 2) $15.00
Roman Catholic Inventions $15.00
Scripture Twisting $15.00
Vatican II and Evangelism $15.00
The Virgin Mary $15.00
What Is Your Authority? $15.00
Is Catholicism a Cult? (Part 1) $15.00
Is Catholicism a Cult? (Part 2) $15.00
How to Witness to a Roman Catholic $15.00

SPECIAL! **Choose any two from this series for just $25.00**

ALSO AVAILABLE:
Debate With a Monsignor (Robert M. Zins vs. Monsignor Ed Jordan)...$15.00

PEACEWAY Productions accepts both *Mastercard* and *Visa*

**PEACEWAY Productions
P.O. Box 9064
Austin, TX   78766**

Also available from White Horse Publications:

Graven Bread:
The Papacy, the Apparitions of Mary, and the Worship of the Bread of the Altar

by Timothy F. Kauffman, 208 p....................$5.95

Quite Contrary:
A Biblical Reconsideration of the Apparitions of Mary

by Timothy F. Kauffman, 192 p....................$5.95

Call 1-800-867-2398 to order.

Mail order:

PO Box 2398
Huntsville, AL 35804-2398

(include $2.00 S&H plus 35 cents for each additional
book to the same address)